Reality Gap

Alcohol, Drugs, and Sex—What Parents
Don't Know and Teens Aren't Telling

Stephen Wallace

UNION SQUARE PRESS
An imprint of Sterling Publishing Co., Inc.

New York / London
www.sterlingpublishing.com

STERLING and the distinctive Sterling logo are
registered trademarks of Sterling Publishing Co., Inc.

Library of Congress Cataloging-in-Publication Data

Wallace, Stephen (Stephen Gray)
  Reality gap: Alcohol, Drugs, and Sex—What Parents Don't Know and Teens Aren't
Telling / Stephen Wallace.
     p. cm.
  Includes index.
  ISBN 978-1-4027-5304-6
  1. Teenagers--Drug use. 2. Teenagers--Alcohol use. 3. Teenagers--Sexual behavior. I. Title.
  HV5824.Y68W355 2008
  613.80835--dc22

                        2008009182

10 9 8 7 6 5 4 3 2 1

Published by Sterling Publishing Co., Inc.
387 Park Avenue South, New York, NY 10016
© 2008 by Stephen Wallace
Distributed in Canada by Sterling Publishing
c/o Canadian Manda Group, 165 Dufferin Street
Toronto, Ontario, Canada M6K 3H6
Distributed in the United Kingdom by GMC Distribution Services
Castle Place, 166 High Street, Lewes, East Sussex, England BN7 1XU
Distributed in Australia by Capricorn Link (Australia) Pty. Ltd.
P.O. Box 704, Windsor, NSW 2756, Australia

Book design and layout by Scott Meola

Manufactured in the United States
All rights reserved

Sterling ISBN 978-1-4027-5304-6

For information about custom editions, special sales, premium and
corporate purchases, please contact Sterling Special Sales
Department at 800-805-5489 or specialsales@sterlingpublishing.com.

CONTENTS

PROLOGUE   ix

A NOTE FROM THE AUTHOR   xv

One   DEFINING THE REALITY GAP: ALL MAY NOT BE WHAT IT SEEMS   1

Two   EPIDEMIC   19

Three   RISKY BUSINESS   75

Four   HORMONES AND HOBGOBLINS   107

Five   CONSPIRACY OF SILENCE   155

Six   WEAPONS OF MASS PERSUASION   183

Seven   WHAT THEY LEARN FROM US   201

Eight   BREAKING DOWN BARRIERS   219

Nine   COMMUNICATION COUNTS   245

Ten   REASON TO BELIEVE   273

EPILOGUE–LESSONS LEARNED   293

ACKNOWLEDGMENTS   297

RESOURCES   299

INDEX   304

ABOUT THE AUTHOR   318

The following charts, prepared by Guideline for *Teens Today*, appear in this book on the pages indicated:

Concerns: Teens vs. Parents	13
Teens and Drugs	25
High-Schoolers Who Have Engaged in Sexual Activity	25
Beliefs About Availability and Opportunity of Drugs and Alcohol to Teens	27
Drug Use by Teens	35
Teens 15 to 17 Engaged in Sexual Activity	39
Teens 15 to 17: Emotional Effects of Sex	41
Teens' Perceptions of Driving Behaviors	45
Biggest Influence on Teen Driving	46
Prevalence of Driving Behaviors	47
Effects of Setting Consequences for Teens' Driving Behavior	50
Follow Through on Consequences: Teens Who Have Never Driven Under Influence of Alcohol or Marijuana	51
Following Through on Consequences: Teens Who Have Driven Under Influence of Alcohol or Marijuana	51
Alcohol Use by School Grade	78
Teens' Reasons for Drinking or Using Drugs	143
Teens' Reasons for Having Sex	144
Teens' Reasons for Abstaining from Sex	144
How Teens Feel About Themselves	151
Risk Types and Consideration of Negative Outcomes	152
Would Not Having a Mentor Negatively Affect You?	210
Do Your Parents Discourage You from Mentoring Activities?	210
Chief Reason Your Parents Discourage You from Mentoring Activities	210
Mentors and Sense of Self	211
Mentors and How Teens Feel About Themselves	212
Highly Nurtured Middle-School Teens and Parents	216

To Ro, who taught us to find love, laughter,
and friendship in the world.

And to Eric, you are missed every day.

PROLOGUE

A 1984 CBS Schoolbreak Special titled "Contract for Life: The SADD Story" shared the moving tale of a high school coach and fifteen of his students who, in 1981, responded to the deaths of two Wayland, Massachusetts hockey players by starting a grassroots organization, Students Against Driving Drunk, to help young people say "no" to drinking and driving. More than twenty-five years later, SADD (now Students Against Destructive Decisions) has evolved into a peer leadership organization dedicated to preventing underage drinking, other drug use, impaired driving, violence, and suicide.

SADD provides an alternate path for young people to follow and helps them to find support for a healthy, positive lifestyle. Some 10,000 SADD chapters across the country—and hundreds of thousands of young people—address the factors that contribute to the development of destructive behavior and instill attributes that promote youth resiliency and wellness. In short, SADD students work as "change agents" in their communities to design, plan, and implement activities and programming in an effort to prevent their peers from harming themselves or others due to destructive thoughts and actions.

I first became involved with SADD in 1985 while working as a school psychologist for a small district outside of Boston. A group of students had heard of the young organization, begun just a few miles to the north, and wanted to start a chapter in their school. The superintendent recommended they ask for my help.

We began by talking strategy: how do we get the word out and start the long, slow process of changing attitudes and, hopefully, saving lives? We sponsored an assembly at the school to talk about the issues, set up a booth at the community fair, and made up T-shirts saying, "Friends Don't Let Friends Drive Drunk." All in all, it was a good start. We got people talking.

Today, as SADD's national chairman and chief executive officer, I am still trying to get people talking.

The Campaign

The small commuter jet banked sharply to the right, descending and lowering its landing gear as I snuck a peek out the window to see the river crisscrossed with bridges that borders this small Kentucky city. Another day, another airport, another hotel.

On this day, however, I was not embarking on some mundane business trip. I was on a campaign. My mission is to keep young people safe and empower their parents by teaching them how they can have strong voices in their children's lives.

This particular stop on my campaign marked my twenty-eighth state in about half as many years. I've spoken in too many school auditoriums to count, in classrooms containing as few as eight people, in gymnasiums before audiences of 2,000, and once in an outdoor amphitheater teeming with some 6,000 kids. The venues and numbers don't matter. I'll talk anywhere, to anyone who will listen. After all, that's what campaigns are all about, right? One person. One vote. One changed mind. And I'm determined to change as many minds as I can about the very real dangers that young people face, and the very real outcomes of the poor choices they make. And as quickly as I can.

Because I am also racing against time. Every day, due to a lack of understanding about what those outcomes might be, our children are putting themselves and other kids in harm's way. Many of them are dying as a result.

The epidemic is happening right under the noses of the people who love these kids the most: their parents, teachers, coaches, and friends. These are some of the minds I need to change. And that is what I will talk about today at a small Indiana high school just across the border from Kentucky. Taking action. This community was desperately crying out for it. Recently, an in-school survey alerted administrators that alcohol had become a prominent fixture in the lives of many of their students. In the brief time it took to execute a strategy to address the problem, tragedy had struck. The life of a promising young man, just a junior, had recently been taken away by an equally promising young woman, a senior set to attend college the following fall. She'd plowed her vehicle into his oncoming car after leaving a school soccer game, allegedly intoxicated.

Thus, in one sense, my arrival at the school is too little, too late. In another, it is an opportunity: a new starting point from which one small community could begin the long process of changing minds. If the students here can turn the tide on a long-accepted culture of substance abuse, we could save lives. But for that to happen, these students need to be prepared to open up about the real world in which they live. They need to be willing to talk to and take care of each other. They need to be willing to communicate with their parents about the decisions they face, the pressures they feel, and the issues that concern them most. And they need to be willing to ask for help. In less than an hour, I will challenge them: "Are you willing to avoid alcohol and drugs when others around you are not?" I will ask. "Are you willing to include other kids who have been left out, bullied, or ridiculed? Are you willing to take the keys out of someone's hand who shouldn't be driving? Are you willing to open up and talk to your parents, to share your world with them, to see them as a part of the solution as opposed to part of the problem? Are you willing?"

The presence of the deceased boy's mother in the auditorium today punctuates the urgent need to act so no other parents will suffer such a monumental, inexplicable loss. And her grieving face will no doubt add a certain poignancy to the moment and the movement, I think. The thunderous applause I anticipated at her introduction told me that the students appreciated her presence here, and I find myself hoping that their response will translate into a determination not to let what happened to her son happen to someone else.

I walked into the school through the main entrance after identifying myself on an intercom, to be buzzed in by a busy woman behind the counter of the cramped main office—such is the state of school security in an era following the shootings at Columbine, Santee, Jonesboro, and Virginia Tech. From here, I was directed to the school's auditorium, where during the last period of this unusually hot March day, some 750 middle and high school students will assemble to hear my pitch: "You can make a difference . . . you just need to be willing to try."

Christine, the school's chapter president of SADD, and her compatriots, Mark, Marcy, and Daniel, are willing to try. They planned this event and raised the money to make it happen.

But it's been an uphill climb for them and not without sacrifices—or at least trade-offs. Christine's mother tells me, "She feels like an outcast," because she's taken a stand against the drinking, drug use, and impaired driving of her classmates. Such ostracism is startling when you consider that the context for it is the recent death of a classmate. It makes me wonder, "How difficult must similar initiatives be in other places, where tragedy has not yet occurred?"

Christine is standing in front of the semicircular stage, nervously practicing her introduction of me as I enter the hall.

"Hey, that's me you're talking about!" I exclaimed, offering a smile and a handshake to try to calm her nerves. Christine didn't appear mollified.

Soon, the bell rang and the students, looking unenthusiastic, filed into the steeply inclined rows. They'd rather go home than listen to the "drug guy."

Nevertheless, these teens and their parents have the same opportunity to create meaningful, positive change in their lives, their families, their school, and their community as the young people of Wayland, Massachusetts did back in 1981.

I tell the audience that it's all up to them. They're silent but listening closely. I tell them that only they can transform tragedy into something positive by committing to themselves and each other that they will do whatever it takes to keep such tragedy from visiting their community again. I wrap up my remarks by quoting Dr. Leo Buscaglia, author of the best-selling book, *Living, Loving & Learning*: "Choose the way of life, choose the way of love, choose the way of caring, choose the way of hope, choose the way of belief in tomorrow, choose the way of trusting, choose the way of goodness. It's up to you. It's your choice."

In the end, I can only hope that a few of them will be encouraged to act. If they are, I can predict the result: they will join me in changing hearts and minds, all the while encouraging others to take action, to be brave, bold, independent, concerned, and caring. To get involved. To make a difference.

Reality Gap

Here among the pages of this book I seek to share not only the grim realities facing American kids today, but also the triumphs in the lives of the thousands of young adults I have met and worked with.

In the migrant sugar cane communities of south Florida, rural mountain towns in Pennsylvania, and the suburbs of Boston, and in both clinical and educational settings, I have witnessed first-hand many of the forces that shape adolescent development and influence decision-making. *Reality Gap* reflects my professional journey and shares the stories of some of the young people I met along the way. Most important, it offers a firm context in which adults can consider, and be empowered to act on, the challenges facing the young people they love.

Through my speaking and writing, I constantly try to make the most of the opportunity to empower young people to look out for each other and to help parents and other caring adults maximize their influence in children's lives. And, in truth, I am privileged to get to know so many wonderful young adults, through SADD; at Mount Ida College, where I teach psychology; and in my work at a summer camp in Massachusetts.

The Cape Cod Sea Camps were founded in 1922 (Camp Monomoy for boys) and in 1939 (Camp Wono for girls) and to this day remain a family-owned enterprise. Each summer, about a thousand children and teens participate in our camps, which include day and overnight programs and activities such as sailing, swimming, soccer, and the arts.

Along with two colleagues, I serve as a "resident camp"—or overnight—director and have specific responsibilities for training our counselors, working with our health center to help kids with any emotional or psychological issues, and overseeing our sprawling teen leadership program. While much of my work with SADD takes place behind the scenes (meeting with the board, raising money, and developing strategy) or at the proverbial 50,000 foot level (giving speeches and conducting media tours) my work with teens and families at camp, and during what I call the "off-season" of September to June, when I also teach and run a marketing and government relations consulting business, keeps me updated on present-day adolescent life.

Much of the information that appears in this book has been gleaned from my years studying developmental theory and applying it to real-life interactions with teens. Where appropriate throughout, I cite other bodies of work and data that have guided my thinking; but I rely most heavily on my own research and on the narratives of the teens and parents who took part. Their voices count most.

A NOTE FROM THE AUTHOR

One way I, and SADD, remain current on teen issues is by gathering information from young people themselves about what choices they face, how and why they make decisions, and who or what influences them. We call this project *Teens Today*, reflecting the freshness and immediacy of our approach.

In brief, *Teens Today* is a study of adolescent attitudes and behaviors conducted from 2000–2006 by SADD and Liberty Mutual Group, a company with a strong interest in keeping young people safe, particularly behind the wheel. This unique coupling of a national not-for-profit organization with a Fortune 100 insurance company (and one of the country's largest auto insurers) has yielded a body of work widely recognized by parents, educators, and other researchers as an important barometer of the world in which our young people live and of the challenges they must tackle.

While all accounts in *Reality Gap* are factually correct, privacy considerations have dictated that I change minor details such as names, cities, descriptions, or ages of the non-professionals referenced. In some cases, dialogue has been paraphrased. I have taken pains to conceal the identity of the young people whose stories appear in these pages. Any perceived identification of a subject of discussion by a reader, particularly their parents, is most surely mistaken. All statistics cited, unless otherwise noted, are from *Teens Today*. Educational materials, tools, and excerpts of published reports and press releases from SADD are reprinted with permission. Opinions offered are those of the author, not of SADD.

Stephen Wallace

Teens Today Methodology (2000–2006)

Each of the annual *Teens Today* studies has involved qualitative and quantitative research phases. The exploratory, qualitative phase of the research has involved focus groups and in-depth interviews (IDIs) with students, and in some years, with parents, in cities across the country, including Atlanta, Boston, Charlotte, Chicago, Dallas, Denver, Los Angeles, Miami, Minneapolis, New York, Phoenix, San Diego, San Francisco, Seattle, St. Louis, and Tampa. These have been followed by quantitative surveys of teens and parents.

In most years, the surveys were self-administered by teens in supervised classroom settings in randomly sampled middle schools and high schools across the United States. The surveys were conducted by web and telephone in three (2 years via phone and one year via web) out of the eight years of the research program. The surveys were conducted to test the research hypotheses developed following the focus groups and IDIs.

Focus Groups/In-Depth Interviews

The first phase of each annual study explored potential research hypotheses. These explorations were conducted in the form of focus groups and one-on-one, in-depth interviews. This research was typically conducted in three cities across the United States. The focus groups and in-depth interviews provided substantial content for the refinement of, and, if necessary, the reformulation of research hypotheses that were tested in the subsequent quantitative, survey phase of the study.

Separate focus groups were conducted with middle school boys, middle school girls, high school boys, and high school girls. Participants were recruited from phone lists identified as having teens in the household, and all groups included 6 to 12 individuals. The groups were conducted at professional focus group facilities and viewed by members of the research team. Participants received a $50 stipend for their contribution to the discussion.

One-on-one, in-person, in-depth interviews (IDIs) were also conducted with a smaller number in each of the cities in which the focus groups were conducted. Additional IDIs were conducted each year in the Greater Boston area. The content of the discussions were similar to those of the focus groups, but offered a different research dynamic, allowing us to compare the results to those obtained in the focus groups. IDI participants also received a stipend for their involvement in the research.

Mail Self-Administered Surveys

The quantitative surveys conducted between 2000 and 2006 were typically self-administered by teens in a paper format under close supervision by teachers in the participating schools. The participating schools were sampled from a national list of schools provided by a business list provider. Each year the school sample was segmented according to the four primary U.S. Census regions and further segmented by size and type of school. The resulting data each year was weighted to reflect the accurate middle school and high school populations by region, grade level and gender. Upon recruitment of the participating schools, each received a package containing an overview of the project, instructions for survey administration, the surveys themselves, and opt-out notifications forms for parents if they did not wish their teens to participate in the survey. The surveys were generally administered in homeroom settings, completed confidentially by the students, and returned to Guideline, a full-service research firm, for processing. In 2003, Roper ASW performed the quantitative research.

Phone

In two years (2000 and 2001) data collection was conducted via phone. In both cases, household lists were purchased targeting families with teens and interviews were conducted with both teens and parents. Data was collected randomly to ensure an appropriate mix of respondents along various demographic factors. Because the targeted teen respondents were under the age of 18, interviewers recruited parents to allow their teen to participate in the interview before actually beginning the survey with the teen. Respondents were not compensated for the interview.

Internet

In 2005, quantitative data collection was conducted by web. Respondents were recruited through the use of an online panel. As with the phone approach, parents were recruited for participation and parental permission was also sought for their teen to participate. The survey itself was programmed and hosted on the web and recruited respondents were sent a link to the survey and asked to complete the interview in a reasonable timeframe. Respondents were not compensated for the interview.

One

Defining the Reality Gap: All May Not Be What It Seems

On a balmy Southern California evening in late March, I sat in a sound-proof observation room peering through a thick pane of one-way glass. I was here as part of a cross-country tour to observe groups of teens—and, separately, their parents—as they answer questions about adolescent behavior, particularly drinking, drug use, sex, and driving. My research team and I were looking for new insights into what compels these young people to make destructive decisions.

Each group of teens and parents, in each city we visit, adds to our understanding of which issues are most important to teens, and just as important, how their behaviors differ from their parents' perceptions of them—this is the reality gap that has given this book its name. I was anxious to hear what this group of West Coast kids has to say, and to learn if their thoughts and opinions differ from those of teens I've observed in other parts of the United States.

For the most part, the teens seemed quiet and visibly apprehensive about the focus group. All of them, except for Jared.

Tall, slender, and blond, this 17-year-old high school senior acted like he owned the room. He slouched in a chair with his long, bare legs stretching a good way across the expanse of open space beneath the table and regaled his peers with tales of his adolescent indiscretions, taking delight in the smirks and smiles of adulation cascading his way. In minutes, Jared was revealing a substantial drug habit and his regular role as his friends' designated driver. He says with a shrug, "I drive wasted better than anyone else."

I left my booth and moved across the hall to peer into another conference room, where I see Jared's mother—who is not privy to her son's monologue about drugs and alcohol—puzzling over her selection for the parents' group.

"I'm not sure why I'm here," she admitted to the moderator. "Jared's not involved in any of these things. He prefers to spend weekends at home, playing Monopoly with his grandmother."

I wanted to bang my fists on the glass and scream, "Wake up and smell the coffee!" Because sadly, in the United States in the twenty-first century, Jared is hardly alone in his involvement in dangerous, even life-threatening behaviors. And his mom is not alone either in her complete ignorance of the destructive forces at work in the day-to-day pursuits of her son. It almost seems impossible that a teen could be so duplicitous that his parents would not suspect the type of behavior that Jared described. Yet, a series of factors often combine to obscure what might be clearer, or even obvious, to others.

In the Oscar-nominated movie *Traffic*, Michael Douglas plays our nation's "drug czar." His character is so consumed with beating back the threat posed to the United States by South American drug lords that he is oblivious to the gulf between him and his teenage daughter, a gulf that ultimately fuels her drug-induced freefall from a comfy Ohio suburb to the gritty streets of downtown Cincinnati. Like Jared's mom, Douglas' character hasn't got a clue.

The movie may be fictional, but it is instructive, nevertheless.

Why? Because it demonstrates how easy it is to believe what we want to believe about our children. Sometimes we even go so far as to ignore the clear, cold evidence of the frightening choices they may be making. We want to believe he's not drinking, so we pretend we didn't see the empty vodka bottle in his closet. We want to believe her when she says it's a friend's marijuana in the pocket of her coat, so we dismiss the more troubling probability that it's hers. We want to believe that condom in his wallet is "just for show," so we skip this very real sign he may be having sex. And we want to believe she's driving safely when we caution "Be extra careful!" each time she heads for the car, forgetting the fact that she often speeds and checks text messages even when we're riding along with her! It's also possible that we miss out on evidence she's being bullied or he's depressed and suicidal, because the thought of it is too difficult to bear.

I understand the pain that parents feel. I get the anxiety. Sometimes the truth hurts. But it also challenges us to better understand, accept, and influence our teens. We may never do or say everything just right, since "perfection" when dealing with a rapidly changing teenager is an elusive goal. But when we at least make the effort to effectively communicate with our teen, we will undoubtedly gain new insights into his challenges and choices. That's what this book is all about. And that's what will make guiding our kids a whole lot easier.

Having our carefully crafted beliefs dashed by a dose of reality can be painful, because hearing not-so-good things about the teens we love makes us question our own effectiveness in counseling them. It also causes us to be sick with worry. Gary, the dad of 17-year-old Jon, looks anguished when he tells me, "I guess, like all parents, I thought my son was perfect. I never believed he would drink at a party." But Jon did, was arrested, and then sentenced by a judge to attend an "impact panel" designed to better educate youth offenders and their parents about the risks associated with alcohol and drugs.

Gary's story is fairly typical. Many of us find it difficult to keep up with all the changes in temperament, interests, friends, and activities our kids go through as they develop. As this new independent life unfolds before us, we tend to become more and more isolated from the inner world of thoughts and feelings that teens suddenly seem to have such difficulty sharing. A sense of powerlessness can easily take hold, and, without a true grasp of a teen's daily concerns and struggles, parents quickly lose perspective on what being a modern-day teenager is all about or assume it's pretty much like what they went through in the '60s and '70s. In some ways it is, but in many important ways it is not. As we will see in subsequent chapters, teens wrestle with many of the same issues we remember struggling with. Yet, they do so at younger and younger ages and in an environment that has grown both more dangerous and more consequential.

For example, the average age for alcohol initiation is now 13, and the potency of today's marijuana is estimated to be 10-to-20 times greater than it was 20 years ago. There is also an increasing emergence of other forms of perception-altering substances, such as inhalants, "club drugs," and prescription drugs, and of dangerous activities, such as cutting and self-asphyxiation, which point to other differences between our childhoods and theirs.

While vices such as LSD, cocaine, and heroin are nothing new, many parents tell me that the most commonly used substances when they were teens were beer, wine, or hard liquor. Perhaps marijuana for some. Getting their minds around the staggering array of illegal substances so readily available and widely used today is a real challenge for many of them. I also hear from them that bullying was more benign in their day— they called it "picking on" someone—and was perceived as mean, but not necessarily cruel (though by today's standards, it may have qualified as such), as are many of the bullying and hazing behaviors today. And oral sex? That was more likely something that came after intercourse, if at all, I am told—certainly not instead of it.

The void between our kids and us is the reality gap that contains our lack of awareness about what teens really think and what they really do. Sixteen-year-old Anniston, a parochial-school sophomore from the Midwest, looks me squarely in the eyes and says in an almost-hushed tone, "My parents know a little, but think they know much more than they actually do. They're so off!"

Most parents have the very best of intentions regarding their kids. But there are so many new hurdles our kids now face, and times really have changed in significant ways since our own adolescence. Sixteen-year-old James says about his parents, "It's amazing how clueless they are!" Unfortunately, this "cluelessness" translates into a parent's powerlessness to influence decisions, and leaves teens ill-equipped to confront increasingly complicated issues.

The task of raising teens is certainly more difficult than we could ever have imagined. Navigating the "command and control" to "advise-and-consent" continuum of parenting in the modern-age requires balance, common sense, and, most important, constant communication. That is easier said than done. In his book *Get Out of My Life, But First Could You Drive Me and Cheryl to the Mall*, Anthony Wolf recounts the following hilarious, hypothetical conversation between parent and teen:

"Well son, what's happening?"

"Not too much, Dad. The usual."

"How's school going?"

"Pretty good, but I'm still having a tough time with algebra. I just don't know if I can ever get the hang of it."

"You know, I felt that way about algebra when I was in high school. I remember really getting down about it. But I hung in there and finally it ended up OK."

"Thanks, Dad, I really like hearing about what it was like when you were in school. Maybe I'll do OK in algebra, too."

When I read this excerpt out loud at student and parent assemblies, it brings no small amount of laughter, as each side knows absolutely that it does not represent real-life interactions between teens and their parents.

And, of course, Dr. Wolf is just humorously illustrating his belief—and one that I share—that good communication between young people and their parents can, and should, take place.

No doubt, many well-meaning parents have difficulty summoning up the courage to confront such hard-to-talk-about subjects as alcohol, drugs, and sex. But not engaging children in meaningful dialogue about critical issues, through commission or omission, leads teens to make poor decisions and to engage in destructive behaviors.

Effectively educating our children about the very real dangers that await them, and intervening when necessary, require that we truly understand the issues for ourselves, and also the factors that drive adolescent decision-making in the first place—I will discuss these in greater detail in Chapters Three and Four. We must also be able to talk about things like drinking, drugs, and sex. Only then can we nurture our children, provide them with a safe place to grow, and offer a moral, ethical framework within which they can make their choices.

Yet, far too often, far too many adults abdicate their responsibility as leaders and role models for their kids in favor of a laissez-faire approach to moral education and discipline. Part of this phenomenon has to do with the busy pace of modern life—a pace that hardly leaves us enough time to fully engage in the lives of our kids—and our tendency to over-commit to people, places, and things. Another part springs from generational differences: namely, our drive to be different from our parents, less authoritarian, and more democratic. But there is a middle ground. We just have to find it—and that's one way this book aims to help. As one teen told me, "We don't need our parents to be our friends; we need them to be our parents." Teens left on their own to "make up" a personal code of conduct have no framework for understanding that each decision they make becomes part of a foundation on which their values are constructed. Without our help to grasp that, they make choices in the "here and now" with little regard for what the longer-term implications of those choices, say drug use or sexual intercourse, may be.

As a child, I was told a story at camp about a wealthy man who, on the day he left for an extended European vacation, summoned his long-time loyal groundskeeper. It went something like this.

"While I am away," he said, "I would like for you to build me a vacation lodge by the lake. I want you to spare no expense. Purchase only the finest wood imported from Canada, baths carved from Italian marble, and rugs hand-woven in Pakistan."

Left unsupervised, and sensing an opportunity to finally make some money for himself, this groundskeeper proceeded to buy not the most expensive materials, but rather the cheapest—cheap wood made to look expensive, cheap marble made to look imported, and cheap rugs made to look hand-made. The change he pocketed for himself. When the wealthy man returned and was presented with the keys to his new vacation home, he handed them back to the groundskeeper and said, "The house you built is not for me, but for you. It is a gift in recognition of your years of loyal service."

Many of our children are building a foundation for themselves much in the same way this man built his house. Left unsupervised, they are constructing a future that is materially weak and morally insufficient. It's a foundation that can easily begin to crumble as our child heads toward adolescence, and collapse altogether under the enormous pressures of being a teenager in today's temptation-filled world.

Ultimately, our kids get to decide what they do, because chances are we won't be there the first time he is offered a drink, passed a joint, or handed a condom. Or when she has a chance to bully, harass, or haze. And sooner or later, our children will drive by themselves, too. So it is only logical that we prepare them the best we can to make the decisions we hope they will make!

Today's Teens

Fundamental developmental differences between children and adults are responsible for the way that information is received—or "framed"— by adults and teens. And the truth is that no matter how mature they may seem to us, our kids need help to accurately interpret the messages that bombard them on a daily basis: *Everyone drinks, drugs are fun, sex doesn't mean anything, and violence is cool.* Young people lack the life-experience and, in many cases, the cognitive preparedness, to sort out fact from fiction, to sift through spin and hype, and to appropriately evaluate what they see and hear and place it in perspective.

As you know all too well, many of these messages fly in the face of the values we work so hard to instill in our children. The media often glamorizes and promotes unhealthy behaviors. For example, in Chapter Six, I discuss some of the alcoholic beverages industry's television commercials which equate happiness, good times, even manliness, with beer. And there are countless music videos, video games, television shows, and movies that promote risk-taking, violence, promiscuity, and more.

Of course, teenagers making bad choices is not a new issue. We can all recall some of our own poor choices that may now make us cringe. So, why all the hullabaloo? Because our children live in a world that is much changed from the one in which many of us came of age. It is a world advanced by technology, yet burdened with information that young people are not always mature enough to fully comprehend. It is a world made ever more dangerous by the dissolution of the extended family: aunts, uncles, grandparents, and neighbors who all once provided a helping hand, a watchful eye. Our children and teens increasingly live their lives in isolation, behind the closed doors of bedrooms, instant-messaging their friends, talking on the phone, or surfing the Internet. Too often, they are separated literally and figuratively from the adults who are best able to guide them. In this new world, young people are, like us, over-scheduled, overtired, and overstressed. These factors can lead them to seek comfort by self-medicating with alcohol, drugs, sex, and other potentially destructive choices.

My friend, psychologist David Elkind, first introduced the idea that we may be pushing children too far in his bestselling book *The Hurried Child*. He warned against the diminution of childhood by imposing too many adult-like demands on kids, detailing the toll that this can take on young lives: low self-esteem, pregnancy, even suicide. Elkind refers to these kids as "miniature adults" and says at the beginning of his book, "The concept of childhood, so vital to the traditional way of life, is threatened with extinction in the society we have created. Today's child has become the unintended victim of overwhelming stress—the stress born of rapid, bewildering social change and constantly rising expectations." Yet still, down the same unfortunate path we march along.

Of course, the definition of "today's child"—overscheduled and stressed—goes back some time. I recall an address I gave to parents one cold February afternoon in the early 1990s at the Snow Library in Orleans, Massachusetts. As one in a series of lectures, my remarks, titled

8

"Where Have All the Children Gone? Our Legacy for Tomorrow," were intended to widen awareness of how times have changed for our children and young adults. I asked the audience members to think back to what life was like when they were teens: *Picture the clothes you wore, remember your favorite kind of music, what dating was like, what rules you lived by, and what the worst thing you could do was.* Then I challenged them to compare what they recalled with their understanding of contemporary teens: *What do they look like? What do they wear? How has dating changed? What rules do they live by? Who influences them most? And what is the worst thing they can do wrong?*

It is an interesting, and often eye-opening exercise to compare our own experiences with those of our children. What I see, as Dr. Elkind saw, are children who more closely resemble adults—at least in terms of behavior—than teenagers. In my speech, I quoted Michael Thomson, author of *Who's Raising Whom*, as saying, "Many high school students are now mimicking the behaviors of college-aged kids . . . drinking, drugging, sexual promiscuity, and acting out." As we will see in the next chapter, we now have middle school students mimicking high school students, and even elementary school students mimicking middle school students. Pushed, pulled, and sometimes just simply left by themselves, many children and teens are choosing adult behaviors they are neither ready for nor that suit their short- and longer-term interests.

In fairness, the rise of dual-income and single-parent families has meant that many parents have little choice but to leave their children and teens in the care of others or to engage them in a staggering array of activities, each bringing with it the promise of safety and supervision. Unfortunately, each new addition to the schedule also charges kids with new requirements and new responsibilities. This can result in kids feeling overextended and overwhelmed. In Chapter Three, I talk about the importance of balancing work with play, allowing young people the time and space to be *young*, and choosing those activities and organizations that promote positive, as opposed to negative, risk-taking. What's most important is the quality of the experiences our children have, not the quantity we can assemble to keep them busy. And, as always, our active participation in those activities will bring us together, building commonalities of experience and new points of reference for conversation.

The Reality Gap in Modern Day Culture

As we will see in later chapters, research indicates that we differ significantly from our teens in our opinion of what is most important to *them* when it comes to things like drinking, drugs, driving, and suicide. They know. We don't. And standing on the far side of the reality gap, we don't even know how to ask.

But, you reasonably inquire, hasn't the reality gap existed forever? To some extent, one could argue that parents have always been a step behind their teenage children in knowing what's new, what's hip, what's hot. Maybe even in knowing some of the choices they were making, as well. After all, we probably all did some things our parents didn't know about and likely worked hard to make sure it stayed that way.

But our modern-day culture has widened the distance and accelerated the harm. More than ever before, there are alarming physical, social, emotional, and legal risks associated with drinking, drugs, and sex, as well as spillover effects, involving bullying, violence, depression, suicide, and dangerous driving. Examples are everywhere. Horrific car crashes and drug overdoses. Gang murders and inexplicable suicides. Teen beat-downs on YouTube and put-downs on MySpace. Violence on middle school, high school, and college campuses. And sex on school buses and in classrooms. These examples only scratch the surface of modern teen culture. Only by knowing about, and addressing, the reality gap will we be able to keep our kids safe throughout the increasingly risk-filled years of adolescence.

Now, there are plenty of parents who understand that destructive behaviors tend to increase as teens grow older. But they frequently attribute those choices to *other* people's children. It's time to set the record straight.

Despite what we may *want* to believe, *our* children may very well be engaging in dangerous, even deadly, behavior. That we don't see it or hear about it doesn't mean it isn't happening. In fact, many of us might be surprised at what our kids admit to when confronted directly.

Compared to what their parents say about them, American high school teens are eight times more likely to say they drink alcohol, four times more likely to admit they use drugs, and twice as likely to report they have had sex. I hear their personal stories everywhere I go.

Carrie, an 18-year-old from the Midwest says, "Exposure to alcohol, drugs, [and] peer pressure sums up the life of a graduating senior."

Scott, from Wisconsin, and also a senior, agrees. "Whether it is to try drugs, or have sex, or even just to smoke, we come across these temptations every day."

But seniors aren't the only ones feeling the heat. Eighteen-year-old Jackie recalls her freshman year of high school this way: "School is a hard place to be—it is away from the comfort zone of your home. I wanted to fit in with all the 'popular' students and told myself that I would do anything to become one. I then starting dating a senior, and he was nice to me at first, but later on in our relationship he pressured me into a lot of things. We would go to parties and drink alcohol and have fun." Jackie is not alone.

In June 2007, I was in New England conducting one-on-one, in-depth interviews with teens in their schools and homes. In Maine, Robert, barely 18-years-old, told me a story similar to the one Jared told back in Southern California: a story of drugs, alcohol, and sexual activity. Robert is, by all accounts from the adults who know him, a superstar. I can see why. Tall and dark, with a chiseled chin and deep-set gray-green eyes, he looks every bit his part: a New England prep-school, ivy-bound, winner-takes-all kid. But behind academic success, athletic prowess, and extracurricular accomplishments lurks another existence that Robert sheepishly confesses includes a number of destructive choices, not the least of which is frequent and heavy drinking.

"My friends and I are afraid we might be alcoholics," Robert admits. And his parents haven't got a clue.

How is that possible? Many kids like Robert evade detection through simple tools of the trade, such as mouthwash to erase the smell of alcohol, or Visine to whiten bloodshot eyes. Others just avoid going home after a night of drinking or drug use by staying over with a friend, for example, whose parents may tend to be less vigilant.

It's not only behaviors like Robert's that separate us from our kids. Many of us don't even know which behaviors to be concerned about in the first place, be they driving, drinking, drugs, sex, or suicidal thoughts. Beyond a mutual concern about HIV and other sexually transmitted diseases, there is very little about which adults and teens see eye-to-eye. For example:

- Eighty-three percent of teens say they are concerned about drinking and driving, compared to just 48 percent of parents.
- Teen suicide barely even registers on parental radar screens, but teens rank it as fifth among the issues they worry about, with nearly 62 percent reporting they are concerned about it (likely because they have thought about suicide or have a friend who has talked about it), compared to only 36 percent of their parents, for whom it falls to number 17 on their list of top issues.

These statistical separations deeply underscore the need to shrink the reality gap. Because when parents are privy to information such as this, they better understand their child's real world and have a better chance of keeping him safe. On the other hand, a parent who remains unaware of the issues teens consider most important misses crucial opportunities to draw them into conversations where they can express their concerns and gain further insights into the decisions their children are inclined to make and why. Michael Thompson's book *The Pressured Child* points to the fact that adults too quickly forget many of their own childhood experiences, particularly the pain and struggles that mark the slow, unsteady march through the school years. Thompson says, "In my experience as a

Concerns: Teens vs. Parents

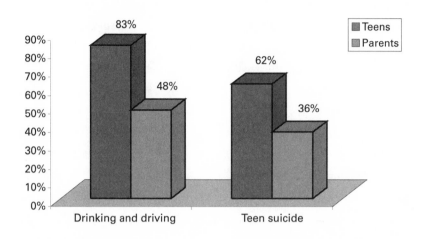

school consultant and psychologist, I see that often parents and teachers have forgotten what school actually feels like for a child, and why children struggle with both their own development and the environment of school." School is, after all, where our children spend the majority of their waking hours (which is why I chose to become a school psychologist as opposed to one of the other types), and thus it is the stage on which their individual physical, social, emotional, and academic growth plays out—often in very visible and transparent ways, subjecting them to constant scrutiny, judgment, and competition.

In addition to forgetting what school is all about for kids, we also tend to forget what growing up is really like. As one Massachusetts teen said, "Just being happy has fallen lower on the priority list." My translation? Survival, physically and emotionally, seems to be the name of the game.

It is true that today's teens live in a world apart from the one their parents and teachers grew up in. And it is also true that the world is much more dangerous. But in many ways, the staples of growing up have remained remarkably similar. Most kids, despite what we may see on the exterior, worry about fitting in, finding friends, pleasing parents, and doing well in school or sports or the arts. They look to the future, as we did, with a degree of anxiety about what it holds for them. *Will I go to college? What will I do for work? Will I have a family? Will I be successful?* In other words, there are probably more similarities between our fundamental experiences as children and young adults and those of our teens than we realize. Thus, while trying as best we can to understand the differences, we must, at the same time, take care not to minimize what is the same. It is the sameness of our life experiences that brings us closer together, shrinks the reality gap, and makes good decision-making more likely.

Effective communication, both at the content level (what we and they are actually saying), and the relationship level (what it really means to both of us), helps to shed light on both perspectives, child and adult, and move the relationship toward reciprocity: I share what's concerning me, you share what's concerning you, and together we work toward a mutually acceptable approach that preserves, or creates, an appropriate balance between legitimate parental authority and a young person's need for autonomy.

But some adults neglect to discuss alcohol, drugs, sex, even driving, with their teens for fear of being labeled hypocrites. After all, for example, they drank then, or they drink now. Scott, the Wisconsin senior we met earlier, says, "I have been told by some parents that, 'We have a hard time telling our children not to do something when we did that exact same thing at their age.'"

Indeed, a mom in Longmeadow, Massachusetts, once approached me after a presentation and asked, "How can I tell my daughter she can't drink when I did in high school?" I explained to her that past behavior is not necessarily a relevant part of the discussion—although current behavior may be. While there are important differences between adult and adolescent alcohol use—just because we do something does not mean that they can—it is critical to remember that we send incredibly powerful messages to our teens through the things we do, even more so than through the things we *did*, or the things we say.

Our choices now, and the examples they set, ring loudly in adolescent ears. As 17-year-old Jack from Westchester County, New York, bluntly put it, "Parents need to look at themselves and see what kind of example they are setting. For any solution to come, both parents and kids need to be willing to give up something and talk to each other more about it, or the problem will just continue to get worse." Jack is pointing out the convergence of what we say and what we do, a topic we'll consider in more depth later in the book.

While intuitively we may know what type of communication best serves our own particular parent-child relationship—"Honesty is the best policy," for example—it is incredibly tempting to let wishful thinking cloud our judgment. After all, self-delusion is a powerful narcotic. When we think the best, it makes us feel good: proud, capable, and successful. The feeling is addictive. When Brad makes the all-star basketball team, or Rebecca aces the SATs, we savor their success, make it our own, and believe that somehow it inoculates them against dangerous behaviors, because they would be incongruous with what we are witnessing with our own eyes. But what's the result of such blind optimism? We too often ignore information that contradicts our positive perceptions of our kids and that might cause us to feel confused, hurt, and angry—even when that information is staring us directly in the face.

Somewhat sheepishly, 21-year-old David, an aspiring doctor and sometimes bartender in northern California, tells me about the time in high school when his single mom walked in on him while he was having sex with an older woman in his bedroom. "She just said, 'Oh excuse me,' and left. She never raised [the issue], so I didn't either." Did she avoid discussing the issue because she was embarrassed, uncomfortable, or maybe afraid David would think she was acting hypocritically? Regardless of her reason, David's mom lost the opportunity to talk with him about important decisions regarding intimate sexual behavior, to share values and expectations, to discuss risks and rewards, and to reinforce family rules for conduct.

In Georgia, Stephanie, whose short stature, soft features, and simple, casual clothing make her look at least two years younger than her 15 years, explains to me that she began to have a physical relationship with her boyfriend Craig during her freshman year of high school, even though, "It felt weird." But Stephanie went along anyway, and by the beginning of sophomore year, she'd agreed to have intercourse.

"I had always told myself I would wait until I was in love, comfortable. But Craig kept asking. Afterward I thought, 'What did I just do? Am I out of my mind?'" As you might suspect, Stephanie's parents were completely unaware of her sexual activity and of the choices she felt she had to make. Unable to intervene, they unwittingly left Stephanie on her own to balance her affection for Craig and her knowing uncertainty about becoming sexually intimate. Had they been able to more effectively communicate about her relationship with him, they would have had the chance to hear what Stephanie was going through and to help her decide what was the right thing to do—for herself and for her family. Instead, they remained oblivious, even in the face of mounting evidence of her affection for him.

Avoiding the truth about our teen's behavior conveniently absolves us from the responsibility of having to do something about it. After all, if we know that Jared is using drugs, that Robert is getting drunk, or that Stephanie is having sex, we have to act, right? But if we don't admit there's an issue, we will have no confrontation and no conflict. That makes dinner time a whole lot more pleasant. Unfortunately, it does nothing to protect our kids from the dangers lurking just outside the kitchen door.

Teens like Jared, Robert, and Stephanie have constructed an alternate reality to offer for their parents' consumption. Jared, who uses drugs and drives impaired; Robert, who thinks he might be an alcoholic; and Stephanie, who is having sex with her boyfriend. Make no mistake about it: The reality gap leaves kids like Jared, Robert, and Stephanie susceptible to ruined health, severed relationships, and greatly diminished chances for success.

If we don't take the time to talk with, and really understand, our teens, how can we expect to know much about the choices they face and the decisions they make? Only when we carve out opportunities to spend time with our teens will we have a fighting chance of finding out what they're all about.

Granted, it's tough to find that time. Most parents I know have incredibly demanding schedules. Early to bed, early to rise doesn't hold much promise when the space in-between is jammed with shuttling kids to and from school, attending teacher conferences, cheering at soccer games, reconstructing calculus problems, and doing laundry—all the while preparing for work the next day. Understanding and influencing teen behavior is time-intensive work, and that time always seems to be scarce. Yet, the more time we spend with our teens, the more we will discover about their world by watching what they do and listening to what they say.

Of course, kids are busy, too. The sheer number of activities in which many teens participate is staggering. By the time they navigate the school day, play in a basketball game, practice piano, attend the SAT prep class, finish homework, plan a class project, and instant-message their friends, there's little time left for idle conversation. One 17-year-old walked me through her schedule in an e-mail: "I've been working on my college essay and homework for the past couple days. I'm applying early. I'm starting my internship at a science lab on Thursday. I've been doing theater out of school and [am] working with disabled adults and teenagers again this year." Her life is hectic, but not all that unique.

Fourteen-year-old Jim writes: "Oh my goodness! This is the first time I have been able to sit down at my computer and write something other than essays for school. Last week, I had baseball practice from 3:00 p.m. to 6:00 p.m., pit band rehearsals for our school play, *Bye Bye Birdie,* from 6:30 p.m. to 10:00 p.m., and a ton of homework. I think I am running on adrenaline from last week."

Family time often takes a backseat in our mutually busy worlds. But finding time to be together and to talk pays off big. Thirteen-year-old Nasha, wearing a bright-green shirt and hoop earrings, tells me she and her mom make the time to talk at home about important things, like drinking.

"My mom does a really good job being a single mom raising a kid. She has told me that I can drink when I am an adult, but not now, even though other kids are drinking." For Nasha and her mom, what little time they have together is clearly time well spent. As a result of it, Nasha understands her mom's expectations for her and is able to talk openly about the appropriate role of, and time for, alcohol in her life. Her mom, on the other hand, understands more about Nasha's environment and the difficult issues she has to face. They've reached agreement that Nasha will not drink until she is 21. Nasha describes her mom as a role model, and it is clear she does not want to disappoint her—a very large factor in influencing our teens and one that parents greatly underestimate. Their conversations have helped her to clarify the type of decisions she wants to make and why she wants to make them.

Even when parents do make the time to talk, they might be reluctant to spend it discussing difficult subjects and, perhaps, inviting argument. This seems to be especially true when we have different views on the acceptability of certain behaviors, like underage drinking or oral sex, because an open discussion about these topics can result in disagreements. And if our time together is brief, who wants to spend it arguing? Unfortunately, this way of thinking is not really helpful to our children in the long run. If we choose to ignore our teens' views about drinking, drugs, sex, driving, bullying, violence, and suicide in order to avoid conflict, we put them at a distinct disadvantage in making healthy decisions. As difficult as it may be, we have a duty to immerse ourselves in our child's adolescence, understanding and communicating about the difficult choices he faces daily. What is the consequence of not doing so? I see it every day. It is a full-scale, and sadly ongoing, epidemic.

Two

Epidemic

The end-of-year senior-class scavenger hunt planned by students at a suburban Boston high school promised points for proof (pictures, for example) of masturbation, oral sex, and intercourse, as well as drinking and using drugs, providing liquor to middle school students, building naked human pyramids, and stealing. Engage in these behaviors, provide the evidence, and maybe you'll win! Apparently, it's a tradition that heretofore had gone either unnoticed or unaddressed by teachers, administrators, or parents. The mother of one student reported that her daughter was embarrassed by what she had heard about the senior romp, but my guess is that most students were hardly surprised. Even the "best" of teens regularly relate to me stories of flagrant drinking, drug use, and sex by classmates, and, sometimes, themselves.

Unfortunately, most parents with whom I talk are blissfully unaware of what is common behavior in their town or for their teen. They tend to believe that their teen is not drinking, using drugs, having sex, driving dangerously, being bullied, or thinking about suicide.

So begins an epidemic, one that remains largely hidden from view, is certainly under-reported, and is mostly unrecognized. Ironically, the truth is not always hard to find, if you simply ask.

In a hot, crowded high school gymnasium, standing before 700 young people and their parents, I posed a series of questions:

"By a show of hands, how many of you know someone who regularly uses alcohol?" Most hands go up.

"How many of you know someone who regularly uses drugs?" Almost as many are raised.

"How many of you have friends who drive impaired?"

"How many of you know kids who are engaged in casual, anonymous, even exploitive sexual activity?" The percentages remain about the same. So, too, when I ask, "How many of you know people who feel lonely, isolated, left out, depressed, or suicidal?"

The parents seem stunned by the kids' responses. This quick, visual display uncovering the epic proportions of risky teen behavior and emotional distress is powerful . . . and all too real. I can see the look of shock on many parents' faces gradually morphing into fear, moving like a slow wave making progress toward shore. The parents are wondering, "Is my kid making these decisions? And, if so, why?" Few of them probably even thought to ask before tonight.

In truth, all kinds of kids make all kinds of decisions—some good and some bad—for all kinds of reasons (many of which are outlined in Chapters Four and Five). And while I go to great lengths in this book to alert parents to the destructive choices of many teens, I want to be cautious and remind readers that many young people are making good, healthy, and safe choices. And it's important to understand the impetus behind both negative and positive decisions.

Just as important is making sure our teens are realistically gauging the extent to which their peers are making good or bad choices. For example, while 63 percent of middle and high school students say they have used alcohol, 37 percent say they have not. At all. If we can point this out to them, we will be helping them remember that there is a peer group out there that is doing just fine without resorting to alcohol, drugs, sex, or dangerous driving to have fun.

When it comes to discussing such difficult issues with young people, we need to have some idea of who our child *is* to know where to start. In other words, if our child is a non-drinker, our messages may be more reinforcing ("I am proud of you for the good choices you are making about alcohol") than they would be if he were experimenting with alcohol ("I'm concerned about you and want to be sure that you understand the risks and consequences of choosing to drink"). Of course, if who he or she really is differs from our perceptions about them, we can easily get tripped up. Telling a drinker, like Robert from Chapter One, for example, "I am proud of you for the good choices you are making about alcohol," would be ludicrous—and pointless.

In order to best predict, and respond to, behavior, I have found that it is helpful to sort teens by what I call "decision type."

Teen behavior, particularly with respect to alcohol and drug use, breaks down into three identifiable categories, according to the *Teens Today* research I have been conducting since 2000. These categories are pretty self-explanatory.

- **Avoiders:** Teens who avoid involvement with alcohol and other drugs.
- **Experimenters:** Teens who occasionally engage in drinking or other drug use.
- **Repeaters:** Teens who regularly drink alcohol and/or use other drugs.

Of course, the same categories can be useful in characterizing other behaviors as well, such as sex or bullying behavior.

Knowing where a teen falls on this continuum of decision-making is crucial, because this information allows us to plan our communication, prevention, and intervention strategies accordingly. Again, knowing that our teen is not smoking marijuana or sneaking prescription meds out of our bathroom offers a different starting point than knowing that he is. Learning that she has had sex with her boyfriend moves us past the discussion of "When" to "What now?"

But sometimes it can be extremely difficult to know. And if we ask, we may or may not get an honest response. Thus, we need to use all our senses and to be keenly aware of the signs and symptoms that trouble is afoot.

Just as knowing *what* our kids are doing is important, so, too, is knowing *why*. Avoiders, for example, may only be staying away from alcohol and drugs for now, perhaps because of a lack of availability, a current crop of friends who don't drink or use drugs—or maybe, optimistically, because of active, involved parents who talk with them regularly about their expectations for behavior. But all three of those dynamics can change, leaving them prone to becoming Experimenters or even Repeaters. These teens need certain types of reinforcement and support to maintain a healthy lifestyle. Other Avoiders may have made a conscious decision that they will not drink or use drugs "no matter what."

* * *

Zach is a 17-year-old honors student in a parochial school in Chicago. The middle of three children (two boys and a girl), he long ago learned the skills of peacemaker. "Go along to get along" seems to be an important part of his strategy.

Because of his open, communicative relationship with his parents and siblings, he has constructed a set of strongly held principles that help him navigate the twists and turns of adolescent life. By all accounts, Zach is the quintessential "good kid." Good son, good brother, good friend, good student. He works hard, but is easy with others. Zach is an Avoider—having long ago made the decision to live out his high school years without alcohol or drugs. He's comfortable with his choices and does not take issue with his Experimenter and Repeater peers. Zach does what's right for him . . . and what he knows his parents would want.

* * *

Melinda, another 17-year-old, is also an Avoider and chalks up her decision to not drink, take drugs, or engage in sexual activity to her religious beliefs. I have found that this is a common reason kids use to avoid potentially destructive behaviors.

* * *

Sixteen-year-old Connor says he stays away from alcohol and drugs because of his parents and concerns about getting into trouble.

* * *

Fourteen-year-old Tracy, a Texas 8th-grader who lives with her mom, dad, and two sisters, describes herself as an Experimenter. "I'm thinking about smoking weed," she tells me, "and I tend to have a drink once in a while."

* * *

Experimenters present the biggest challenge for parents and other adults. Why? Much as in a political campaign where you secure your base, forget about the far extremes of the party, and focus on those who are still undecided, the big battle in prevention might be thought of as a fight for the hearts and minds of those kids for whom decisions about alcohol, drugs, and sex are fluid and likely to change, depending on the circumstances. Their behavior is difficult to predict and is easily influenced by others. Experimenters need active, communicative, and vigilant adults in their lives who engage fully in their world of decision-making in order to help them steer clear of trouble.

Repeaters, on the other hand, are the most worrisome group of the three. These teens have chosen a lifestyle that is riddled with illegal and potentially destructive behaviors. Too often, these behaviors are brushed aside, treated as a "phase." Parents and other caring adults need to recognize Repeaters for what they are: kids in need of immediate parental intervention, and, in some cases, professional help, such as drug or alcohol counseling.

Whether a teen develops into an Avoider, Experimenter, or Repeater is determined mostly by the expectations, guidance, and involvement of his or her parents. Teens who have close relationships with their parents, who spend time with them, and who talk with them about drinking, drugs, and sex are much more likely to be Avoiders than Repeaters. The flip side is that teens whose parents are uninvolved in their lives and leave them to make up their own minds about behavior are significantly more likely to be Repeaters than Avoiders.

Zach and Melinda are Avoiders. These are kids no one has to really worry about when it comes to sex, drugs, and alcohol.

In a *Teens Today* survey of thousands of teens from across the country:

- Eighteen percent classified themselves as Avoiders.
- Fifty-three percent called themselves Experimenters.
- Twenty-nine percent considered themselves Repeaters.

That means a whole lot of teens out there are still drinking, using drugs, and having early, and often unprotected or unwanted sex. The statistics for each of these behaviors are surprising and discouraging. *Teens Today* data reveals that:

- close to 80 percent of high school students report having consumed alcohol,
- at least one-in-three of 7th- to-12th-graders have used or are using drugs, and
- fifty-three percent of high school students report having had sexual intercourse or having engaged in other sexual activity, including oral sex.

Despite the heartening stories we hear from Avoiders, by almost any definition of the word, we are facing an epidemic of teen drinking, drug use, and sex. Rates of bullying, hazing, sexual assaults, and suicide are equally alarming. And incidences of impaired, distracted, and dangerous driving aren't much better. Our children are engaging in destructive behaviors in staggering numbers, whether it is only to try something once, or to take part in it every month, every weekend, or every day. Despite all our best efforts at education and prevention, drinking, drug use, impaired driving, and early sexual behavior are occurring at significant rates.

This epidemic knows no boundaries of race or socioeconomic class. I hear strikingly similar tales from white kids, black kids, Asian kids . . . wealthy kids, poor kids, and kids from communities as diverse as rural farmlands and urban centers. No teen, no parent, no family is immune to the epidemic, and the physical, psychological, and social problems it causes.

Teens and Drugs

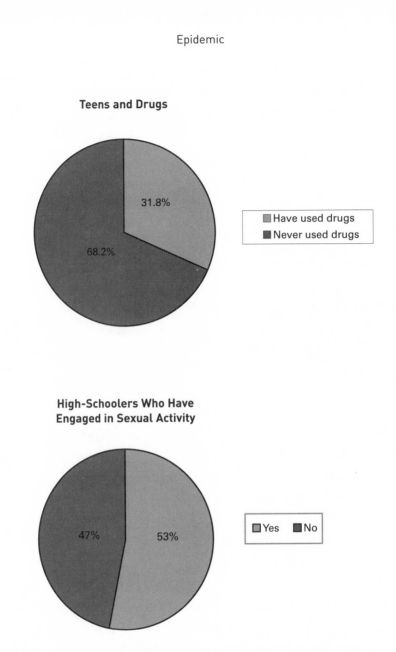

31.8%

68.2%

■ Have used drugs
■ Never used drugs

**High-Schoolers Who Have
Engaged in Sexual Activity**

47%   53%

■ Yes   ■ No

Sadly, many adults fail to recognize the epidemic proportions of these problems, because they have come to view adolescent risk-taking as inevitable, almost like a rite of passage: "They're teenagers, so, of course, they're going to drink, use drugs, have sex, and drive like crazy people!" I hear this all the time. And the offshoot is: "So why should I bother trying to stop it? It's going to happen anyway." Parents may feel similarly help-less to combat teen violence or to cope with teen depression.

If we believe these behaviors are a normal and inevitable—even neces-sary—part of the adolescent experience, we are less likely to pay much attention to them. They become part of the background noise of life—we know it's there, but its familiarity keeps it hidden, almost in plain sight. But even that familiarity can be deceiving. Because as I've said before, things are not what they used to be. Substance use is not confined to alcohol and marijuana . . . or even "harder" drugs like cocaine, Methamphetamine, or heroin. It now frequently takes the form of inhalants (including solvents like paint thinners and office supplies, gases from aerosol cans, and nitrates), over-the-counter and prescription medications, and synthetic drugs such as Ecstasy and GHB. So, if Melinda's parents learn about her marijuana use and assume the problem starts and ends there, they are likely deceiving themselves.

There for the Asking

Most of the teens I talk with say alcohol, drugs, and sex are "everywhere," easily accessible, there for the asking. Their parents imagine something quite different, believing that it is much more difficult for teens to get alcohol or drugs than it really is, or that intimate sexual activity is reserved for "steady" relationships.

On the issue of alcohol, for example, parents significantly underesti-mate how easy it is for their teens to purchase or otherwise get their hands on something to drink. Only half of parents—50 percent—believe it is easy for teens to get alcohol, compared with almost three-quarters—72 percent—of teens who say it is easy. Similarly, only 60 percent of parents believe their teen can easily find an opportunity to drink, while 81 percent of teens say this is the case.

A Massachusetts police officer, talking about the problem of underage drinking, says, "A lot of teens in this community are buying at local liquor stores using fake IDs. They just walk in and it's a fifty-fifty shot." Similarly,

Beliefs About Availability and Opportunities of Drugs and Alcohol to Teens

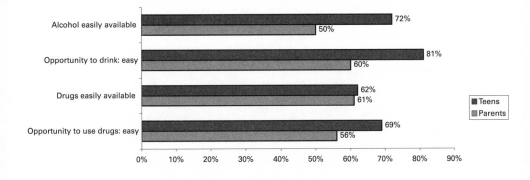

in Arizona, 18-year-old Rafael tells a detective who stopped him for speeding which local supermarkets are most likely to sell beer without carding.

When it comes to access to other drugs, parents correctly estimate their availability (61 percent of parents and 62 percent of teens say it is easy to purchase or obtain drugs), but slightly underestimate the opportunity to use them (65 percent vs. 69 percent, respectively).

According to a study by the National Center on Addiction and Substance Abuse (CASA) at Columbia University, 80 percent of parents believe that neither alcohol nor marijuana is usually available at parties their teens attend. But 50 percent of teen partygoers say they attend parties where alcohol, drugs, or both are available.

After observing or conducting focus groups with middle and high school students across the country between 2000 and 2006, I came to the conclusion that opportunities for sexual behavior, for both boys and girls, are no less plentiful than for drugs and alcohol. One 15-year-old teen shrugs off his access to multiple sex partners by describing a typical Friday afternoon outside of his school: "People just go out and sort of pair-off, go home, and have sex," he says.

It is not enough to hope our kids won't have to face choices about drinking, using drugs, having sex, or riding with an impaired driver. That is wishful thinking through and through, as the boy's story above demonstrates.

Chances are high that they will be confronted with these choices or, in many instances, already have been. Our families are not immune to the epidemic; they are the targets. This is why education and intervention are imperative.

Cognitive Dissonance

Studies that contradict one another confuse parents about how big the problems really are. We are hopeful about our children and their choices, and so we gravitate toward the good news and ignore the bad. In psychological terms, that tendency is due to "cognitive dissonance." Cognitive dissonance refers to a discrepancy between what we believe or want to believe, and evidence that suggests something different, resulting in an unpleasant, even anxious state of mind. If I buy a new car and see an article about its poor ratings for highway performance, for example, I'll probably skip to the sports section! Reading it would cause too much dissonance, or conflicting information, and probably leave me feeling frustrated, or even angry.

A similar process of cognitive dissonance is at work when it comes to our kids. We tend to overlook information that conflicts with our perceptions of their choices or actual decisions. We don't want them to be asked to drink, smoke weed, have oral sex, or get into a car with a driver who has been drinking. And we certainly don't want to believe they might say yes. Similarly, we don't want them to be ridiculed, ostracized, or picked on by other kids—or to act that way toward others. So we pretend none of this could be happening.

When bad news is balanced by good news, too often we receive the good news and discard the rest. I call this the "NIFTY syndrome": "Not In My Family This Year," not unlike the much-hyped "NIMBY ("Not In My Backyard") syndrome," related to everything from power plants to pedophiles.

Truthfully, there's both good news and bad.

While some recent percentage drops have been noted with regard to teen drinking, drug use, sexual behavior, and dangerous driving, other troubling trends have emerged. In many ways, trends in negative behaviors act much like a balloon: Squeeze it smaller here, and it gets bigger over there. Some studies suggest, for example, that rates of underage drinking are going down, while others show an increase in the rate of "binge," or high-risk drinking, among youth. There is also information that suggests "first initiation"—the age at which a young person starts drinking—is earlier than ever before. These days, a significant spike in drinking takes place between the 6th and 7th grades. The average age for first initiation is an alarming 13. And by the 12th grade, more than three-in-four teens are drinking.

When it comes to drug use, the University of Michigan's 2006 *Monitoring the Future* (MTF) study reveals a decline in marijuana and hallucinogen use, but points to a rise in the illegal use of prescription drugs. According to the Office of National Drug Control Policy (ONDCP), Oxycontin, a powerful pain medication, saw an increase in use among 8th-, 10th-, and 12th-graders in 2006, with "past-year use" rising 30 percent, from 3 percent in 2002 to 4 percent in 2006. ONDCP also points out that use of sedatives among high school seniors increased 11 percent from 2001 to 2006 (from 9 percent of students to 10 percent).

Similarly, regarding sexual behavior, while rates of teenage pregnancy have declined steadily since the early 1990s, there's been an explosion of sexually transmitted infections occurring in the United States—approximately 19 million new cases a year, about half of which occur among 15- to 24-year-olds. And according to federal data released in March of 2008, 1 in 4 teens ages 14 to 19 are infected with at least one sexually transmitted disease.

In terms of youth violence, the Centers for Disease Control and Prevention report that in 2003, 5,570 young people ages 10 to 24 were murdered—an average of 15 each day. Of these victims, 82 percent were killed with firearms. In 2004, more than 750,000 young people ages 10 to 24 were treated in emergency departments for injuries sustained due to violence. And, in a 2004 nationwide survey of high school students, 33 percent reported being in a physical fight one or more times in the 12 months preceding the survey, and 17 percent reported carrying a weapon (e.g., gun, knife, or club) on one or more of the 30 days preceding the survey. Finally, they report, an estimated 30 percent of 6th- to 10th-graders in the United States were involved in bullying as a perpetrator, a target, or both.

Here's a clear look at some of the most prevalent destructive behaviors plaguing our kids today, the thorny issues that arise from attempting to squelch them, and some common-sense advice for parents to follow.

Teens and Drinking

No matter how you tally the statistics, alcohol remains a significant health and safety risk to young adults. It is used more frequently, and more heavily, by teens than all other drugs combined! Alcohol remains the "drug of choice" for American adolescents. As a colleague told me recently after observing a focus group of high school boys in a small town in the Southwest, "Forget all that other stuff, these kids are drinking beer . . . and a lot of it." Despite her work in the field of prevention, she came away from that group feeling alarmed. "It's so disturbing," she told me. "Drinking is just so embedded, so deep. And these are really great kids." Some of the boys told her that they view high school as sort of a training ground for college.

"We have to learn how to drink now so that we don't embarrass ourselves when we get to college," offered one.

"It really sucks when you throw up in a girl's mouth," stated another.

It is not all that different from other communities I regularly visit across the country.

According to the Federal Office of Legislative and Policy Analysis, by the time they reach the 8th grade, nearly 50 percent of U.S. adolescents have had at least one alcoholic drink, and more than 20 percent report having been "drunk." Approximately 20 percent of 8th-graders and almost 50 percent of 12th-graders report having consumed alcohol within the past 30 days. Among 12th-graders, almost 30 percent report drinking on three or more occasions per month. Approximately 30 percent of 12th-graders report having engaged in heavy-episodic drinking, or "binge" drinking— that is, having at least five or more drinks on one occasion— once within a two-week period. It is estimated that 20 percent do so more frequently.

Despite its prevalence, the whole issue of underage drinking has long taken a backseat to anti-drug efforts because of a number of serious, and interlocking, social, economic, and political pressures, and, likely, a common perspective that it's not that big of a deal. But that may be changing.

The STOP Campaign

Legislation signed into law by President George W. Bush on December 20, 2006, marked the first step toward a concerted national response to the problem of underage drinking. The Sober Truth on Preventing (STOP) Underage Drinking Act, passed in the final hours of the 109th Congress and nearly three years after its introduction, allocates $18 million toward solving this problem, including funding for some of the policies and programs recommended in the National Academies' September 2003 report to Congress ("Reducing Underage Drinking: A Collective Responsibility"). This is an important step and one that SADD worked hard to make happen.

In fact, hundreds of SADD students from across the country met with their Congressmen and women in Washington, D.C., to add youth voices to the debate and to push for the bill's passage.

George Hacker, director of the alcohol policies project at the Center for Science in the Public Interest (CSPI), a strong supporter of the bill, said, "Passage of the STOP Act represents a long-overdue acknowledgment of the need to do more as a nation to address the harm caused by underage drinking. Unlike illicit drugs, there has been no credible national plan to combat alcohol problems, the greater health and safety drag on our nation. That is a huge gap that must be filled, and the STOP Act is a step in the right direction."

The bill includes money for annual media campaigns about underage drinking, grants for communities and colleges to aid prevention efforts, and research to better understand and evaluate the problem.

Other officials are stepping up as well. In March of 2007, the office of the U.S. Surgeon General issued its first "Call to Action" to try to stop

America's 11 million underage drinkers from consuming alcohol and to prevent other young people from starting to drink in the first place. At the time, acting Surgeon General Kenneth Moritsugu laid out recommendations for government and school officials, parents, other adults, and young people, saying, "Too many Americans consider underage drinking a rite of passage to adulthood. Research shows that young people who start drinking before the age of 15 are five times more likely to have alcohol-related problems later in life. New research also indicates that alcohol may harm the developing adolescent brain. The availability of this research provides more reasons than ever before for parents and other adults to protect the health and safety of our nation's children."

In concert with the National Institute on Alcohol Abuse and Alcoholism (NIAAA) and the Substance Abuse and Mental Health Services Administration (SAMHSA), Dr. Moritsugu identified six goals in combating teenage drinking, including fostering changes in society that facilitate healthy adolescent development by engaging parents, schools, communities, all levels of government, and all social systems, as well as youth themselves, in a coordinated effort to prevent and reduce underage drinking and its consequences. This is the "it takes a village" approach, and I cannot state strongly enough that everyone needs to work together on addressing this critical issue.

Rare is the teen these days whose life is not in some way impacted by alcohol. Even if they themselves avoid it, they inevitably have to deal with friends or parents who don't. These teens also have to make difficult decisions regarding their social lives, because having them usually means accommodating the destructive choices of others.

Trey, 15, says, "Last Saturday night I was the only kid in the dorm that wasn't drinking or drunk. I hate it." Other teens face challenges about getting into cars with driv-

> Sixteen percent of 6th-graders report drinking, and more than 8-in-10 (82 percent) 12th-graders do. Seventeen-year-old Jack, commenting on his school's homecoming dance, where nearly 200 students, some as young as 14, showed up drunk, tells me, "It's pretty simple, kids drink."

ers who have been drinking or using drugs. One Massachusetts teen says, "I would not get into a car with someone who's completely wasted. [But] if they had a couple of drinks, I might get into the car." Still other teens wrestle with even attending parties where kids might be engaging in dangerous, illegal behavior. Despite these prevalent and persistent problems, we, as a society, are still not speaking with one voice about the issue of underage drinking, almost as if we can't really make up our minds as to whether it's acceptable or not.

Boston Globe reporter Peter Schworm interviewed me for a March 2007 story he was writing about local teens suspended from extracurricular activities, including sporting events, for attending a party where alcohol was being consumed by underage youth—a violation of the school's disciplinary policy. The parents of one of the students successfully prevailed upon a judge to issue an injunction against the school, thus permitting her to compete in a track meet. Schworm reported that in her ruling, the judge was differentiating between "active" and "constructive" possession of alcohol, the former applying to teens seen either drinking or holding an alcoholic beverage and the latter applying to those merely present where alcohol is being served.

But increasingly, school administrators and police officers see things a different way, maintaining that even being in the company of friends who are drinking constitutes possession. I said to Schworm that, in my opinion, every community needs to decide for itself what rules make sense for their schools and what steps are necessary to keep their kids safe. There is no single approach that is failsafe. However, once those decisions have been made and the rules are in place, everyone needs to be informed of them . . . and then they need to be enforced!

The disparity of opinions among adults leaves teens in a bind, once again receiving mixed messages about what is appropriate and inappropriate behavior. It also forces them, in many instances, to choose between being able to socialize with their friends and the less-appealing option of staying home, even though they themselves may choose not to drink.

What You Can Do

Working together, parents and teens can plan and execute substance-free activities and events, providing meaningful and fun social outlets for young people to get together, enjoy their friends, and have a good time, without placing themselves at risk. SADD's 2006–2007 National Student of the Year, Daniel Vocelle, and I conducted a national television media tour in the spring of 2007 to promote an innovative fund-raising program offered by Boston Market to fund such initiatives. *Time for Your School* makes available up to 40 percent of a day's sales at a local Boston Market restaurant to be used for supervised, substance-free parties for teens after proms, graduations, or at other times of year. This type of initiative is notable in that it reflects an understanding that adults need to do more to help kids do what we are asking of them: "Stay away from alcohol and drugs." Teens can help, too, and SADD offers a 52-page Event Planner that has all the tools to help you and your teen make your party a huge success, including suggestions for fun themes, such as "Around the World," "Late Night at Your High School" (stupid human tricks and all), and "Clue: An Old Fashioned Whodunit." As Daniel told one of the interviewers, "A lot of kids just want to have a place to go to be with their friends and have a good time. They don't want to have to make decisions about whether to drink or not." My experience tells me the same thing.

Teens and Drugs

Overall, more than one-third (35 percent) of teens say they use drugs. And, as with drinking, drug use tends to rise as teens get older. For example, only 3 percent of 6th-graders report drug use as compared to almost half (46 percent) of 12th-graders. That having been said, the average age at which teens begin using drugs, like drinking, is the same staggering 13.

More so than with alcohol use—which is *truly* epidemic—there appears to be almost a personality or dependence split between those who use drugs and those who don't. As 18-year-old Matt puts it, "I hate

Drug Use by Teens

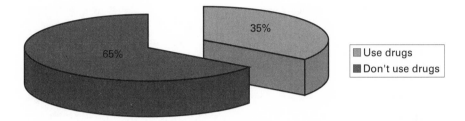

high kids. They are annoying, lazy, worthless lumps on a log. There are a lot of kids who smoke in our school; it sucks. The people who drink can have a fun time without alcohol. But the people who smoke, can't. I don't know why, but that is my experience. Potheads are always looking for someplace and someone to smoke up with. I really don't have any tolerance for it, because usually high kids are high all the time and that sucks because you can't talk to someone who is high all the time. I feel bad for most of them, because they really don't think they are doing any damage to themselves." Indeed, a group of nearby high school boys say that the majority of kids are smoking weed, "Once you do it once, you want to do it every day." Who says it's not addictive!

While most teens admitting to drug use cite smoking marijuana, there has been an alarming rise in the use of other drugs, including opiates, which are popular painkillers. The Drug Abuse Warning Network (DAWN), which monitors the medications and illegal drugs reported by emergency departments across the nation, found that opiate pain relievers are some of the most frequently reported prescription medications in drug-abuse-related cases. Since 1988, the number of deaths among young people ages 15 to 24 using opiates has tripled. Eleven percent of teens report using prescription drugs to get high!

On Friday night, April 10, 2004, in the Boston neighborhood of Charlestown, a 17-year-old high school student walked his girlfriend to her door, walked himself home . . . and died. His mother found him in his bed the next morning when she went to wake him up. A combination of the opiate painkiller Oxycontin and the sedative Klonopin ended the life of this hockey star and left his girlfriend, a sophomore who had also consumed both drugs, clinging to life in the hospital. This is a tragic story, but not a rare one. *The Boston Herald*, citing police statistics, reported that in the preceding year, 41 drug overdoses, 11 of them among people under the age of 25, were recorded in this community, encompassing one square mile, home to the U.S. Constitution and the Bunker Hill Monument.

In increasing numbers, young people are turning to prescription drugs—smoked, snorted, chewed—to get high. They call it "pharming." In many instances, prescription drugs are easier to get, readily available in a parent's medicine cabinet, or from an illegal online pharmacy, and are perceived by young people to be "safer" because, after all, a physician has doled them out. But they certainly are *not* safe when used without a doctor's consent and for the express, intentional purpose of getting high. In December, 2007, I was invited to the White House for an event during which the president highlighted a "Monitoring the Future" study showing gains in reducing youth drug use (860,000 fewer young people using illegal drugs today than there were in 2001), but warned about escalating and illegal use of prescription drugs, particularly painkillers, by teens.

As the Office of National Drug Control Policy (ONDCP) points out, when teens intentionally abuse these drugs to get high, it's not just with a prescription dose of two pills, or an extra swig of cough syrup. In some cases, teens are ingesting anywhere from a few pills to dozens or more a day, or drinking up to five bottles of cough syrup, or mixing either pills or cough syrup with alcohol.

And some of these prescription drugs aren't even meant for humans. Just a couple of days after the fatal overdose in Charlestown, the *Boston Globe* reported the overdose of two rural teens who had ingested a veterinary medication intended to sedate horses.

Of course, marijuana and prescription medications are just some of the drugs plaguing young Americans. Heroin and cocaine are taking their toll as well, with 1-in-10 teens indicating they have used these types of drugs. Also alarming is the use of so-called "club" drugs used at clubs, bars, or all-night parties, such as Ecstasy, GHB, Rohypnol, Ketamine, Methamphetamine, and LSD. Some of these drugs, like Ecstasy, are promoted as aphrodisiacs, making people more affectionate, trusting, and open. Used in combination with alcohol, which they often are, these drugs can be even more dangerous because of the cumulative effects. Their colorless, tasteless, and odorless nature has also led to their use as "date-rape" drugs, placed in the drink of an unsuspecting victim to render him or her defenseless against sexual assault.

What You Can Do

The sheer number and type of drugs readily available to young people are staggering and overwhelming. There are just so many ways for kids to get high that it's hard to imagine any ways to stop them. Yet, there are some strategies that can be effective.

First, educate yourself about drugs—what they look like, what their risks are, and how they work.

Learn about the effects and how kids on drugs might look and act. Second, talk with your teen. Get to know his perspective on drug use, her perceptions of the risks, and the degree to which the kids he hangs out with use drugs. Third, don't be afraid to take action if you believe your child is at risk. I've spoken to way too

The Office of National Drug Control Policy has a lot of great information accessible on their parent Web site, www.theantidrug.com.

many parents who wished they'd acted sooner, perhaps by seeking professional help.

Teens and Sex

Drugs and alcohol aren't the only teen issues about which parents don't have a clue. Seventeen-year-old Ben from the Pacific Northwest muses about the copy of the sex book his mother gave him for graduation, saying she feared that the "abstinence-only education" offered at school may have left him with the wrong impression about having sex. She didn't want him to miss out on one of life's great pleasures. What she didn't know was that Ben had been sexually active since age 14 and began having intercourse starting at age 15. Apparently, no conversation, with her or Ben's father, edged close enough to the subject to prompt his disclosure, although Ben did marvel at the fact that he and his girlfriend were often upstairs together, alone in his room with the door closed. "I don't know what they *thought* we were doing," he says.

Fifteen-year-old Trey is sexually active as well, but now wishes he had waited. He says he started having oral sex with girls just because, "I thought everyone else was doing it." He would have benefited from a candid reminder from his mom or dad that not everyone was (almost 40 percent aren't)! And, as we saw earlier, Stephanie made a decision about intercourse she later regretted.

Choices about sexual behavior have an important impact on the health and well-being of teens, and our kids are making them earlier than ever before. *Teens Today* reveals that sexual activity is reported by one-quarter of middle school students and almost two-thirds of high school students. A majority of teens ages 15 to 17 report having engaged in sexual activity other than kissing (60.9 percent), including more than half who report having had intercourse (52.1 percent).

Why is this of concern? After all, if kids are using condoms during intercourse to protect themselves, where's the harm? The younger a girl is when she has sex for the first time, the more likely she is to have had

Teens 15 to 17 Engaged in Sexual Activity

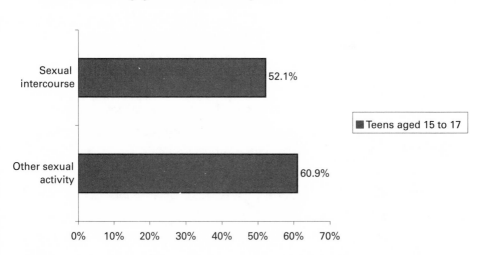

unwanted or forced sex—almost 4 in 10 girls who had first intercourse at 13 or 14 have experienced one or the other. Older girls, like 15-year-old Stephanie, can feel the same way. We also know that the earlier a teen (or child) has sex, the more partners they tend to have and thus the more likely it is they will contract a sexually transmitted infection or disease (STI or STD)—the number of cases of which continues to rise dramatically worldwide.

In this country, about eight million of the 12 million annual diagnoses of STIs are among young people under the age of 25. (Condoms do not necessarily prevent against these, or pregnancies.) According to the National Campaign Against Teen Pregnancy, nearly 4 in 10 young women become pregnant at least once before they reach the age of 20—nearly one million a year—and 8 out of 10 of these pregnancies are unintended. Yet, according to *Teens Today*, only about one-of-six sexually active teens feels strongly that young people who have sex are likely to develop STDs (16.1 percent). This statistic alone points out how important it is that we redouble our efforts to educate young people about the real consequences of certain behaviors. That's why SADD points out the facts to teens: Teen pregnancy affects the mother, the father, the baby, and the families of the teen parents; teen mothers are less likely to complete high school (only one-third receive a high school diploma) and more likely to end up on welfare; the children of teenage mothers have lower birth weights, are more likely to perform poorly in school, and are at greater risk for abuse and neglect; and that a sexually active teenager who does not use contraception has a 90 percent chance of becoming pregnant or causing pregnancy within one year.

Perhaps just as alarming is the apparent connection between early sexual activity and feelings of inadequacy, stress, and depression. According to *Teens Today*:

More than one-third of sexually active 15- to 17-year-olds say having sex often leads to depression (30.7 percent) and loss of self-respect (38.8 percent).

Almost one-third of sexually active 15- to 17-year-olds says that the decisions they make about sex cause them to feel stressed (29.7 percent).

Also concerning is a report by the Heritage Foundation that links teen sexual intercourse with suicide:

- Of girls, 14.3 percent of those who have had sex have attempted suicide, compared with 5.1 percent of virgins.
- For boys, 6 percent of those who have had sex have attempted suicide, compared with seven-tenths of one percent who were virgins.

Of course, with survey research, there is always the "chicken and the egg" question. Which came first? In this case, is the sex causing the depression or is the depression inciting the sex? It's hard to know—but SADD believes it is important to give kids as much information as possible so that they and their families can make informed decisions about what is best for them.

There are also a host of potential long-term social-emotional consequences of early, intimate behavior. In large part, this may be because even though sexual behavior among adolescents is not new, what is surprising is the casualness and frequency with which such "hooking-up" takes place.

Teens 15 to 17: Emotional Effects of Sex

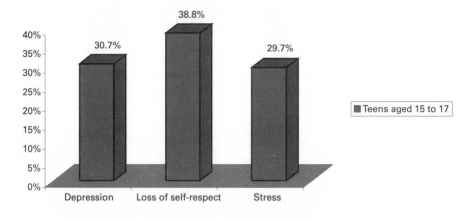

People often ask me what I see as the biggest change in teen behavior over the past 10 or 20 years. The answer is easy: Sex, or "sexual behavior" (since most teens now reserve the term "sex" for just intercourse). Earlier and earlier, teens, even pre-teens, are talking about and engaging in all kinds of sex. A 34-year-old colleague of mine at camp who teaches at a New England boarding school says, "My 9th-graders are all having sex. When I was in 9th grade, it was like, 'Sex? Nah . . . let's talk about base-ball.'" And most any middle school student can fill you in on "who's doing what with whom." Boys are quick to ask for oral sex, and girls aren't as inclined to say "no" as you might think. Hang around a handful of 7th-graders long enough, and you're likely to hear speculation about who's getting it and who's not. Even reports of middle school sex parties have become commonplace.

This change from relationship-based (relational) sex to just hooking-up (recreational sex) has many experts in the fields of psychology wondering if some young people are jeopardizing their ability to form significant emotional attachments and healthy adult relationships in the future.

In *Unhooked, How Young Women Pursue Sex, Delay Love, and Lose at Both*, author Laura Sessions Strepp speaks to those concerns, saying, "The need to be connected intimately to others is as central to our well-being as food and shelter. I hope to encourage girls to think hard about whether they're 'getting it right,' whether their sexual and romantic experiences are contributing to—or destroying—their Sense of Self-Worth and strength. Their studied effort to remain uncommitted convinces me only of how strongly they want to be attached."

But it's not only girls who may be giving up important pieces of themselves with a casual, careless approach to intimate sexual behavior. Boys, too, require intimacy and for all the bravado about just wanting to "get laid," many find little lasting value in cheap and easy hook-ups. When 18-year-old Danny found intimacy in intercourse with a long-time girlfriend, he questioned the significance of his earlier oral-sex escapades with a variety of girls he didn't even know. "This is so much more meaningful," he said. Similarly, 17-year-old Alex says he stopped going to parties and hooking-up for oral sex (something he says his single mom knew nothing about, but would be very upset to hear) once he was in a committed relationship. He now expresses some skepticism about his previous choices.

Exploring the phenomenon of recreational sex, I asked a group of North Carolina middle school boys to expound on the subject of "sex bracelets" worn by some girls at school. They told me that the plastic or rubber bracelets vary in color according to which sex acts the wearer is prepared to perform if a boy breaks the bracelet. Though a bit inconsistent on which color meant what, the boys were unanimous, and enthusiastic, about the popularity of this particular form of sexual marketing.

"Black means a blow job," offered 12-year-old Brandon, a 7th-grader. Adam, a 12-year-old 6th-grader, added, "Another [color] means you eat a girl out and do sixty-nine."

In her book *Nothin' Much, Just Chillin,'* journalist Linda Perlstein posits that, while middle school teens are quick to talk about sexual behavior, they are somewhat more reluctant to actually get involved with it. Still, while older teens are more likely to report being sexually active than are younger teens, nearly one-quarter (24 percent) of 6th-graders report some type of sexual activity other than kissing (compared with 73 percent of 11th-graders and 78 percent of 12th-graders). Says Hannah, a 12-year-old 6th-grader, "I know a lot of kids who are pregnant because they have had sex." In 2000, there were 75 pregnancies per 1000 females ages 15 to 19. And while that rate of pregnancy is significantly less than it had been a decade earlier (117 pregnancies per 1000 females in 1990), the United States has the highest rates of teen pregnancy and births in the Western industrialized world.

For parents to believe that young teens are not sexually aware and are not talking about sexuality and sex with their friends is to miss important opportunities to help them learn about sexuality and sexual behavior. This leaves them at risk of not having the information they need to fully understand their own feelings about their emerging sexuality or about engaging in intimate sexual behavior.

Fifteen-year-old Kenny tells me about his first genital sex experience the year before: "We were hanging out in my room, you know, just kissing. Then she unzipped my pants and just started rubbing it—I didn't even know what she was doing!" Kenny returned the favor, even though that was more mystifying: "She did it to me, so I figured I should do it to her. I had no idea how."

For sure, kids like Trey and Stephanie (and maybe Kenny) became sexually active before they really wanted to, risking infection or pregnancy because of unfamiliarity with protection. Also, silence from parents does nothing to help kids understand family expectations or to establish their own values around this important part of human development.

The onset of puberty brings with it a heightened awareness of sexual feelings and increased likelihood of sexual contact, even in early grades. In our society, sex, in all its forms, is hard to escape, even for very young people. They are bombarded with messages and information about sex from an early age. Adults must be proactive in discussing sex and sexuality with teens. We can serve as an important filter through which information flows, and an important resource for children as they absorb and seek to understand what they see and hear so much about—even if they don't always make the choices we wish they did. Sixteen-year-old Brenda had been cautioned by her mom about having sex too young, but decided on intercourse with her high school boyfriend, a senior, anyway. "He wanted to, so I wanted to," she tells me. "I wanted to make our relationship closer."

Fourteen-year-old Steve, casually clad in blue jeans, a white T-shirt, and sneakers, talks about the pressure he feels when it comes to sex. "It's the guys in the locker room," he says. "They're like, 'What are you thinking? Why didn't you do this? You should have done that.' It's like you're gay if you didn't hook-up." Steve rates becoming sexually active his number-one source of stress, but he is lucky enough to have parents who talk with him candidly about both the issue and their expectations for his behavior. He says his parents are influential in his thinking about sex, although he points out that it "all boils down to what I think, since they won't be there." Even so, he listens to what they have to say. "They want me to be in a relationship if I decide to have sex," offers Steve. "They don't want me to do it with some random person." And he thinks they are right: "For oral sex or intercourse, I would have to be going out with the person," he says. A year and a half later, Steve is sticking to his guns—he's engaging in mutual genital touching ("You've heard of friends with benefits, right?" he asks me) with a classmate, but nothing more.

Teens and Driving

Parents certainly do not know the whole story about teen driving, either. Teens report drinking and driving, drugging and driving, and driving without seat belts, in numbers that would surprise most adults . . . and maybe even some teens themselves.

There is an interesting disconnect between teens' self-perceptions as drivers and what they are actually doing on the road. Nearly 9 out of 10 teens (89 percent) describe themselves as safe drivers. Yet, many engage in risky behaviors, such as speeding and talking on a cell phone,

Teens' Perceptions of Driving Behaviors

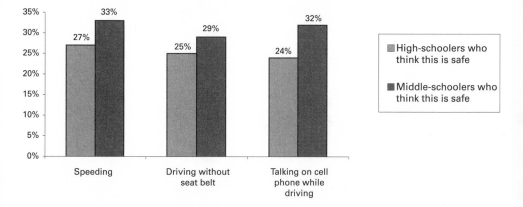

that often lead to crashes. Others neglect to use safety belts, which greatly increases the likelihood of injury or death in the event of a car crash.

You may be asking, Why? The fact is that many teens just don't view these behaviors as dangerous. Consider this:

- Twenty-seven percent of all high school students and 33 percent of middle school students think speeding is safe.
- Twenty-five percent of all high school students and 29 percent of middle school students say driving without a safety belt is safe.
- Twenty-four percent of high school students and 32 percent of middle school students say talking on a cell phone while driving is safe.

Interestingly, high school and middle school students overwhelmingly say their parents are, or will be, the biggest influence on how they drive (almost 60 percent and 69 percent, respectively). That's the good news. The bad news is that they also say many of their unsafe driving behaviors mimic what they see their parents doing! For example, almost two-thirds (62 percent) of high school teens say their parents talk on a cell phone while driving; almost half—48 percent—say their parents speed; and 31 percent say their parents don't wear a safety belt.

Biggest Influence on Teen Driving

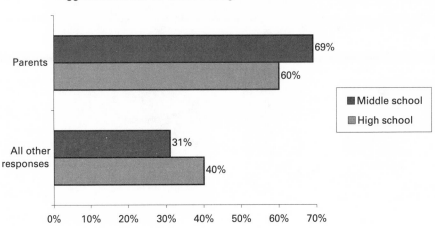

Perhaps, then, it is no surprise that teens say they behave the same way, in roughly the same percentages. Case in point: Sixty-two percent of high school drivers say they talk on a cell phone while driving, and approximately half of high school teens who do not yet drive (52 percent) and middle school students who do not yet drive (47 percent) expect they will engage in this behavior when they begin driving; also, 67 percent of high school drivers say they speed; and 33 percent of high school drivers say they do not wear their safety belt while driving.

Seventeen-year-old Johnny says, "The majority of the people at my school drive dangerously; they speed, and they speed dangerously. I'm not talking 5-to-10 miles an hour over. I'm talking about 30-plus. Combine that with the handful of kids who drive after drinking, well, you've got a dangerous combination there. Honestly, though, I think the parents have a big part in their kids driving dangerously, more so than people think. Brand-new Audis, BMWs, and Mercedes are seen in every row of the parking lot [at school]. One girl in my grade totaled (yes, totaled) two Mercedes during *test drives*, and her dad bought her a third one! Even my best friend has a problem driving fast. He's a nice, responsible kid, but he can't help but speed. When his dad bought a brand-new

Prevalence of Driving Behaviors

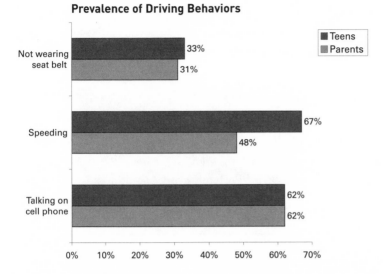

BMW, they offered him a Z4 at a dirt-cheap price (about half-off), so he took it and gave it to his son. Now, let me ask you this—what teenager is going to have a Z4 and *not* speed? He doesn't even drive that dangerously compared to my classmates—he'll go 10 mph over the speed limit, but that's about it. However, he's already crashed two cars this winter—he bashed the front end of the Z4 by running into a ditch after slipping on black ice. Not two weeks later did he crash another car (again on ice). When I tell him to slow down, he says he's fine, he's not going that fast, etc., etc. He says it wasn't his fault that he crashed two cars because he was going the speed limit."

Astonishingly, teens say that their parents are often in the car when they are driving dangerously! For example, teens speed (almost 50 percent of the time), talk on their cell phones (about 20 percent of the time), and eat or drink while driving (almost 20 percent of the time), even though a parent is present. Clearly, some parents are not exercising appropriate influence over their teen

The National Highway Traffic Safety Administration (NHTSA) reports that, on average, more than 300,000 teens are injured in car crashes each year, nearly 8,000 are involved in fatal crashes, and more than 3,500 are killed.

drivers, even though their influence can be quite profound, both in setting a good example for driving behaviors and in setting rules and enforcing consequences when teens aren't safe behind the wheel.

Few things are as anxiety-producing for parents as when their teen heads out the driveway in a car. They know all too well the potential outcomes of a split-second distraction, such as changing the radio station or answering the cell phone. And they fear that he does not. *How do I know he's driving safely? And, even if he is, what about the other drivers' on the road—is he watching out for them?* Probably every parent dreads "the phone call"—*Mrs. Smith, this is Sergeant Jones. There has been an accident . . .*

What You Can Do

These numbers highlight how important it is that parents set the example they wish their children to follow, minimize teens' temptations to drive dangerously by resisting the inclination to provide cars that are designed for speed, and enforce their own rules when riding with their child. Parents should not be afraid to establish expectations for their young drivers, discuss those expectations frequently, and ensure they are being met. Teens who have regular communication with their parents about expected behaviors are less likely to make destructive decisions, including ones related to driving.

Setting expectations and following through on consequences may very well help prevent teens from getting into car crashes, which are the leading cause of death for American teens—more than drugs, guns, or any disease combined.

Family rules about driving might include
- no driving after 10:00 p.m.
- no use of alcohol or other drugs
- no eating, changing CDs, handling iPods, or putting on makeup
- no cell phone use or text-messaging

Impaired Driving

Susannah, a high school senior from the Midwest, recalls a tragic event that took place just two years earlier but will likely resonate with her forever.

"The fall of my sophomore year," she says, "I had three friends, one very close friend and neighbor, get killed in a car accident. They had all been drinking and ran a stop sign. A truck t-boned their car, killing all three instantly. My closest friend Dan was in the backseat. He wasn't wearing his seat belt and was thrown around the inside of the car. Losing those three hit me really hard. When you are 16, you don't think about losing your friends to such a little thing as running a stop sign. You don't think that a few drinks will hurt."

Sadly, Susannah's story is all too common. Recent data reveal that one-in-five teen drivers drives under the influence of alcohol. And 40 percent of teens admit to riding in another teen's car while drinking and driving is taking place. The results of this slice of the reality gap are demonstrable. For the

> Automobile crashes remain the leading cause of death among young people, and a significant portion—about 28 percent—of them are alcohol-related.

first time in almost two decades, the number of teen deaths in alcohol-related car crashes is on the rise. Perhaps it's not surprising that a group of teens in suburban Minneapolis estimated that 1 out of every 10 kids who get drunk at parties drives himself home.

Even though teens are actually less likely than are adults to drive after drinking, their fatality rates are dramatically higher. This is especially the case with low and moderate blood-alcohol levels and probably has to do with teens' relative inexperience with driving.

Replacing the public discourse on drinking and driving with other, even less important issues has clearly had an impact on the frequency and content of messages delivered to young people about its risks. The fact that the issue remains important to youth, more so than to their parents, suggests that the kids have it right . . . and are just waiting for help from the bench.

Teens rank drinking and driving as their number two concern (right after HIV/AIDS and sexually transmitted diseases), likely because they are driving impaired, know someone who is driving impaired, or have been a passenger of someone driving impaired. They often go along because of peer pressure and a fear of being ostracized.

Some kids, like 18-year-old Connecticut senior Cody, have volunteered their time to "safe-rides" programs, in an effort to curb deaths and injuries among their classmates who find themselves in a situation where they are unable to safely navigate their way home.

Sadly, and despite the best of intentions, such a spirit of volunteerism only fuels the problem. It enables bad choices by putting undue burden on those who actually obey the law and live up to the expectations of their parents and other caring adults who discourage underage drinking and other drug use. Cody tells me, "At first, I thought that it would serve a good purpose. It works in theory, but not in practice. I thought that I would be helping the community by keeping drunks from driving home after a party, but what I found was that it is just a taxi service, driving people from one party to the next. It is a reason to drink—it removes the consequences. 'Don't worry, it's cool. I'll just call Safe Rides.'"

Disabusing ourselves of the notion that this problem has been solved once and for all will go a long way in reminding us to put it back on the table for regular discussion with our teen. And establishing clear ground rules (no drinking or drug use, no riding in a car with someone who has

Effects of Setting Consequences for Teens' Driving Behavior

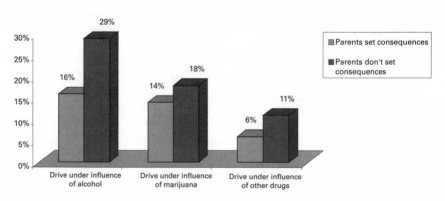

Follow Through on Consequences:
Teens Who Have Never Driven Under Influence of Alcohol or Marijuana

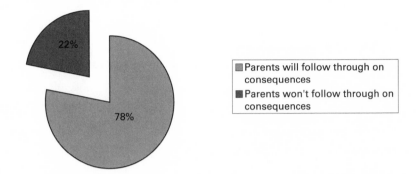

Follow Through on Consequences:
Teens Who Have Driven Under Influence of Alcohol or Marijuana

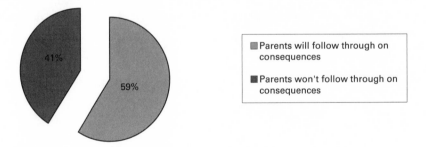

been drinking or using drugs) will go a long way in reminding our kids what choices we expect them to make.

Teens say parents who set expectations with clear consequences for them about breaking the law while driving are less likely to have driven under the influence of alcohol (16 percent vs. 29 percent), marijuana (14 percent vs. 18 percent), or other drugs (6 percent vs. 11 percent) than are teens whose parents do not set any consequences.

And teens who have never driven under the influence of any illegal substance are a third more likely to say their parents will follow through with consequences than are teens who have driven under the influence of either alcohol or marijuana (78 percent vs. 59 percent).

According to ONDCP, while many teens know full well the dangers of drinking and driving, many are unaware that marijuana also impairs driving. More than half of the teens who drove after using marijuana claimed that it did not affect their ability to drive safely, mirroring a prevalent view among youth that drugging and driving is a safe alternative to drinking and driving.

Nearly One-in-Eight Teens Is Driving Under the Influence of Marijuana
As 18-year-old Robert says, "There's definitely a misconception that you can still drive under the influence of pot." Another teen says, "People smoke weed and drive. They think less about it than they do with alcohol, because they think they can control it. Also, the message, 'don't smoke and drive' hasn't been out there." Perhaps, but it's starting to resonate.

In December of 2004, I joined U.S. drug czar John Walters and Secretary of Transportation Norman Mineta at a press conference in Washington, D.C., to announce a renewed effort to educate parents and teens about the risks of combining marijuana and driving. Walters said in a statement, "Unfortunately, many young drivers don't yet understand the risks associated with marijuana and driving. Marijuana impairs driving and leads to risky decisions. Parents of new drivers can use the milestone of earning a driver's license to discuss the dangers of marijuana and being responsible behind the wheel."

More recently, in December of 2007, deputy drug czar Scott Burns and I conducted a national satellite television and radio tour highlighting research showing that 13 percent of high school seniors reported driving while high on marijuana. That's nearly equivalent to those who reported driving drunk (14 percent), even though far more teens report using alcohol (17 percent) than marijuana (7 percent) in the last 30 days.

Why are so few people talking about this? As mentioned in the previous chapter, a majority of parents are unaware of the degree to which their teens have access to drugs. Also, many parents who are aware seem unconcerned, perhaps underestimating the potency of today's weed (estimated to be 10 to 20 times stronger than the marijuana of yesteryear) or the possible consequences of its use.

Nevertheless, the majority of licensed teen drivers who use drugs regularly also drug and drive (68 percent), and this tendency is more prevalent than driving after drinking (47 percent of those who drink regularly). More than one-third of teens who are using drugs regularly are not concerned about riding in a car with a driver who is using drugs (38 percent).

What You Can Do

To reverse this gruesome trend, it is important for parents to hold to a zero-tolerance rule for young people. According to *Teens Today*, greater parent involvement, clear rules, and parental supervision are associated with less-risky behavior, such as marijuana use and driving while high or under the influence of alcohol. After all, if teens aren't drinking or taking drugs in the first place, alcohol- and drug-related car crashes won't be an issue.

But some of us may be so focused on the dangers associated with impaired driving we forget the important first step regarding drinking and drug use and either overtly or covertly send the message, "If you are going to drink, at least don't drive." That is a powerful loophole for young people inclined to look for a chink in the armor—a signal, no matter how subtle, that some alcohol use, for example, is acceptable.

In the spring of 2007, a reporter interviewed me for a story about a decision by administrators at Lexington (Massachusetts) High School to ban students from traveling to and from prom in cars and limos, instead requiring that all attendees be transported home by bus from the school parking lot. He summarized some parent objections this way: "They're going to be drinking beforehand, so how are they going to get to the school without driving?" I responded, "Aha . . . well now we are getting down to the real issue." It's not buses or limos, or really even impaired driving that should be our primary focus. It's the fact that parents know about, perhaps expect, and even condone drinking before prom, and have purposefully or unwittingly put their seal of approval on it.

"It took two lives," said the sad woman standing before me in the lobby outside of a school auditorium where I had just completed another presentation. "My best friend's son was killed by a drunk driver. And the driver later committed suicide at age 21." The enormity of this tragedy, like so many others I hear about on the road, only underscores the urgent need to better educate our children about impaired driving.

Bullying

Believe it or not, bullying is a significant problem affecting children and teens—and it takes place in many forms and in many places. Young people are often reluctant to talk about the bullying they see for fear of being labeled "snitches." They may be even more reluctant to report being bullied themselves because they feel weak or ashamed. This makes it all the more important that bullying be a subject we include on our checklist of things to talk about with our kids.

According to the American Medical Association, bullying occurs when one child repeatedly picks on another child who is weaker, smaller, and more vulnerable. Girls as well as boys can be bullies. The bully picks on other children by teasing, threatening, or attacking them. Bullies can also exclude their victims from activities or start rumors about them. Bullies often pick on children who make them feel powerful by reacting emotionally or giving in to their demands.

Thirteen-year-old Jasmine, a 7th-grader, says she sees a lot of bullying.

"It's not necessarily physical. Sometimes they just tell someone they're ugly. When I see that, I feel bad for the person. It hurts me that some people have to deal with that. Bullies should be put in that position so that they can see what it feels like."

Matthew, a 15-year-old 9th-grader, fidgets nervously as he describes to me his place in the social strata at school. Wiry and seemingly uncomfortable in his own body, Matthew's gray pants, dragon-buckle belt, and gray sport shirt buttoned all the way up to his neck make him look out of step with his peers. He says he's different from the other kids, and as a result, gets bullied a lot—made fun of, pushed, and laughed at. High school has been a tough experience thus far and he doesn't like it. But he feels he has little wherewithal to fight back. As we will see in a moment, he's wrong. Matthew and others like him have the ability to protect themselves and their friends. They just need some help in figuring out what to do and to whom they can turn for help.

Unfortunately, bullying is a dangerous staple of many adolescent environments.

A study by the Kaiser Family Foundation and Nickelodeon found that 74 percent of 8- to 11-year-olds and 86 percent of 12- to 15-year-olds say teasing and bullying occur at their school, and most characterize those behaviors as "big problems."

Another study by the Families and Work Institute reported that two-thirds of young people have been teased or gossiped about in a mean way at least once in the past month, and almost half of young people have been hit, shoved, kicked, or tripped.

In *Raising Cain: Protecting the Emotional Life of Boys*, psychologists Dan Kindlon and Michael Thompson note that boys, as a group, are more aggressive (and violent) than girls, representing what they call a "culture of cruelty." For boys, they assert, aggression is often more defensive than offensive. In other words, boys may see the world as a more threatening place than girls do and respond by being aggressive in order to protect themselves. Kindlon and Thompson say, "Despite collegial appearances, all boys live with fear in this culture of cruelty. They also adhere to its code, and are loyal to its tenets, even though they may not feel as if they fit in, because they view it as a test of their manliness."

Of course, girls bully, too, although it often takes place in more covert ways than the bullying behavior of boys. In *Odd Girl Out: The Hidden Culture of Aggression in Girls*, Rachel Simmons points to a double standard in America that tolerates open aggression by boys but not girls. Sharing the same human emotions, such as anger, as boys, girls resort to what Simmons calls "alternative aggressions" that capture the concepts of relational aggression (ignoring or excluding other girls or sabotaging their relationships with others, for example), indirect aggression (inflicting harm without confrontation, such as spreading rumors), and social aggression (meant to damage a girl's social standing). Simmons says, "Some alternative aggressions are invisible to adult eyes. To elude social disapproval, girls retreat beneath a surface of sweetness to hurt each other in secret. They pass covert looks and notes, manipulate quietly over time, corner one another in hallways, turn their backs, whisper, and smile."

And, as if age-old methods of bullying weren't bad enough, the Internet has brought with it a new wave of "cyber-bullying." Increasingly, boys and girls use e-mail, instant-messaging, and Web logs ("blogs") to spread rumors and engage in other bullying tactics (including the dissemination of pictures and videos) designed to embarrass and humiliate their targets. For example, a story making its way around the media circuit in November, 2007, shared the news of a 13-year-old girl who was photographed by a friend with a cell phone emerging from the shower. The photo was apparently text-messaged to a boy on the school football team, who in turn texted it to other kids. Not surprisingly, the photo ended up being posted on the Internet.

In some ways, this type of bullying is even more tempting than traditional methods, as it can preserve a degree of anonymity.

Matthew is just one of countless teens who endures bullying and abusive behavior on a regular basis. He is understandably feeling scared and anxious. Beaten down psychologically, he is in need of guidance.

What You Can Do

First, check-out your teen's school policy. Be certain they address the issue of bullying and set firm limits on this type of aggressive behavior.

Second, teach teens when and how to ask for help from adults. Some victims of bullying believe they deserve to take abuse, or that it's all just part of growing up. Parents need to help teens understand the difference between good-natured ribbing and bullying behavior that can leave them at risk physically, psychologically, and certainly socially.

Third, help kids to understand how bullying hurts other children. One good way to reduce bullying behavior is to sensitize kids to its effects, discussing some of the emotions bullied kids often feel, including anger and humiliation. They also need to understand that the emotional scars of being bullied can last a very long time . . . even a lifetime.

Fourth, encourage kids to support others who may be bullied and to report incidents of bullying behavior. Be sure they understand where they can go for help and assure them—and make sure of this yourself—that they will be protected against retribution by the bully. Here again, the policies of the school, club, or team are important, because if there are no consequences for the bully, other kids will be less likely to report bullying the next time they see it. And, finally, remind teens that bullying affects everyone, whether they are the bully, the one being bullied, or even a bystander. This is because bullying fundamentally changes the ways in which people interact with each other in a school or group setting, drawing artificial lines between individuals and groups and making people feel on-edge and threatened.

Adults other than parents also have an important role to play in ensuring that bullying is not tolerated. After all, much of the bullying that takes place occurs out of sight of parents, often at school. School administrators, teachers, and coaches are key monitors of behavior and are often best-able to educate young people in the classroom, in the schoolyard, or on the practice field about bullying, to intervene when it occurs, and to exact consequences against its perpetrators. These professionals are key stakeholders in the health and safety of our children and should be called upon to protect and defend them. They also need to be identified as some of the adults available to talk with teens being bullied or to those witnessing aggressive acts. And it goes without saying that parents learning of aggressive, bullying behavior should immediately notify the appropriate authorities. Simply put, bullying cannot be allowed, and bullying behavior must be treated with the seriousness of other "major" offenses as it places children at risk, physically, emotionally, and socially.

Despite a heightened sensitivity to the issue of bullying these days—as depicted in movies like *Welcome to the Dollhouse* and *Napoleon Dynamite*—it remains somewhat misunderstood by adults. The following ten myths about bullying appear in SADD's Chapter Manual. They attempt to correct the record regarding what bullying is all about.

THE MYTH: *Bullies suffer from insecurity and low self-esteem. They pick on others to make themselves feel more important.*
THE RESEARCH: Most bullies have average or above-average self-esteem. They may instead experience aggressive temperaments, a lack of empathy, and poor parenting.

* * *

THE MYTH: *Bullies are looking for attention. Ignore them, and the bullying will stop.*
THE RESEARCH: Bullies are looking for control, and they rarely stop if their behavior is ignored. The level of bullying usually increases if it is not addressed by adults.

* * *

THE MYTH: *Boys will be boys.*
THE RESEARCH: Bullying is seldom outgrown; it's simply redirected. About 60 percent of boys identified as bullies in middle school commit

at least one crime by the time they are 24. Also, plenty of girls are bullies, and victims of bullying, too.

* * *

THE MYTH: *Kids can be cruel about differences.*
THE RESEARCH: Physical differences play only a small role in bullying situations. Most victims are chosen because they are sensitive, anxious, and unable to retaliate.

* * *

THE MYTH: *Victims of bullies need to learn to stand up for themselves and deal with the situation.*
THE RESEARCH: Victims of bullies are usually younger or physically weaker than their attackers. They also may lack the social skills to develop supportive friendships and cannot deal with the situation alone.

* * *

THE MYTH: *Large schools or classes are conducive to bullying.*
THE RESEARCH: No correlation has been established between class or school size and bullying. In fact, there is some evidence that bullying may be less prevalent in larger schools, where potential victims have increased opportunities to find supportive friends.

* * *

THE MYTH: *Most bullying occurs off school grounds.*
THE RESEARCH: Although some bullying occurs outside of school or on the way to or from school, most bullying occurs on school grounds: in classrooms, in hallways, and on playgrounds.

* * *

THE MYTH: *Bullying affects only a small number of students.*
THE RESEARCH: At any given time, about 25 percent of U.S. students are

the victims of bullies and about 20 percent are perpetrators. The National Association of School Psychologists estimates that 160,000 children stay home from school every day because they are afraid of being bullied.

* * *

THE MYTH: *Teachers know if bullying is a problem in their classes.*
THE RESEARCH: Bullying behavior usually takes place out of sight of teachers. Most victims are reluctant to report the bullying for fear of embarrassment or retaliation, and most bullies deny or justify their behavior.

* * *

THE MYTH: *Victims of bullying need to follow the adage "Sticks and stones will break your bones but names can never hurt you."*
THE RESEARCH: Victims of bullying often suffer lifelong problems with low self-esteem. They are prone throughout their lives to depression and other mental health problems and even to suicide.

* * *

From an early age, parents and other adults can protect children from bullying by simply not tolerating it, as mentioned before. Setting the ground rules from the get-go is important. So, too, is moving quickly when bullying occurs. As Dr. Joel Haber, an expert on bullying, says, "Policies are great, but you need action." One key action step is to be sure the perpetrators of bullying are punished according to the rules that are in place.

At camp, we train our counselors to spot bullying behavior by identifying some of its common forms (such as name-calling, gossiping, shoving, hitting, and threats) and where it may occur (such as in bathrooms and showers or on buses). We also ask them to make clear to the kids that when bullies are identified, we will respond aggressively to be sure the behaviors don't continue, often engaging the bully's parents in the discussion and application of consequence.

Another important step is to recognize and reward kids who stick up for the bullied. Verbal praise, such as, "I really admire the way you stuck up for your friend when he was being made fun of," or "You did exactly the right thing in letting us know that she was being gossiped about online," are effective ways to remind young people that they have a responsibility to each other when it comes to bullying behavior. We also need to be sure to let them know they can remain anonymous, as many children fear that speaking up will place them at risk, too.

Finally, as Dr. Haber points out, we need to encourage all kids to say something when a peer is being victimized. He says, "There are no innocent bystanders." Witnesses have a duty to act! Otherwise, bullies will continue to be bullies and victims will continue to suffer the embarrassment, shame, and hurt doled out by the perpetrator.

SADD offers advice to young people who, although they may not be the ones being bullied, witness the bullying of others. Here's what you can say to your kids:

- *Maybe you're not being bullied, but you know someone who is. Have you ever stood around when someone was being bullied, but you weren't sure what, if anything, you could do? Maybe you figured that nothing you could do would make a difference. You can!*
- *Refuse to join in. Don't laugh at mean jokes or crowd around someone who is being harassed.*
- *Correct classmates. If you hear an untrue rumor, correct the people who spread it and ask them to stop repeating it.*
- *Try to be a friend to the person being bullied. That person needs to know that people will be supportive through this difficult time.*
- *Keep an eye on bullied kids. When bullying becomes too much to bear, victims may choose destructive behaviors themselves to avoid the bully and the situation. If you see any of these signs, tell a parent, teacher, counselor, coach, or any other adult who is close to the situation.*

- *Don't question the victims. Kids get picked on through no fault of their own. Be careful not to unintentionally make a victim feel as though he or she did something to encourage the bullying.*
- *Let a teacher or other adult know what's happening. Adult intervention can stop bullying before it escalates into violence.*
- *Don't fight the bully yourself. It may not be safe to fight back, and you do not want to be labeled as a snitch! Tell an adult instead.*

Hazing

Hazing represents a particularly vile form of bullying and often occurs as part of ritualistic "induction" activities passed from one class to the next, one team to another, one generation to a later generation. High-profile examples of hazing include the three varsity football players from Mepham High School on Long Island, accused of sodomizing three freshmen during a pre-season training camp, and senior girls from Northbrook, Illinois, who, under the influence of alcohol, led a violent, demeaning hazing of their 11th-grade classmates, punching and kicking them, covering them with feces and urine, and forcing them to eat dirt and pig intestines. More recently, the mother of a 13-year-old Georgia boy alleged that her son was injured in a violent hazing episode on a school golf-team bus ride when older students held him upside down by his boxer shorts and punched him in the groin and stomach. It was an "initiation" ritual, they said.

According to "Initiation Rites in American High Schools," a study performed by Nadine C. Hoover, Ph.D., and Norman J. Pollard, Ed.D., at Alfred University, close to half of students (48 percent) report being subjected to activities that are considered hazing. They also report that 10 percent of students steer away from joining activities such as athletics or cheerleading or joining church groups for fear of being hazed. Conversely, 29 percent of students said they did things that are potentially illegal in order to join a group.

Harmful initiation rites are also prevalent among gangs, with 73 percent of members being hazed, according to Hoover and Pollard. SADD points out that gangs provide identity and social relationships for young people who feel lost and frustrated in their economic, social, and/or cultural environment. That may lead them to believe that the humiliation is the key to entry—the price they have to pay to belong.

Like bullying, hazing can have serious long-term effects for its victims. Hoover and Pollard report that 71 percent of the students subjected to hazing reported negative consequences, such as getting into fights, being injured, fighting with parents, doing poorly in school, hurting other people, having difficulty eating, sleeping, or concentrating, or feeling angry, confused, embarrassed, or guilty.

Stophazing.org seeks to sort out fact from fiction about hazing by posting a set of myths and truths.

MYTH #1: *Hazing is a problem for fraternities and sororities primarily.*
FACT: Hazing is a societal problem. Hazing incidents have been frequently documented in the military, athletic teams, marching bands, religious cults, professional schools, and other types of clubs and/or organizations. Reports of hazing activities in high schools are on the rise.

* * *

MYTH #2: *Hazing is no more than foolish pranks that sometimes go awry.*
FACT: Hazing is an act of power and control over others—it is victimization. Hazing is premeditated and *not* accidental. Hazing is abusive, degrading, and often life-threatening.

* * *

MYTH #3: *As long as there's no malicious intent, a little hazing should be OK.*
FACT: Even if there's no malicious "intent," safety may still be a factor in traditional hazing activities that are considered to be "all in good fun." For example, serious accidents have occurred during scavenger hunts and

kidnapping trips. Besides, what purpose do such activities serve in promoting the growth and development of group team members?

* * *

MYTH #4: *Hazing is an effective way to teach respect and develop discipline.*
FACT: First of all, respect must be *earned*—not taught. Victims of hazing rarely report having respect for those who have hazed them. Just like other forms of victimization, hazing breeds mistrust, apathy, and alienation.

* * *

MYTH #5: *If someone agrees to participate in an activity, it can't be considered hazing.*
FACT: In states that have laws against hazing, consent of the victim can't be used as a defense in a civil suit. This is because even if someone agrees to participate in a potentially hazardous action, it may not be true consent when considering the peer pressure and desire to belong to the group.

* * *

MYTH #6: *It's difficult to determine whether or not a certain activity is hazing—it's such a gray area sometimes.*
FACT: It's not difficult to decide if an activity is hazing if you use common sense and ask yourself the following questions:
- Is alcohol involved?
- Will active/current members of the group refuse to participate with the new members and do exactly what they're being asked to do?
- Does the activity risk emotional or physical abuse?
- Is there risk of injury or a question of safety?
- Do you have any reservation describing the activity to your parents, to a professor, or university official?
- Would you object to the activity being photographed for the school newspaper or filmed by the local TV news crew?

- If the answer to any of these questions is "yes," the activity is probably hazing.

What You Can Do

The good news is that parents can play a vital role in protecting young people, just as with bullying. Educating teens about what is appropriate and inappropriate behavior—and when to ask for help—is a good first step. Remember, what might seem obvious to us may be less clear to them. So, we serve kids well by fully informing them about the problem of hazing, offering real-life examples, such as the ones in New York and Georgia, and letting them know that such behavior is *never OK*—and that they are not weak or less of a group or team member to report it. If Bobby hears stories on the first day of practice about the "traditions" that will take place at an upcoming team training camp and/or Sarah witnesses some of the older girls on the field hockey team mistreating younger members because, "This is what we had to go through," they should know that it's time to look for an adult they can talk to.

Parents can help teens steer clear of hazing by raising the subject, acknowledging the increasing importance of groups at adolescence, and talking about what is and is not an appropriate price to pay for membership. Teens need adult guidance to establish boundaries. Like so many areas of decision-making, they benefit from the opportunity to think through situations ahead of time and to develop a response plan, including notifying parents or other adults that hazing is taking place. Just as is the case with bullying, it is important that young people know who they should approach to anonymously report aggressive, violent behavior. We can also help teens to establish acceptable rites of passage, even initiation, and to develop feelings of belonging that are absent of destructive, debasing, humiliating, and often illegal, behavior.

Of course, teens (not unlike many adults) "go along to get along." Remember the preeminence of the peer group at adolescence—

"membership" in a group helps young people attain feelings of freedom, power, and fun. Belonging is an important part of being a teenager. Participating in activities, groups, and teams helps teens to establish their social identities, build relationships, and learn such important skills as problem-solving and conflict resolution. But "belonging" should not come at such huge expense.

There are many organizations that offer teens alternative venues and social groups where they can find camaraderie and fun without fear of being bullied or hazed, or being faced with peer pressure around using alcohol or drugs. If we want to eradicate these behaviors, it is critical that we understand their role so that we can create meaningful alternatives for fun, freedom, and belonging.

It is on their peer group that teenagers increasingly rely to define and evaluate how they are doing socially, academically, and athletically. The importance of having friends cannot be overstated. Yet, sometimes we just assume that our children have an innate sense of how to make them. Some do, some don't. Some will wrongly assume that they must go along with all sorts of negative behaviors—including hazing—in order to belong. In any event, many children and adolescents will learn their socialization skills by observing their parents' interactions with each other and with people outside the family. We serve teens well by modeling such relationship-building and maintenance strategies as listening to others, sharing our own thoughts and feelings, developing interests that connect us to others, and tolerating differences. A mom or dad who shows teens how to make and keep friends by setting a good example in their own social relationships can be enormously helpful.

Suicide

Suicide, as evidenced by SADD's *Teens Today* research, is an important issue and a considerable threat to teens. As such, it is something that adults need to be on the lookout for, screening kids for any sign that they might be considering harming themselves and teaching them how to ask for help if they feel depressed or suicidal. So significant is the threat to young lives, that SADD has made suicide one of its core issues—seeking to bring much-needed attention to the problem and the solutions.

In his book *More Than Moody*, Dr. Harold Koplewicz reminds us that during adolescence, "being moody and crabby are as much a part of the territory as pimples and proms," but depression among young people is a serious illness too often dismissed as just some passing developmental phase. Citing new clinical and biological findings, including brain research conducted in at the National Institute of Mental Health, Koplewicz says, "Now we know that serious depression is the most common mental illness among teenagers."

Indeed, while automobile crashes account for the most deaths among young people, suicide ranks third, right after homicides. And after years of decline in teen suicides, the numbers are now dramatically surging, according to the Federal Centers for Disease Control and Prevention. Citing a CDC report released in February, 2007, The Associated Press reported that:

Teens rank suicide as number 5 on a list of 25 issues that cause them concern. Parents, on the other hand, rank it 17th on the same list. This disparity may help explain the high rates of suicide we see among young people. Why? Because if the most important adults in teens' lives are not particularly concerned about suicide, they very well may miss its warning signs!

- The suicide rate climbed 18 percent from 2003 to 2004 for Americans under age 20 (from 1,737 deaths to 1,985). And most suicides occurred in older teens.

- By contrast, the suicide rate among 15- to 19-year-olds fell in previous years, from about 11 per 100,000 in 1990 to 7.3 per 100,000 in 2003.

- Suicides were the only cause of death that increased for children through age 19 from 2003 to 2004.

While most teens seem to recognize suicide as a hugely relevant issue, many parents often do not.

This example of the reality gap is arguably the most disturbing. If parents do not grasp the saliency of suicide in the lives of their teens, they will be hard-pressed to identify suicidal thoughts, intentions, or gestures. And that can have devastating results. Many of these young people will die, many of them will try, and many more will suffer from the debilitating effects of depression.

* * *

Blond and somewhat disheveled, Billy resembles a rock star—a comparison that would no doubt make this rambunctious guitarist smile. At age 15, he has already found his calling: music. "I was put here to write and play music for others," he explains, his sharp blue eyes steadfastly fixed on me. Popular with his peer group, academically and athletically adept, this youngest of five children from an affluent northern California family seems to have everything going for him. Except, perhaps, confidence in himself. Sitting across from me on a small couch, looking uncomfortable, Billy cautiously concedes having been depressed. "I even wrote a suicide note," he said, declining to reveal its contents. "Let's just say that my parents had no idea. But music has been my salvation."

It is often difficult to quickly identify the foundation of suicidal thoughts—a predisposition reflective of particular brain chemistry or something more situational and perhaps transitory. In Billy's case, he believes it stemmed from a somewhat contentious relationship with his mom, whom he feels is always on top of him.

* * *

Another young person who finds some solace in music is Davey, an 8th-grader from Florida, whom I met after I gave a presentation in his community. He e-mailed me later that night to say, "I just wanted to say again that your speech was very compelling. I look at a lot of what goes on in my school and see what you mean . . . I guess the part that meant the most was talking about suicide. I have talked with a few people who have had bad childhoods or lives, or have bad views of themselves. And being a person deeply rooted in music, I find stuff that gets me by and encourages others."

* * *

Seventeen-year-old Adam, a high school student from Missouri who was struggling academically and failing to meet his parent's high expectations, also reached out to me one evening, saying that he wanted to end it all. Sadly, his parents were completely unaware of his suffering. And on the most devastating end of the spectrum, so were the parents of 15-year-old Meghan, who used a gun to end her life in her bedroom at home while her parents slept in the next room. Her father tells me, "You just don't know." But in reality, you can. Meghan had been cutting herself—we'll discuss this behavior next—and this was an obvious sign that she had experienced distress prior to her suicide.

> According to the National Mental Health Association (NMHA), 4 out of 5 teens who attempt suicide have given clear warnings. The signs include:
> - both indirect and direct threats
> - obsession with death
> - poems, essays, and drawings that refer to death
> - dramatic changes in personality or appearance
> - irrational behavior; an overwhelming sense of guilt or shame
> - changed eating or sleeping patterns
> - a severe decline in school performance
> - the giving away of prized possessions

Many parents are caught completely by surprise when a young person contemplates, attempts, or commits suicide.

The American Academy of Pediatrics offers a helpful list of questions to ask yourself if you believe your teenager has become depressed.

- Has his personality changed dramatically?
- Is he having trouble with a girlfriend (or, for girls, with a boyfriend)?
- Is he having trouble getting along with other friends or with parents?

- Has he withdrawn from people he used to feel close to?
- Is the quality of his schoolwork going down?
- Has he failed to live up to his own or someone else's standards (when it comes to school grades, for example)?
- Does he always seem bored, and is he having trouble concentrating?
- Is he acting like a rebel in an unexplained and severe way?
- Is she pregnant and finding it hard to cope with this major life change?
- Has he run away from home?
- Is your teenager abusing drugs and/or alcohol?
- Is she complaining of headaches, stomachaches, etc., that may or may not be real?
- Have his eating or sleeping habits changed?
- Has his appearance changed for the worse?
- Is he giving away some of his most prized possessions?
- Is he writing notes or poems about death?
- Does he talk about suicide, even jokingly? Has he said things such as, "That's the last straw," "I can't take it anymore," or "Nobody cares about me?" (Threatening to kill oneself precedes 4 out of 5 suicidal deaths.)
- Has he tried to commit suicide before?

The CDC says that the first step in stopping suicide is understanding what factors make it more likely that someone might harm themselves. These include such things as previous suicide attempts, a history of mental disturbances, alcohol or drug abuse, a family history of suicide, child maltreatment, hopelessness, aggression, feelings of isolation, and local epidemics of suicide.

Professional help in dealing with physical, psychological, or substance problems, family support, training by parents or counselors in problem-solving, and cultural or religious beliefs that discourage suicide are all seen as factors that make suicide less likely.

Once we see some or all of the listed signs, there is a lot we can do to help. Often, though, we are afraid to directly address the issue of suicide for fear of planting an idea in a child's head. The mother of a 14-year-old boy I was counseling asked, "How do you know that talking about suicide isn't going to make him think about doing it?" But if we have any reason to suspect a child or teen is depressed, we have an obligation to talk about it. The American Foundation for Suicide Prevention counsels, "If your friend or loved one is depressed, don't be afraid to ask whether he or she is considering suicide, or even if they have a particular plan or method in mind. And NMHA points out, silence is deadly. Suicidal thoughts should not be handled with silence as though they don't exist. Suicide is an extremely relevant part of the teenage landscape and claims far too many young lives each year. Again, the *Teens Today* research reveals that young people already know about it, talk about it, and worry about it.

Depressed, suicidal teens need our encouragement to open up and share their feelings without concerns that we will judge them, lecture them, or respond with panic. Adam didn't want to tell his mother because, "She'll just freak out and focus on finding me the best possible doctor." He really just wanted to talk, to *her* . . . and eventually he did.

Once we have created and nurtured an environment of acceptance and communication, teens will feel more comfortable opening up about how they are feeling. We can then better determine the need for, and urgency of, professional intervention. When talking with kids about suicide, I ask them to rate the magnitude of their depression, then their suicidal thoughts, on a scale of one to ten. I ask them if they have a plan. And I try to ascertain if they have the resources (such as access to a gun or sleeping pills) to carry out the plan. Each of these is a key indicator of the seriousness of the threat. If the threat to our teen seems real, we need to do everything in our power to guarantee their physical safety, including seeking immediate professional help, even hospitalization.

Depressed teens often have difficulty asking for help, instead hoping against hope that a significant adult in their life will intervene before destructive thoughts and behaviors turn deadly. Others don't believe intervention is possible—or at least that it will make a difference in relieving their suffering. Lacking sufficient life-experience to know that there is a "light at the end of the tunnel," many teens believe the way they feel is the way they will always feel.

Cutting

Not lethal, but still enormously disquieting, is the practice of cutting. This behavior represents an alarming trend among adolescents, particularly girls. Cutting oneself with razors, knives, even nail files or sticks, serves as a means to release emotion and offers a sense of control, relief, and, strangely, peace for its practitioners. Cutting signals severe internal distress, sometimes in response to a negative event or action, and warrants immediate intervention. While the act of cutting is rarely seen as a suicidal gesture, it can convey a level of impaired psychological functioning consistent with possible suicidal ideation.

Children and teens who cut feel hurt inside. They may have a history of problematic relationships with caregivers, such as parents, and may not have learned how to successfully cope with feelings of anger or sadness. They are also more likely to be abusers of drugs and alcohol. And a high percentage of cutters (approximately 50 to 60 percent) have been physically or sexually abused.

For these teens, cutting gives them some control over their own pain. It's a jolt that ends feelings of helplessness and numbness, and replaces them with a dramatic form of self-expression: *I am hurting. I am in pain.* In that way, cutting makes external what had previously been only internal and offers the sufferer a physical alternative to psychological distress.

Bobbie, a 12th-grader from Delaware, shares her story of pain. "High school can get tough and teenagers can make mistakes. Sophomore year was mine. It was a hard time in and outside of school. I chose to turn to alcohol to forget everything going on around me. Every weekend I was drunk. I was depressed because of everything in my life and had been cutting myself for years. Alcohol was not helping because it is a depressant, but I did not realize that. It was just one of those times that nothing was going right. I felt like things were never going to be right again and I just gave up. Cutting was not enough, so I tried to overdose on some pills. Fortunately, I was not successful. After that night, I got some professional help."

Teens who cut need professional help, just as Bobbie did, to identify and express the emotions behind the cutting and to begin learning more adaptive responses to emotional distress. They also need their parents to recognize their pain and talk about it: *I know you are hurting and I want to help.*

The most disturbing trend surrounding cutting, suicide, and all the other destructive teen behaviors we've outlined here is the lack of parental awareness—the reality gap itself, rearing its ugly head. A "not-my-kid" mentality captures even the most well-intentioned parents, tempting disaster and leaving young people without a true understanding of the risks they face when they choose to drink when they are underage, use drugs, drive impaired, or engage in a host of other destructive or potentially destructive behaviors, including cutting and other forms of self-injury. The risks are significant and, unfortunately, too often underestimated by young people. And sometimes by their parents, as well.

Three

Risky Business

In 2006 I wrote an Op-ed piece for the *Arizona Republic* detailing the unique work of the Phoenix Police Department's Youth Alcohol Squad. This unit of specially trained detectives spends weekdays in schools educating young people about the dangers of underage drinking and alerting them about weekend policing in their areas. I had recently joined them on patrol, along with SADD's executive director and our Arizona state coordinator.

It had been a hot desert day that quickly turned into a cool, moonlit night as we crisscrossed the city in the detective's nondescript dark-blue Suburban, its tinted windows obscuring us and the detection technology we were carrying. The easy, playful banter among the officers belied the seriousness of the job ahead. It was more than a routine patrol. It was a mission to protect young lives.

Perhaps emboldened by the feeling of liberty offered by Spring Break, some area teens had ignored that advance notice of the crackdown on illegal purchase and consumption of alcohol. Kids were out "cruising" in search of the next six-pack, the next party. A corner gas station, a mini-mart, and a grocery store all pose possibilities for underage purchase, offered up the first kid arrested that evening, Rafael, an 18-year-old male whose erratic, high-speed driving nearly claimed the life of an innocent motorist right in front of our eyes. He had been surprised that we had pulled him over.

Minutes after Rafael was issued a slew of tickets and had driven off, we made our way across town to a rambunctious house party hosted by a girl whose parents had gone to Hawaii. The upscale neighborhood was choked with vehicles, hastily abandoned by teens anxious to get to the punch bowl or the beer funnel.

About half the partygoers managed to escape through open doors or windows by the time we entered, but some 40 others, ages 15 to 18, remained inside. They were huddled together on the living room floor, many appearing dazed or high. Some were confused, some upset, others simply angry. None of them had planned on getting caught. But then, who does?

What's your name? How old are you? Where do you go to school? How much have you had to drink? What's the legal age to use alcohol? These were some of the rapid-fire questions posed to each teen just before he or she was administered a blood-alcohol content test, known as the Breathalyzer (BAC). The open bottles of vodka and rum sitting nearby suggest the ultimate, unfortunate results. Only about one-quarter of the kids passed the BAC, and my job was to hand them back their drivers' licenses and tell them they can go. Not a bad assignment compared to writing up citations or talking with upset parents.

"You're criminalizing behavior that isn't criminal," said one girl to a detective. Another confidently asserted, "You can't do this." Maybe one day these kids will be lawyers, but this evening, they were completely misinformed about several suddenly pertinent points of law.

In the kitchen, 17-year-old Tim had insisted that he was 21, while he arrogantly and impolitely refused to produce any corroborating identification.

"I'm going to give you one more chance," offered the detective, clearly exasperated, "and then I'm taking you to jail."

"I don't care what you do," countered Tim, the disdain nearly dripping from his mouth. In the end, he was arrested, handcuffed, and taken to a juvenile detention facility downtown.

Sleepy parents, summoned by the police—or in some cases by the teens themselves—arrived at the crime scene.

"I'm completely stunned," exclaimed the mother of a 16-year-old boy, who had no idea he was a drinker. He, on the other hand, was incredulous at my suggestion that the five beers he claimed to have consumed were a lot. Across the walkway, a girl implored her father to believe her:

"I haven't been drinking!" But faced with the evidence (a BAC suggestive of six or seven drinks), she claimed that she didn't know the punch was spiked. This is a popular defense tonight at this party gone wrong.

"This is so unfair! They should have just told us to go home," another teen wailed plaintively to no one in particular.

A little later, as I waited with Tim in the detention-center holding room, he complained, "I am going to lose my parents' trust, my license, my car, and my job. I can't believe it." He lived in Mesa, where his parents believed that he was just down the street at a friend's house, and not partying miles away in Phoenix. Or sitting in jail, handcuffed to a wall.

A lack of information and understanding about the real risks—including legal ones—attached to certain situations, such as the one facing Tim, increase the likelihood that teens will make poor choices. Some teens believe they won't get caught or won't be held accountable for the decisions they make. Many more simply believe they won't get hurt. Without relentless reminders from parents about all the potential outcomes of poor choices—especially short-term ones like being arrested, which they can easily get their minds around—teens slide into a social world where little, if any, consideration is paid to what might very likely happen if they break the rules and the law. A group of 11th- and 12th-grade Massachusetts boys participating in a focus group for SADD made the point: *We need to hear about the immediate legal consequences.*

The Arizona teens are actually incredibly lucky. Nobody was hurt, nobody was killed. Yet, their lack of awareness of even the most basic of laws that apply to them underscores the staggering knowledge vacuum that helps perpetuate destructive decision-making.

Parents need to guide their children's choices by regularly talking about the dangers and potential outcomes of behavior, and then holding their kids accountable by enforcing family rules and imposing punishment. When we fail to do this, we fail our children. We need to remind them early and often of the risks associated with their behavior. This chapter gives a fuller look at some of the most common risky behaviors (specifically underage drinking, other drug use, impaired and distracted driving, and early sexual behavior) and their short- and long-term effects.

The Risks of Underage Drinking

Underage drinking is enormously consequential, both in terms of the damage that can be done by alcohol itself, and because of its close connection to other destructive behaviors, such as impaired driving (obviously), drug use, unprotected sex, sexual assault, and other forms of violence, like hazing. It is also closely linked with depression (after all, it is a depressant!). Since it's simply illegal, it can also result in fines and arrest.

Yet, the statistics (63 percent of middle and high school students have used alcohol, including 16 percent of 6th-graders, 41 percent of 8th-graders, and 75 percent of 11th-graders) show us that young people—and many of their parents—routinely underestimate the risks of underage drinking.

One Friday night, sometime after 9:00 p.m., I was walking home after having dinner with friends at a local Boston restaurant. Passing by a liquor store, I heard a young boy's hushed voice, "Hey sir, if I give you

Alcohol Use by School Grade

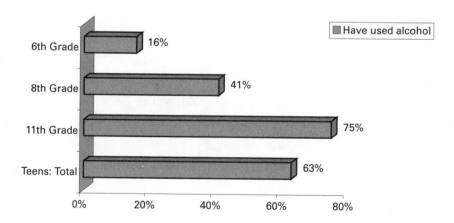

some money, can you buy me something inside?" He looked to be only 12 or 13. My first thought was, "Wow, did this kid ask the wrong guy!" Of all the people in the world he could have stopped, he asked the chairman of SADD! When I relate this story in my presentations, people invariably say, "Wait! What did you do?" "I took his money and ran!" I reply, bringing laughter to the room.

In truth, I declined, but it seemed useless to engage this child in a discussion about the risks of underage drinking while standing on a dark sidewalk outside of a liquor store. He was unlikely to be receptive to what I had to say (as we'll see in Chapter Eight, timing our conversations is important)—or maybe I was just in a hurry to get home. It's possible I missed an important opportunity—a "teachable moment."

My second thought, however, was a little more sobering: This happens, every Friday and Saturday night, in almost every community across the country. And so often the answer from adults is "Yes."

The propensity of adults to buy alcohol for teens is addressed in the National Academies' report and reflects their lack of awareness about the very high price of underage drinking. Even in their own homes, parents often allow their teens to drink.

At a junior class parent-teen assembly in Cambridge, Massachusetts, one mom's hand is raised higher than most during the Q&A segment.

"Don't you think it's better for them to be drinking in my home where it's safe and I've taken all the car keys away than off somewhere in the woods?" she asks.

Sigh. I am asked this question all the time, but never feel that I am making much headway among those who ask it. They're a hard group to sway, those parents who believe that allowing their children and their friends to drink at home somehow keeps them safe, or means they are less likely to drink somewhere else the next time—or drink and drive. But I give persuasion the good old college try.

"Actually, no, I don't," I begin. "There are scores of stories about kids who die of alcohol poisoning or alcohol-related accidents in the home.

Plus, even if you think it is right to allow your child to drink, what gives you the right to decide for someone else's child?"

The crowd stirred as controversy took hold. You could have cut the tension with a knife as parents heatedly began to weigh in on one side or the other. It's funny to me that no one even mentioned the illegality of the whole issue of underage drinking. The comments focused solely on the safety, and the moral and ethical undertones of purchasing alcohol for, or allowing drinking by, young people.

But across the country, states are enacting new legislation to crack down on underage drinking and to hold accountable adults who provide young people with alcohol.

- In Georgia, a woman was charged with five counts of contributing to the delinquency of a minor for purchasing a keg for her son's eighteenth birthday party.
- In California, a mom and wife of a police officer was arrested for serving alcohol to teens in her home.
- In Wyoming, police arrested 23 high school seniors in a raid on a sunrise party. They said a parent had purchased the beer they'd been drinking.
- In Virginia, a woman and her ex-husband were sentenced to more than two years in jail each for hosting an alcohol-included 16th birth-day party for their son and his 15- and 16-year-old friends in 2002.
- In Massachusetts, the father of a 15-year-old girl was charged with involuntary manslaughter, following the alcohol-induced death of his daughter's friend. The dad was accused of purchasing a 1.75-liter bottle of vodka for the girls.

In all of these cases, adults are subjecting themselves to legal consequences for providing alcohol to minors.

Many parents purchase alcohol for their teens, because, like the mom in Cambridge, they believe it's safer to allow them to drink at home and that it makes it less likely their child will drink elsewhere. Others believe it "de-mystifies" alcohol, making its use less appealing by removing the allure of doing something you're not supposed to do. Despite these motivations, the data shows that parents who allow their teens to drink at home are merely setting the stage for drinking later on. More than half (57 percent) of high school teens who report that their parents allow them to drink at home, even just on special occasions, say they drink with their friends, as compared to just 14 percent of teens who say their parents don't let them drink at all.

Why this carry-over effect? Because teens have brought their drinking behavior in-line with what they perceive their parents' attitudes to be—*my drinking is not such a bad thing after all!*—regardless of what their parents actually say. The message they take away with them is *It's OK to drink with my friends since I drink at home!*

It is also common for teens to see things in absolutes, in black and white, particularly when it comes to justifying personal behavior: *If adults drink to celebrate the holidays, why shouldn't I?* Cognitively speaking, they have limited experience with thinking abstractly and capturing the nuances that differentiate adult drinking (and celebration) from that of young people. One of the most common complaints I hear from parents is that other parents allow alcohol-included social gatherings in their homes. According to a national survey of 2,019 adults conducted by Harris Interactive and *The Wall Street Journal* in May 2004, 23 percent of adults say parents in their areas allow teens to attend such parties. One mom contacted by the paper said, "My son had really struggled in high school, and I had promised him when he graduated he could have a party. He asked me, 'Can we drink at the party?' I said, 'Hell, yeah. And we'll do shots to everyone who ever said you wouldn't graduate.'" On a similar note, an upstate New York mother actually tended bar for her teen's high school graduation party and reportedly encouraged binge drinking. One teen died the next day as a result of acute alcohol poisoning, and the mom was arrested. She pled guilty to criminally negligent homicide and was sentenced to jail time and five years of probation.

Stories such as these are frighteningly prevalent, even though many parents say they are opposed to the idea of adults providing alcohol for teens. For example, a report from The Century Council, a not-for-profit organization funded by the distilled spirits industry to fight drunk driving and underage drinking, shows that of 1,000 parents and non-parents surveyed, most believe it is wrong for parents or other adults to provide alcohol to underage youth. Ninety-six percent of adults said it is unacceptable for another adult to provide alcohol to their teenager without their permission. Further, all survey respondents said that if they learned another parent or adult provided alcohol to their teenager without their permission, they would consider taking legal action against them. Given the increasing propensity of most courts to hold at least adults legally accountable, they probably would have a case.

Of course, as we have seen, parents need not be complicit for teens to find and drink alcohol. Fifteen-year-old Brian says, "I have tried drinking and kind of regret it. At the same time, I know it will happen again. The first time was with my cousin, who is older. She sort of pressured me into it. Now I drink with my friends probably about once a month. I feel bad because my parents don't want me drinking, but they don't bring it up."

So what's the big deal?

Alcohol used by teens is inextricably linked with falling grades, failing relationships, automobile crashes, sexual assaults, suicide, and hazing. In fact, if you take almost any issue or problem afflicting young people and add alcohol to the mix, you can clearly see the additive effect that underage drinking has on a host of other social and legal pitfalls. The following are some of the issues—physical, social, and legal—surrounding underage drinking that parents need to know about so that they can better guide their kids.

The physical risks associated with drinking involve the impact of alcohol on an evolving brain. In short, drinking can impair cognitive functioning, impede memory, and result in academic difficulty. There is also the issue of dependence, as with most any drug. The chronic disease known as alcoholism marks alcohol dependence. And much like adults, teens and younger children can suffer from this disease. Alcoholics crave alcohol and often continue to use it despite the repeated physical, psychological, and interpersonal problems that occur. Many alcoholics have difficulty meeting obligations to work, school, family, and friends. And as you might guess, they often encounter legal difficulties related to alcohol, such as being arrested for underage drinking, illegal possession of alcohol, or impaired driving.

The emotional risks of alcohol use include irritability, sadness, and depression. Alcohol can also induce behavior, including sexual activity, that might later cause emotional distress and suicidal thoughts. As we have seen, many teens engage in, and later regret, sexual behavior under the influence of alcohol. Sixteen-year-old Trevor tells me he regrets engaging in numerous oral sex episodes at parties where he had been drinking. And 17-year-old Randy says he was drunk when he allowed a girl he describes as "skanky" to perform oral sex on him in a bedroom at a party. Right in the middle of the act, he realized his error in judgment, pulled his pants back up, and left.

There are also a number of developmental risks associated with teen drinking. Adolescence is a time when young adults are encountering significant social and psychological changes, which we will examine more closely in Chapter Four.

Unfortunately, alcohol is often used to avoid dealing with—or to mask—important emotions brought about by a lot of "first-time" situations (such as a romantic breakup or the death of a relative or friend) and decision-making. Avoiding those feelings rather than learning to use them effectively to solve problems can stunt healthy emotional development.

There are some important questions kids need to ask themselves regarding alcohol use, including *What decisions will I make to feel that I have status or standing in a group of peers? How will I deal with stressful or painful situations or periods in my life? Am I comfortable interacting with others, even those I don't know?* All these demand the question: *Can I do it without alcohol?*

Fourteen-year-old Tracy tells me, "I drink because I am lonely and depressed." She also wonders if using other drugs might help take her mind off her problems. But Tracy is merely numbing her pain— temporarily. It will be back once she sobers up. Drinking is not a constructive alternative to experiencing loneliness, anxiety, stress, or loss. It only delays the inevitable struggle to identify, understand, and communicate about these powerful emotions.

Alcohol use also exposes teens to a number of personal risks, like jeopardizing relationships with peers and parents. On the peer front, qualitative research by SADD reveals that a powerful motivator for teens not to drink is a fear of doing something in front of their friends under the influence of alcohol that would be embarrassing. When it comes to parents, drinking by teens can precipitate a breach of trust that might damage teen-parent relationships, because lying and deceit often go hand-in-hand with alcohol use by young people. Eighteen-year-old Robert, the high school senior from Chapter One who thinks he and his friends might be alcoholics, laments the impact that his drinking has had on his relationship with his parents. "It forces me to lie," he tells me. "That has pushed us apart. We aren't as close as we used to be. I feel bad about that." Robert has placed his relationship with his parents, whom he admires and loves, in jeopardy—all in the interest of getting drunk.

For many teens, drinking also interferes with important personal goals, such as academic or athletic performance. Alcohol use then becomes a hindrance to activities that can bring reward, fulfillment, fun, and positive feelings about oneself. Remember that alcohol is a drug and it can easily diminish our ability to function optimally, whether taking an exam, maintaining peak physical condition for sports, or preserving the mental acuity required for a musical recital.

Finally, there are the legal risks associated with alcohol use by teens. The effect of a police record on college admissions or an employment application—not to mention personal reputations in school and throughout the community—can be devastating. Our teens need to be aware that even one drink can cause them to fail a Breathalyzer, potentially leading to the loss of a drivers' permit or license and fines or jail time.

What You Can Do

Knowing all this, what can parents then tell their kids about using alcohol? First and foremost, that drinking alcohol will affect their body, their brain, and their chances to successfully meet their personal goals—perhaps even permanently. It leads to a loss of coordination, diminished reflexes, distorted vision, and memory lapses, even blackouts. Alcohol impairs the central nervous system, lowers inhibitions, and impairs judgment. As such, it is a contributing factor in a vast array of dangerous, even deadly decisions, such as driving under the influence or having unprotected sex. Drinking can also lead to death from alcohol poisoning.

It is important to point out to young people that they don't necessarily have to be the ones drinking to get hurt. Just being with others who are drinking leads to increased risk of being involved in a car crash or the possibility of being otherwise adversely affected—such as being hurt in a fight that can easily come about when people are influenced by alcohol. As we saw with the Massachusetts case, there is also the risk of being arrested because they are in the presence of alcohol and may be charged with illegal possession.

It cannot be said enough that we have a responsibility to our teens to point out in clear, concrete terms the potential outcomes of poor choices, including ones involving alcohol. Stories from everyday life abound and can be effective in starting dialogue and bringing to life once hypothetical, abstract notions of risks and rewards.

It doesn't get much clearer than the vivid play-by-play (see box below) of what happens in an accident. Yet, as we will see in Chapter Four, a structural reorganization of gray matter and brain circuitry during adolescence, and continuing at least into the early twenties, hinders judgment when it comes to clearly sorting through the potential risks and rewards of a decision such as whether or not to use alcohol—and then get behind the wheel of a car. Further, alcohol appears to affect how that neurolog-

Here's one example that will help teens comprehend what actually happens in a car crash and how quickly it can all unfold. Studies at Yale and Cornell Universities provide a dramatic split-second chronology of what happens when a car going 55 mph rams into a tree, showing that it only takes .7 of a second to kill a person in an automobile crash. Here's how that chronology unfolds:

At .1 second, the front bumper and grillwork collapse.

At .2, the hood crumbles, rises, and smashes into the windshield, and the grillwork disintegrates.

At .3, the driver is sprung upright from his seat, his broken knees are pressed against the dashboard, and the steering wheel bends under his grip.

At .4, the front of the car is destroyed and dead-still, but the rear end is still plunging forward at 55 mph. The half-ton motor crushes into the tree.

At .5, the driver's fear-frozen hands bend the steering column into an almost-vertical position, and he is impaled on the steering-wheel shaft. Jagged steel punctures his lungs and arteries.

At .6, the impact rips the shoes off his feet. The chassis bends in the middle, and the driver's head is slammed into the windshield. The car's rear begins its downward fall, as its spinning wheels churn into the ground.

At .7, the entire body of the car is twisted grotesquely out of shape. In one final agonizing convulsion, the front seat rams forward, pinning the driver against the steering shaft. Blood spurts from his mouth. Shock has frozen his heart. He is now dead.

ical re-wiring takes place and how the brain will process information in adulthood. This means that young people desperately need parental intervention to fully understand and appreciate the many dangers associated with alcohol use.

The Risks of Other Drug Use

For many teens, drugs other than alcohol are becoming the preferred way to get high. Ironically, our efforts to limit youth access to alcohol—while at least partially successful—has led some young people to conclude that it's simply easier to get their hands on substances other than beer, wine, or liquor (although their ability to procure alcohol is still easier overall).

For example, 72 percent of teens say it is easy for them to get alcohol, while 62 percent say it's easy for them to obtain other drugs. Parents report believing the opposite, with 61 percent saying it's easy for their teens to obtain drugs compared to 50 percent who say that about alcohol.

Another trend driving drug use is that the effects of marijuana and pills are easier than alcohol to conceal from adults. As one Texas boy tells me, "I can't get drunk and go home because my parents will know. But I can get high and they'll have no idea." Why? Because the visible effects of getting high (say, odor or bloodshot eyes) are more readily "fixed" than may be the ones associated with alcohol, such as trouble walking or speaking, and vomiting. An 8th-grade Florida boy says that at least half of the kids he knows smoke pot, more than the number who drink. "A drunken person is more apt to get into trouble than a stoned person," he explains.

Unfortunately, as is the case with alcohol, many parents tend to seriously underestimate the ease with which teens can find ways not only to procure drugs, but also to use them. Indeed, teens have a greater opportunity to use drugs than their parents believe, with nearly 7 in 10 (69 percent) saying they do, compared with only 56 percent of parents.

Also like alcohol, other drugs are frequently used by young people to mask significant problems and "anesthetize" themselves against the pain they feel. Nancy, a high school senior from North Carolina, says, "By the age of 13, I had already tried more drugs than the average 25-year-old. My home was an unstable roller-coaster of emotional and physical abuse. I escaped the crazy atmosphere by associating with older kids who introduced me to destructive tactics to cope with my despair. Young, naïve, and looking for a cure, I tried any drug presented to me."

One of the most popular drugs among teens continues to be marijuana and, contrary to popular belief (or perhaps wishful thinking), it can be both addicting and a "gateway" drug. According to the National Institute on Drug Abuse (NIDA): "Long-term studies of high school students and their patterns of drug use show that very few young people use other illegal drugs without first trying marijuana. For example, the risk of using cocaine is much greater for those who have tried marijuana than for those who have never tried it. Using marijuana puts children and teens in contact with people who are users and sellers of other drugs. So, there is more of a risk that a marijuana user will be exposed to and urged to try more drugs."

In that sense, smoking marijuana is a lot like playing Russian roulette. The Office of National Drug Control Policy (ONDCP) says that marijuana is addictive and cites a statistic from the Substance Abuse and Mental Health Services Administration pointing to the fact that more teens are in treatment with a primary diagnosis of marijuana dependence than for all other illicit drugs combined. Of the 4.3 million Americans who meet the diagnostic criteria for needing drug treatment (criteria developed by the American Psychiatric Association), two-thirds are dependent on marijuana.

Regardless of its likelihood to incite experimentation with, or use of, other drugs—or even its addictive qualities—we know scientifically that marijuana directly affects the brain in the same way that alcohol, cocaine, or heroin do. THC, the active ingredient in marijuana, changes the way in which sensory information is received by and acted on by the brain, specifically the hippocampus, which is a part of the limbic system that is crucial for learning, memory, and the integration of sensory experiences involving emotions and motivations. THC suppresses neurons in the information-processing system of the hippocampus.

In addition, researchers have discovered that previously learned behaviors also deteriorate. As such, marijuana can impair the ability of young people to stay alert, to concentrate, and to retain information, making learning extremely difficult. As you might guess, smoking marijuana also increases the risk of developing lung cancer and can limit the body's ability to fight off infection.

Of course, marijuana affects timing and the ability to do things that require coordination, like drive. Not surprisingly then, marijuana use is linked to tens of thousands of serious traffic accidents each year. Yet, as we have seen, many young people don't see the danger of mixing weed with driving.

In Chapter Two, I discussed the increasing abuse of prescription drugs, such as painkillers and antidepressants, as well as over-the-counter drugs, such as cough syrups and allergy medicines. These, too, present considerable physical and emotional risk to teens. Misusing drugs that depress the central nervous system, such as ones used to treat anxiety or sleep disorders, especially in combination with other drugs such as alcohol, can lead to respiratory failure. Stimulants, on the other hand, such as ones used to treat attention deficit disorders—Ritalin, for example—can result in an irregular heartbeat, dangerously high body temperatures, and possible cardiovascular failure or seizure. And we know from self-reporting and news accounts that, not infrequently, kids may be abusing the Concerta or Ritalin they have been prescribed for an attention deficit— or may be selling it to a friend, thereby putting themselves or someone else at risk for physical distress.

Teens using Methamphetamines, such as crack cocaine and heroin, can experience anxiety, depression, or paranoid or delusional thinking. In addition, they leave themselves susceptible to irreversible damage to blood vessels in the brain, permanent psychological damage, heart attacks, and strokes.

The use of inhalants, such as aerosols, to get high can result in instantaneous death. Period. Aerosols starve the body of oxygen and force the heart to beat irregularly and more rapidly. Inhalant abusers can also suffer liver, lung, and kidney problems. According to the Alliance for Consumer Education, 1 in 5 children will abuse inhalants by 8th grade. Their Web site, www.inhalant.org, links to news stories highlighting the tragic toll of "huffing," like this one: In May 2007, KUSA-TV reported on an Englewood, Colorado, mom who found her 15-year-old son dead in the bath after he huffed from an aerosol can meant to clean dust from computers. "I never suspected this. I've never heard of it. Didn't know anything about it," Dana Acker told the news station. "They think it's a game and it's not. My son's gone from it." She now visits schools to talk to students and parents about the dangers of inhalants.

Last but not least, it is critical that adults and young people familiarize themselves with the legal risks of illicit drug use, whether the drug is marijuana, cocaine, heroin, a club drug, or some other illegal substance. Punishments for violating both federal and state laws pertaining to the sale and possession of marijuana, cocaine, Methamphetamine, and Ecstasy generally relate to the substance itself, the quantity of the substance, and the type of offense (sale or possession). Past offenses may also be taken into account. Because of the differences from state to state and offense to offense, it is difficult to capture here the likely outcomes of any particular drug offense, but information available online from ONDCP and reports such as "Illicit Drug Policies: Selected Laws from the 50 States," prepared for the ImpacTeen Illicit Drug Team, offer a compelling glimpse of the rates of arrest and incarceration, and a snapshot of relevant state laws, respectively. Familiarizing young people with the laws that apply to them is an important component of an overall strategy parents can employ to tip the balance of decision-making toward healthy, safe, risk-free choices.

Obviously, there are many critical effects of using drugs that young people need help to understand. SADD's Web site (www.sadd.org) offers valuable information for kids about these many damaging effects—as well as some of the related issues we have been discussing, such as depression, cutting, suicide, bullying, and hazing.

As we know, too often teens believe they are indestructible—something I'll cover in greater detail later on—and therefore not vulnerable to long-term damage, death, or legal consequences resulting from the illicit use of marijuana or other popular drugs. That makes both knowing and passing on this information so vitally important.

The Risks of Distracted and Impaired Driving

The National Transportation Safety Board (NTSB) has long been concerned with the issues of distracted driving and novice drivers, and recommends that all states prohibit holders of learner's permits and intermediate licenses from using cell phones or pagers while driving. Some states, such as New York, already ban handheld cell phone use for all drivers, young and old alike. Part of the concern stems from an emerging trend among teens who use their cell phones to text-message while driving. In fact, teens cite instant-messaging and text-messaging as their biggest source of distraction while driving, with more than 1 in 5 saying they use an electronic device with a screen while operating a motor vehicle.

A 17-year-old boy interviewed for a Motor Week segment on PBS weighed in on the topic: "It distracts your eyes from the road; you pay less attention to what's going on around you." But he does it anyway. Another teen told the interviewer, "I usually have the phone next to the steering wheel. I can see the steering wheel [and] I [can] look up and see the road. It's not that hard." And one teen I talked to told me, "I sometimes do text while I drive, although I know I probably shouldn't. Personally, I think it's more dangerous than talking on the phone when driving, because it requires you to take your eyes off the road most of the time. Texting has become so popular that I'm surprised it wasn't made illegal. But, I've been texting for so long that I don't really have to look at the screen, so it isn't as dangerous for me."

What teens like these don't expect is, well, the unexpected. Taking your eyes off the road, even briefly, presumes that everything you think is going to happen—such as the car in front of you continuing straight ahead or the car on the side street not pulling out into oncoming traffic—is going to happen. As any seasoned driver knows, such a presumption is a grave error in judgment.

Teen drivers are far more likely than other, older drivers to be involved in fatal crashes because they lack driving experience and tend to take greater risks. The very youngest drivers are most likely to engage in risky behaviors such as speeding and tailgating. Because of their inexperience, beginners are least able to cope with hazardous situations, such as a blown tire, black ice, and other unpredictable incidents along the roadway. This lack of experience combined with an aggressive driving style, results in a high crash rate.

When it comes to driving under the influence, teens themselves are far more concerned about the issue than are their parents.

- Only 5 percent of parents think their teen would drive after drinking, but 21 percent of teens say they have.
- Forty percent of teens admit to riding in the car of another teen who has been drinking.

And that can have serious consequences, as was the case of Massachusetts high school student Melissa Smith. According to a police report cited by the *Boston Globe*, Melissa was seriously injured in a car crash in the early morning hours of September 13, 2005, after leaving a party with 15-year-old Meghan Murphy and her sister 17-year-old Shauna Murphy, who was driving under the influence of alcohol. The sisters were killed.

The legal risks of impaired driving may not be as significant as the fatal consequences, yet they still need to be well understood by teens who drink. Ranging from mandatory alcohol counseling, to loss of license, to incarceration, the penalties can have both short- and long-term effects on a young person's ability to meet their personal goals and function effectively.

From any angle, driving under the influence of alcohol or other drugs is simply too consequential. It kills, shatters families, and oftentimes destroys the lives of those who commit the crime—as we saw in the suicide death of the 21-year-old man who had killed someone while driving drunk.

The Risks of Early Sexual Activity

The short-term impact and long-term consequences of early sexual activity are among the least-understood outcomes of teen behavior. The recent explosion of non-intercourse sexual activity (including oral sex) among young people and the lack of much longitudinal data on its effects make predictions about any long-term outcomes difficult. That said, there exist enough anecdotal and statistical data to suggest there are plenty of reasons to define sex among teens as risky behavior.

Some (if not most) teens are *physically* ready to engage in sexual activity before they are *emotionally* ready. Unfortunately, many young people (and probably older people as well) confuse sexuality with sex—meaning that to prove one's manhood or womanhood, to themselves or others, boys and girls sometimes believe they must do sexual things. Understanding and coming to grips with individual sexuality is an important part of adolescent identity formation. It helps pre-teens and teens to learn about themselves and prepares them for one day becoming sexually active.

Consensus around teen sexual activity is hard to achieve. Each family has its own take on what is appropriate, when it is appropriate, and why. Attempting to craft, or at least communicate, a "best approach" for parents guiding teens would be an impossible task. That is why, unlike issues such as underage drinking, illegal drug use, or impaired driving, for example, SADD has not adopted a "policy" or even a particular point of view when it comes to teen sex. Rather, it serves as a forum, a meeting place really, where young people and their parents can find information pertaining to risk and, hopefully, use that information to inform dialogue with one another about what makes most sense for their family. Beyond the straightforward presentation of common consequences of early, intimate sexual contact (such as teen pregnancies and transmittal of STDs/STIs and HIV/AIDS), much of what I discuss here, and throughout the book, reflects my own experiences in counseling youth, rather than an official point of view of the organization I chair.

Sexual activity is not an inherently negative behavior, and should not be presented to teens as such. They know that's not the truth. They understand that it should be a positive experience, bringing with it great physical pleasure and feelings of being close to, and loved by, another person. The discriminating criteria with which teens often struggle are when and why to become sexually active. To help them grapple with these issues, teens need unambiguous messages from us about the risks, because in the end, they get to decide what to do sexually with their bodies and will generally do so when we are not around! In this way, sexual behavior differs somewhat from, say, illegal drug use, or cutting behavior, or violence, where we are more inclined to actively intervene. When it comes to sex, our hope is often that, with our guidance, our teen will be able to sort out the pros and cons of becoming sexually active and make choices that are best for her.

When sexual activity is appropriate relates to emotional maturity and the ability and preparedness of the participants to fully appreciate the many—and often complicated—emotions involved with sexual behavior. Teens are not immune to the human inclination we all have to believe we know what's best for ourselves at every age and stage of development, even if we realize later that we were mistaken.

By its very nature, sexual activity (particularly oral sex and intercourse) is intimate. Teens need help to fully appreciate that with intimacy come many tricky consequences, including relinquishing a part of themselves to someone else. Many young people do so before they've even figured out who they are, and that makes sexual contact even more consequential, because just the act of engaging in intimate sexual behavior can become defining in and of itself. It says much of the values we hold, and how we treat other people. If Tommy accepts oral sex from anyone who offers or Michele sleeps with as many boys as possible, it probably says something about who they are—if not to themselves at least to others.

Intimacy also implies some level of responsibility to the other person. A teen needs to consider whether his *when* synchs with her *when*. One teen may feel ready for some level of intimacy and, spoken or not, may influence the decision of a partner who is not. This often happens because a young person may be afraid of losing her boyfriend if she senses urgency on his part to have sex. Of course, the roles here can be reversed.

Much like drinking or drug use, sexual activity may come with some emotional baggage as well. As we have seen, there is clinical and statistical evidence showing that early sexual behavior is linked to a loss of self-respect and depression among many teens.

It's probably not surprising that boys are considerably less likely to associate sexual behavior with negative emotional outcomes, probably because of the gender stereotypes. Although boys can feel bad, too. Sixteen-year-old Jon, for example, regrets that feeling depressed about school led him to engage in intimate sexual behavior, including oral sex, he thought would make him feel better. It didn't.

Often, teens seek solace in sexual activity only to learn later that the temporary diversion doesn't really fill the emotional needs they were trying to meet. Realizing they have surrendered something so personal with so little to show in return can add to feelings of anxiety, depression, or worthlessness. Sadly, most girls and boys who have been sexually active wish they had waited.

Tom, an 18-year-old senior, expressed sadness and disappointment at having been tricked into having sexual intercourse in the backseat of a car with a girl he had known for only two weeks. He thought she cared about him, but, as it turns out, she really only wanted sex. "I regret the whole experience with her. It wasn't real. Something in me knew she didn't care about me, but I tried not to listen to that, and I felt bad when I realized she was just in it for sex. That's not what's important to me. In the future, I'll have to know a lot about the person, love the person. Now I know what can happen."

Other teens may just feel they have no choice.

Peter is 15 years old and barely into his sophomore year at a suburban high school. Lanky, though not yet exactly tall, he prides himself on his athletic prowess and fills our available time together with the latest facts and figures from professional sports. His general disinterest with other matters (such as schoolwork) is typical—and endearing in a youthful sort of way. Not a drinker, smoker, or other drug user, Peter is an admitted partygoer, where those sorts of activities are regularly in full swing. But he knows from his parents and teachers the potential impact of substance use on his still-developing body and fears for the toll it would take on his athletic performance.

But one night at a party at a schoolmate's house, it was a performance of another sort that caused him concern. Approached by some friends, Peter was instructed to go to the basement; there was someone down there who wanted to talk to him. So, down the stairs he went to find a finished room, carpeted and furnished, and occupied by another teenager, a girl. Condom in hand, she asked Peter to have sex.

"I was scared," he says. "I mean, even being naked with a girl seemed weird." Fearing returning upstairs with the deed undone, Peter reluctantly removed his shirt, pants, and underwear . . . and had sex for the first time. He says he felt raped. When it comes to sex, who is doing what to whom can involve tangled issues of compliance and control. Like Peter, most teens inherently understand the value of their bodies and their sexuality. For either boys or girls to casually give it away is a mistake that often comes back to haunt them.

Another thing that is clear is that the earlier a person engages in sexual acts, the more likely he is to contract an STD.

This happens both because teens tend to have more partners the earlier they begin engaging in sexual activity, and also because of differences between girls and women in the types of cells that cover the cervix, which leaves girls more at risk for infection.

Dr. Meg Meeker says that parents may not realize STDs have changed and may not be quickly curable by a shot of penicillin. It also seems to be the case that there is insufficient evidence to conclude that condoms offer protection from all STDs, such as gonorrhea, HPV, herpes, chlamydia, and syphilis, especially when they are not used correctly—

> It has been estimated that 1 in 4 sexually active teens has an STD, according to Dr. Meg Meeker, a pediatrician specializing in adolescent medicine and author of *Epidemic: How Teen Sex Is Killing Our Kids.*

which can only be expected from kids who are new to sexual activity. She says, "If used correctly and consistently, condoms rarely fail to prevent the passage of a virus or bacteria in bodily fluid. The problem is, not all STDs are transmitted through fluid." Meeker points to HPV and herpes as viruses that are actually passed through skin contact. "Condoms only prevent contact with some bodily fluids and only the skin of the genitals themselves," she says.

Many teens tell me that they engage in oral sex because it is a "safe sex" alternative to intercourse. Fourteen-year-old Luke asked, "Is it true that you can't get an infection from oral sex? That's what a kid at school told me." What Luke—and his friend—didn't know, and clearly need to know, is that STDs and HIV *can* be transmitted through oral sex. Many sexually transmitted infections such as oral herpes, syphilis, gonorrhea, and HPV are conveyed without intercourse, through mouth-to-penis contact. On the other hand, 14-year-old Alan wondered if his girlfriend might get pregnant because he had ejaculated in her mouth. He needed some education as well.

Last but not least are potential legal consequences of intimate sexual behavior—a consideration many teens seem unaware of, such as state statutory rape laws or having sex with a partner who is under the influence of alcohol or drugs and may later claim they had not given consent.

On a January night in 2005, a group of five varsity hockey players, ages 16 to 18, at a prestigious New England prep school, finished dinner and stopped by the boys' locker room where, according to the head of school (as reported in the *Boston Globe*), they each received oral sex from a 15-year-old girl in a shower area. The boys were expelled and would eventually be charged by the district attorney under Massachusetts statutory-rape laws for engaging in a sex act with a child under the age of 16. According to a school investigation, this was just one of at least four instances in which the girl engaged in sex acts with boys on- or off-campus.

And in June of 2007, The Associated Press reported on the release from jail of a former high school football—and academic—star after serving more than two years of a 10-year sentence he received upon being convicted of aggravated child molestation for having oral sex at age 17 with a 15-year-old girl at a 2003 New Year's Eve party involving alcohol and marijuana.

As if all this weren't compelling enough evidence about the benefits of waiting to become sexually active, teens also need to be wary about the motivations behind sexual requests. Sometimes a sex partner can have a rationale of which they are not immediately aware, or are unwilling to share, including power, control, or revenge. This can simply add to the emotional upheaval that can come with early sexual behavior.

There are a lot of influencers in our society that promote unhealthy motivations for sexual activity. For boys, the message is usually that being a man means having sex . . . early and often, with as many girls as possible. Sex, then, becomes just a series of conquests that can leave boys feeling empty inside. For girls, the message is that being sexually active is what is expected and will make them more popular, more accepted, even more loved. And, after all, everyone else is doing it.

In our society, media images that portray sex as casual and unimportant create a false sense of acceptability in the minds of young people already predisposed to test limits and take risks. As 17-year-old Zach put it, "If you watch TV, you just assume everyone is having sex." These messages reflect stereotypes that teens don't always measure up to. And parents may have a hard time dispelling these notions both because of a reticence to wade deeply into a discussion about teen sex and also because of the sheer power of media images on teen perceptions and, in some cases, behavior.

It may well be that we have a naturally occurring disinclination to, and discomfort with, discussing sex with our children. Whatever the case and the cause, too many parents neglect to talk about sex with their kids. As difficult as it may be for parents, talking with young people about sexuality and sexual behavior is an incredibly important job. While other adults, such as teachers, counselors, or coaches, may also have occasion to talk with teens about sex, either formally (as in sex-education classes) or informally (as in answering questions teens may pose during office visits), parents are best-positioned to ground dialogue in important family values and to convey expectations for behavior.

Although teen sex is nothing new, the context in which it is taking place is different from 30 or even 10 years ago. Very different. Younger and younger, teens, even pre-teens, live in a world where intimate sexual behavior, including oral sex and intercourse, is standard fare, barely causing a raised eyebrow among boys and girls just on the cusp of puberty. Most report teen sex to be widespread and, frankly, not all that significant.

Sixteen-year-old Mark says he started dating Marci in 7th grade. Soon after, they became sexually active. Mark recalls, "We were going out a long time and I felt like I should. It was not romantic or sexual or anything. Neither of us knew what we were doing. We didn't really even talk about it. We just started kissing, I went up her shirt, and then she went down my pants. It was painful, the worst thing ever." By the start of 8th grade, Mark and Marci were having oral sex, and on Valentine's Day in the 9th grade, they had intercourse for the first time. Even Mark admits it was probably too early for his own good.

Of course, some teens voice no regrets at their choices regarding sexual behavior. Sixteen-year-old Toby and his 17-year-old girlfriend Ashley decided to become sexually active at their half-year anniversary—starting with oral sex and moving on to genital sex and, ultimately, intercourse.

Toby says they talked about it ahead of time, discussing "staying together" afterward, as well as concerns about pregnancy and disease. Toby says he did his homework, surfing the Internet in search of answers about condoms and other birth-control and safety measures. While Ashley's parents knew of their decision (Ashley was on "the pill"), Toby was less open with his. "They would probably be angry at first," he offers. "But, they know it's a serious, stable relationship." And remember Brenda from Chapter Three who had sex with her boyfriend after talking with her mom? She, too, had no second thoughts, even after he broke up with her.

Teens like Toby, Ashley, and Brenda tend to say they have sex to feel good, have fun, and to please their partner—although for many of them, these outcomes are elusive. Of course, peer pressure also plays a role as do societal stereotypes—maybe especially for boys, but increasingly for girls, as well.

Katie is a friendly, confident girl, with the dark hair and dark eyes of her half-Hispanic heritage. Though 14 and a freshman in high school, she is slight in stature but well-groomed, wearing jeans, a pink T-shirt, and sandals. She looks more like a 7th-grader than a high school student. Katie is wary about sexual behavior, pointing out that it is fraught with risk, such as STDs, getting pregnant, or being emotionally hurt. It can also damage a girl's reputation. "Guys would think they're easy, and other girls might think they're a slut." Even so, she estimates that 65 to 70 percent of her classmates are having oral sex or intercourse. She plans to wait for marriage.

Katie's story points to the enduring stereotypes that surround sexual behavior by teens. So, too, does a line attributed to comedian Robin Williams, "Boys are born with a brain and a penis, but only enough blood to operate one at a time."

Those stereotypes say that boys want—and should seek—"all the sex they can get"—and can't control their sexual urges—while girls better be careful or risk bearing a backlash of peer (and adult) disapproval. As 17-year-old Danny puts it, "The way sex is viewed, guys can have sex as much as they want; it's just another fling; it makes them more popular." Indeed, *Real Boys* author William Pollack points out that society creates an image of boys as "sexual machines." As for the girls, Danny says they're seen as "the whore."

Both stereotypes hurt teens. Boys, because they feel pressure to be sexually aggressive and active whether they want to or not (17-year-old Neil says, "I'm not going to say no as a guy"), and girls, because they often cannot safely discuss or explore their sexuality. Psychologist Mary Pipher, in her bestselling book *Reviving Ophelia: Saving the Selves of Adolescent Girls*, bemoans the double standard that still exists, saying, "The same girls who are pressured to have sex on Saturday night are called 'sluts' on Monday morning."

Most stereotypes, including these, don't always fit. "Teachers think it's the boys trying to get sex, but now it's the girls trying to get sex," explains Justin, a 14-year-old 8th-grader. Seventeen-year-old Neil agrees, "They're like guys now, pointing out the guys they had sex with, 'I did him, I did him, I did him.'"

But, teens who rush toward sex often fail to identify the emotional element attached to such behavior—one that doesn't disappear just because they want it to. Despite what popular culture and the media would have us believe, teens need adult guidance to understand that sexual contact means something. At its best, it is about expressing love, or affection, or at least making a physical connection with someone they care about. When someone has sex or "hooks-up" for self-gratification only, it devalues both partners.

In her book *The Sex Lives of Teenagers*, psychiatrist Lynn Ponton makes the case that sex is a fact of life for all young adults, even if only in fantasy. That view, of course, reflects a reality that children, like adults, are sexual beings. From an early age, children are sexual and sexualized, largely by our popular culture. In her book *Dilemmas of Desire*, author Deborah Tolman writes, "As early as middle school or even the waning moments of elementary school, girls and boys are relentlessly exposed to a set of rules, principles, and roles that are mapped out for the production of 'normal' heterosexual relationships and sexual behavior." *Epidemic's* Meeker says, "No discussion of teen sex would be complete without a detailed understanding of the impact of sexual messages (whether through words or visual imagery) on the tender adolescent psyche. And the impact is profound." She points to three "primary lessons" teenagers learn from the sexual messages they absorb: Sex is big; sexuality is the largest dimension of a person's personality; and cool people are promiscuous." As I do in Chapter Six, Meeker explores the role of movies, music, television, the Internet (the 800-Pound Gorilla), and advertising in promoting teen sexual behavior. She even shares the story of a 15-year-old female patient coming to an appointment carrying a copy of *Cosmopolitan* and giggling at the titles on the cover, such as "Seven Bad-Girl Bedroom Moves You Must Master."

Judith Levine, in *Harmful to Minors: The Perils of Protecting Children From Sex*, argues that sex is not inherently a bad thing for kids; rather, it is the stigmatizing of it that really hurts children. She says, "In America today, it is nearly impossible to publish a book that says children and teenagers can have sexual pleasure and be safe, too." But, Levine is not dismissive of the real risks that exist, such as HIV or STDs, and acknowledges that, "Of at least one phenomenon we have plenty of evidence: Kids are having sex they don't want." All the more reason, as I say throughout this book, that we need to engage teens in even the most difficult-to-have conversations to help them make the decisions they *do* want to make.

Regardless of where a parent stands on the questions of if and when, why and how, indiscriminate, sometimes indiscreet, and often exploitive sexual behavior by school children, some not yet old enough to even drive, points to forces at play that go beyond normal human development. Disturbing reports of early, casual, and sometimes public sexual behavior among young teens are most often met with surprise, even horror, by parents and school officials. Others see it as par for the course. Whatever the case, the fact is that these types of incidents seem to be happening with increasing frequency in all types of communities all across the country.

In the spring of 2003, a yellow school bus bumped its way along its appointed route in the southeast suburbs of Boston. On board, a middle school girl performed oral sex on a high school boy, classmates cheering them on. One year later came another sexual encounter on a school bus from the same community, this one involving two middle school students. A mom told a local paper, *The Enterprise*, "I find it shocking that I'm not shocked. It seems this type of behavior is no longer a big deal." Another parent said, "This is why I and a lot of other parents drive our kids to school. It's because of what happens on the school bus." She advocated stricter standards for the types of clothing worn to school, citing examples of thongs, and short shirts or shorts, all of which create a climate of sexuality.

More recently came a report of two 6th-graders engaging in sexual intercourse inside their St. Louis classroom while some friends looked on. And then there is the tale of two prep-school kids who, as sophomores, were having sex in various venues around campus, including the wrestling room and a laundry room in the school chapel.

Stories such as these leave many parents bewildered, trying to make sense of a sexual culture that may vary considerably from the one they encountered in high school—let alone in middle or elementary school.

Today's teens, on the whole, appear less inhibited about sexual behavior than teens a generation ago. Hidden behind the explosion of intimate sexual behavior lies a pervasive attitude that, short of intercourse, sex—if you even call it that—just doesn't matter. Sex with a friend, sex with a stranger, sex in private, sex in public. It all boils down to just having fun. It's no big deal. Some of the students interviewed about one of the bus incidents seemed nonchalant about the event, as though it was expected or happens all the time. Seventeen-year-old Kelly, interviewed by another local paper, *The Patriot Ledger*, had this to say about oral sex: "There are people that I know who think it's just another thing. It's just not a big deal. One night it will just happen and it's not a big wow. It's just what we did Friday night."

Recently, much attention has been paid to the concept of "buddy sex," or "friends with benefits" (remember Steve who was having genital sex with a classmate). A newspaper cartoon depicting a boy saying to a girl, "Sure, I'll sleep with you as long as it means absolutely nothing," reflects the way many teens view sexual behavior these days. Eighteen-year-old Kevin, a college freshman, says, "My suite-mate will just knock on my door in the middle of the night. I know she's not here to talk."

Such "recreational" sex—not to mention the casual public incidents mentioned before—concerns developmental and relationship experts who fear that these young people may have difficulty forming lasting attachments down the road precisely because sexual behavior—a healthy component of committed, adult relationships—has become devalued to the point where it may not mean much of anything other than "having fun" or "feeling good." Meeker spells out four main reasons she believes teenagers have sex, none of which, she says, are healthy or lead to good relationships: for fun, excitement, and thrills; to be accepted by peers or society at large; to have their needs met (15-year-old Adam, a 9th-grader, tells me he started doing sexual things with his girlfriend the year before. "It was pretty cool," he said, describing their genital touching at the movies. "She said, 'I want to fuck you,' and it made me feel wanted."); or to lose themselves (as in self-medicating).

Many teens admit to feeling some urgency around the whole issue of sexual behavior. Thus, they may become sexually active less because they want to than because they believe it's time they did. This may be especially the case for boys. Blair says, "I must be the only 18-year-old on the planet who hasn't had sex." Eighteen-year-old John says, "My friend kept saying, 'Come on, get in the game.'" Thirteen-year-old Bryan says, "I just want to do it all at once and get it over with so that I can focus on just having a relationship with a girl." And 16-year-old Connor, after exchanging genital touches with a girl following a dance, expressed relief, "I finally did it!"

What You Can Do

While friends and older siblings are, of course, important influencers of teen decisions about sex, with patience and no small amount of courage, parents can help young adults better understand the physical and emotional risks of sexual behavior, the responsibilities that come with mutually caring and respectful relationships, standards for acceptable behavior, and the role that alcohol and other drugs can play in impairing judgment when it comes to making decisions about sex.

It also seems to make a difference regarding who does the talking. One report cited in *Puberty, Sexuality, and the Self: Boys and Girls at Adolescence*, by Karin A. Martin, reveals that when moms talk about sex, their children—boys and girls alike—are more likely to put off intercourse. Interestingly, the reverse is the case when dads talk to boys. Why? Well, according to a first-year psychology student of mine, "It's a pep rally!" Fifteen-year-old Tyler says, "My dad just bought me some condoms when we were in the drugstore. He kind of made a joke about it." Other dads only warn their sons not to get a girl pregnant.

It is critical that we evaluate the messages we are sending teens about our expectations for sexual activity. While it may be good advice to use a condom so as not to get a girl pregnant, or, less likely, to prevent an STD, Tyler is left without any meaningful input from his dad on how to make decisions that are appropriate for him regarding sexual behavior. He also has no inkling of what choices his dad might hope he will make. To the contrary, the message conveyed to him was "Do what you want as long as it doesn't produce a baby."

Teens need help from their mom and dad to understand the many physical and emotional ramifications of sexual behavior and to make the important link between actions and outcomes. They also need straight talk from us about the responsibilities that come hand-in-hand with relationships, such as respecting the other person's emotions and protecting them from physical or psychological harm.

And, finally, learning self-control, even overpowerful sexual urges, is an important part of psychosocial development. It teaches us how to delay self-gratification and certainly not to seek it at the expense of someone else's physical, emotional, or social well-being. More to the point, it is a really healthy thing for kids to postpone sexual behavior until they are certain that they understand and are ready to accept all of the outcomes that can result.

Four

Hormones and Hobgoblins

As an adult narrating the experiences of his youth, Kevin Arnold, the protagonist in the '90s hit television show, *The Wonder Years*, noted, "Growing up is not so much a straight line as a series of advances and retreats." Every parent, of a child of any age, knows that no truer words have ever been spoken. What parents may not realize is that understanding these ebbs and flows is absolutely critical in recognizing the challenges young people face in their daily lives. For parents, taking the opportunity to discover what they don't know is an important step in closing the reality gap.

Some people tend to think of maturation as linear, beginning at point A and ending at point Z. In reality, as young people mature, they move back and forth along a continuum of growth, showing demonstrable signs of progress one day, only to awaken the next day seemingly further behind. This phenomenon marks both their uncertainty about all of the physical, social, and emotional changes they are going through and their antipathy toward the whole developmental process. As we know from our own experiences, growing up isn't easy—and there's some reason to believe it's harder than ever before.

Staring into the abyss of impending independence, 17-year-old Ben, a wiry south Florida teen with dark, curly hair and an easy laugh, tells me about his recent retreat to the local baseball field to think through a rather painful breakup with his girlfriend. He says he likes going there because it's always a place where he can block out the day-to-day struggles of growing up and simply focus on one of his favorite pastimes, baseball. This time, though, the tactic didn't work, and Ben says he finally knew that the little boy was gone.

It's like when I was teaching sailing last summer," he explains. "Across the water, I saw these parents in a boat towing a kid on a raft. It reminded me of sailing with my parents when I was a kid. He even looked like me! It made me sad."

As evidenced by Ben's stories, it is not without a degree of regret and a sense of loss for what came before that teens face the nevertheless exciting prospect of becoming an adult. The awkward dance of adolescence affords teens the opportunity to try out new identities, new decisions, and new relationships before returning to the safe harbor of childhood predictability. Some call it regression. I call it shelter.

Moving backward toward a safer place (a bedroom, a favorite chair, or a beloved stuffed animal) offers kids a brief respite from the unrelenting push to become smarter, stronger, more mature, more responsible, and more prepared for adulthood. It helps to ease the stress of three most important tasks a teen must master: figuring out his own identity, achieving a degree of independence from his parents, and building more adult-like relationships within his peer group. When budding teens can rely on their parents for a consistency of care, no matter how disruptive or distasteful their behavior might become, it helps them find the confidence they need to move forward. This is an important result to keep in mind as adolescence continues and our teens come to seem more and more distant from us. We are an anchor for our children. Even when they can't show it, teens need us to be present, vigilant, concerned for their welfare, and caring about the people they are and are becoming.

Who Am I?

In terms of a child's physical, cognitive, and social-emotional growth, the period of adolescence offers many developmental dilemmas. Chief among these is establishing an identity to call his or her own. In his book *Identity: Youth and Crisis*, famed developmental psychologist Erik Erikson refers to identity as a "subjective sense of invigorating sameness and continuity." The shorthand for a teen might be "knowing," on a consistent basis, who he or she "is." Remember Billy, our rock-star friend from Chapter Two? He is well on his way toward establishing at least one part of his identity (vocation): musician!

Erikson maintains that to adequately assess their emerging identities, young people rely on the image projected back to them by the significant adults in their lives. In other words, much of what teens think of themselves is a reflection of how they believe we see them.

> *You are competent, capable, and loveable* are three messages we want to send to our growing teens—regardless of how much they might be driving us crazy!

To paraphrase Erikson, to experience wholeness, young people must feel continuity between how they think of themselves and how they believe others think of them. It is really this commonality and consistency of self-definition that helps teens figure out their identity.

In truth, the process and challenge of acquiring an identity has been pondered and written about for generations. The enormity of the task and its rather transparent manifestations in the everyday lives of teens make it unmistakable, remarkable, and incredibly fascinating. Watching our teens change before our eyes, acting like one person one day and another the next, might seem bewildering, but if we view this frenetic behavior through a developmental lens, thereby remembering what all of this is actually about, we can better understand and appreciate what we see. This makes our relationship with them stronger, our communication easier, and the reality gap smaller.

Sigmund Freud, who co-founded the psychoanalytic school of psychology, maintained that identity attainment results from a process by which an individual incorporates the characteristics of another person. He said that identification is "invariably based on an emotional tie with an object," typically the parent.

Psychologist James Marcia sees identity in a slightly different way, as a self-structure built of drives, abilities, beliefs, and individual history. Marcia says that the better constructed the identity, the more likely it is that the individual will recognize both his own uniqueness from and similarity to others. Both components are important for growing teens. Individuality helps them cement their very own place in the world and their particular ability to contribute to the people and places around them. Similarity nurtures sociability and, importantly, empathy.

Regardless of whose theory we most relate to, there have been scores of studies that substantiate the existence of an adolescent developmental process leading to an expanded and more comprehensive personality. And while that process actually begins long before adolescence, it is during the teenage years that this struggle becomes crystallized into an active quest to answer the question, "Who am I?"

In her relentless search for identity, a teen will "try out" different modes of behavior, dress, and speech. This accounts for much of the almost-daily, and sometimes confusing, changes we see in our teens involving such things such as dress, hairstyles, speech patterns, and even personalities. She is searching and searching for just the right identity, the right fit. And what she finds, and decides to hold on to, will have significant implications for her entire life.

Emerging Independence

While on the one hand looking to parents to clarify who he is, a teen will at the same time seek some degree of separation from mom and dad. This is also a critical piece of identity formation, the very basis of the march to independence. For teens to truly understand who they are, they need to find a self-definition that has nothing to do with their parents. In a sense, they start becoming "Mark" or "Mary," as opposed to "Richard's son, Mark," or "Collette's daughter, Mary."

Achieving independence is no easy task, and it does not happen all at once. For most of their adolescence, teens will have one foot out the door and the other planted firmly within. In this way, they are testing the outside world without fully committing to entering it—knowing all the while that they can retreat to the safety of the familiar, protective world of home and family. This toe-in-the-water approach to finding independence helps young people alleviate some of the stress associated with transition.

The process of separation is accompanied by a fair amount of trepidation for teens and parents alike. Teens are charting a new life-course, excited yet anxious about testing out their new identities and the limits of their capacity to handle what the world will throw at them. Parents, on the other hand, sense their teen's anxiety and understand the potential dangers of too much freedom, too early. This creates a conflict for us, on the one hand knowing the importance of becoming independent and on the other hand realizing that doing so exposes our teens to greater risks. In many ways, the challenge for parents is akin to walking a tightrope, carefully trying to maintain the proper balance so as not to falter and fall one way or the other. Lean too far to the left, and we can smother our child. Lean too far to the right, and we might leave him unprepared to make the tough calls of adolescence.

Our natural inclination, of course, is to hold on to our children as tightly as possible and never let go! Wouldn't it be great if we could really protect them that way? But the trick of successful parenting is finding a balance between holding on to teens while gradually, systematically letting them go. It is a vexing task, perhaps the most difficult part of raising or loving teens.

As they grow, young people want a longer leash, but feel compromised by having no leash at all. They, perhaps better than we, understand their limitations and find comfort in the structure that comes with expectations, rules, and consequences. As 17-year-old Tommy says, "Sometimes I just want my parents to be parents," reflecting his belief that his mom and dad abandoned their parenting role a bit too soon. Teens can be scared when we let go too quickly, because they may not yet be developmentally ready to chart their own course. They want the safety and security that comes with knowing that there are boundaries, both literally (as in curfews) and figuratively (as in what constitutes appropriate behavior, such as saying no to alcohol).

Given teens' desire for our continued involvement, we may be surprised that our attempts to nurture them are often met with rejection. This is because such "interference" is the antithesis of what they are trying to accomplish, and thus our best attempts to be part of their lives are sometimes met with expressions of annoyance and disgust, despite the fact that involvement really is what they want from us! This only adds to the emotional toll the behavior of growing teens takes on aging parents, placing them in a seemingly no-win situation.

Letting go when we should be holding on, and holding on when we should be letting go. Many parents understandably have trouble discerning when to do what. Finding the proper timing and balance in parenting teens is a delicate undertaking. And it requires lots of information, lots of verification, and no small amount of courage.

By working with our teens however, we can find that balance, even if the equation keeps changing. Letting go should happen in small doses, matching a teen's preparedness for independence and decision-making. Holding on is just as critical, especially when teens are struggling with choices about personal behavior. As I discuss throughout this book, teens grappling with developmental tasks related to identity, independence, or relationships with peers need and appreciate our help. So, too, do teens facing other life challenges, such as academic struggles, injury or illness, boredom, loneliness, anxiety, stress, and depression. It's all part of the package of parenthood and the incumbent responsibilities of other adults who work with and care about teens.

Often we allow ourselves to be deluded into thinking, "We're done," or maybe even, "They want us to be done." But it is at our child's peril that we let our guard down just because our teen suddenly looks or acts older. Normal development is a marathon, not a sprint, and the rapid-fire changes of adolescence require our full attention. They develop quickly, happen suddenly, and then give way to yet even more change, like a sudden summer thunderstorm that gives little warning, arrives with great ferocity, and disappears just about the time we finish preparing for the onslaught!

Patricia Hersh, in her book *A Tribe Apart*, documents what she calls her "journey into the heart of American adolescence." She concludes that adults have abandoned teens in droves—at least in the social/emotional sense—leaving them to their own devices to find the behaviors and attitudes that "work" in their world. Unfortunately, too often what "works" has to do with what is "cool" or "in," regardless of whether it's "good" or "smart." Referring to the students at a school where she spent some time, Hersh says, "The school is saturated with the aura of self-conscious posing among middle school students. They walk around hyper-alert to what is cool and what is not, who to be like, who is or is not one's friend, what to wear, what to do, how to act."

So strong is the draw to the modern-day teen culture that it often obscures the danger inherent in choices about alcohol, drugs, sex, driving, bullying, and hazing. That's why we need to continue to pay attention! But, as a colleague of mine at SADD says, "Parents reach a point where they just give up!" That can have unintentional, dangerous consequences. A Carnegie Council on Adolescent Development study predicts, "If the nation continues to neglect this age group, millions of young adolescents will become lifelong casualties of drug and alcohol abuse, teen pregnancy, AIDS, suicide, and violence."

Our interference will often seem unwanted, making the prospect of participating in the lives of our teen a daunting one. But we must persevere in paying attention—and talking—to these people we love the most, lest they create what Hersh refers to as a "sub-culture" of teens un-nurtured and uninfluenced by the values we cherish.

The title of Anthony Wolf's popular book (which we mentioned in Chapter One), *Get Out Of My Life, But First Could You Drive Me and Cheryl to the Mall?*, succinctly captures the duality of longing and need balanced by most teens. In truth, teens need parents for more than rides to the mall or money for the movies. They require a finely textured level of support and guidance that cannot often be found in the transitory peer relationships of adolescence. But don't expect them to ask for it. Their studied indifference suckers many a parent into believing they have been vanquished to the outer perimeter of meaning in a young adult's life. But again, nothing could be further from the truth.

Jimmy is a typical teen, somewhat awkward, but with signs of manhood, like the stubble on his chin, beginning to emerge on his decidedly adolescent exterior. Jimmy is conflicted about his relationship with his parents, and they are equally confused. Jimmy wears two faces. At home, it's still easy for his parents to connect to the playful, affectionate boy they have known for all of his 16 years. Outside, when he could be "caught" by his friends, Jimmy rejects any public displays of affection and recoils in horror at his parents' verbal expressions of love or support. Jimmy's walking that line between dependence and autonomy, hoping his parents don't show up for his soccer game, while covertly scanning the crowd of onlookers to make sure they have! Gone are the days of enthusiastic recognition and affectionate affirmation (at least outside the concealing walls of home). They have been replaced by a new loyalty to what might be called a "code" of adolescence: Friends come first.

Jimmy is doing what teens do best, pushing parents aside in favor of a freshly minted peer group. After all, it is the peer group against which he must now increasingly judge his value and worth. At the same time, however, he's just as likely to be pulling his mom and dad close for support, especially during times of crisis (such as the death of a relative or a serious injury or illness) or perceived crisis (such as the ending of a "romantic" relationship).

Generations of teens have tentatively reached for adulthood, while still holding tightly to the safety and security of the childhood they're not yet completely sure they want to leave behind.

Fourteen-year-old Ian, eschewing parental involvement, also sounds like the average teen. "I spend as little time with my parents as possible," he tells me, with a look of disgust. "It's just not fun anymore. I think, 'Please stay away.'" But there's something in his demeanor, his body language, that tells me there's sadness just beneath his façade of disdain.

Slowly but surely, Ian reveals what's really going on: "Lately, I don't get along too good with my parents, even though we used to be pretty close. There's a lot of fighting between them at home. I kind of hope they'll split up and get it over with. They don't even sleep in the same room anymore. I think my mom has gone insane, and I think my dad has an anger problem." What Ian is saying is that he wants to move on, find independence, and be on his own. At the same time, his distress about his parent's relationship belies his continued reliance on them for support, guidance, and counsel, which the problems between them are making scarce. It also serves as an important reminder to us that no matter our own personal circumstances, we need to be sure we are carving out the time to care for our kids, even though they may seem all grown up and self-sufficient.

Changes in the parent-child relationship, such as what Ian experienced with his parents, can signal that something has gone awry. Holding on then becomes even more important so that parents and teens can understand the dynamics that impede healthy family interaction. In this way, they can work together toward solutions that promote intimacy rather than divisiveness.

Teens and Their Peers

Establishing healthy, adult-like relationships with peers presents the third developmental challenge of adolescence. The peer group takes on particular significance during the teenage years and, for many young adults, becomes their strongest influence. This is especially true when it comes to decision-making: While parents are the number-one reason why kids make good choices, peers are the number-one reason they don't!

Suddenly, the peer group is paramount. Especially during adolescence, it is through friends that kids "rate" themselves and see how they stack up. Generally, teens believe that other teens see the world from their perspective and thus provide a more realistic gauge of skills and abilities than do parents, other family members, or other adults.

For example, when Kevin's teammates applaud his performance at the foul line, it probably means more than the very same accolade coming from his mom or dad. Or when Julie's best friend says, "Wow, I love your haircut. You look beautiful!" she's likely to place more stock in that being an accurate evaluation of her attractiveness than in similar comments by her parents.

Peers also serve as a filter of the attitudes and values promoted by the adults in a teen's life. Hopefully, they will have absorbed what we have to say about everything from bullying, to violence, to drugs, to sex. Now it's time to do some comparison-shopping to ascertain what these suddenly more important people believe. *What do you think?* or even, *What do your parents say?* are questions, spoken or unspoken, that many teens have on their minds as they talk with their friends about issues like drinking, drugs, and sex.

Parents can support a healthy transition away from the family and toward the peer group by recognizing it as a critical step toward adulthood, encouraging close peer-to-peer relationships, and monitoring the behavior of those with whom their teen is spending time. This last step makes it more likely that their child will make good decisions. Not surprisingly, young people with friends who make poor choices (such as using drugs) are more likely to do so themselves.

Teens believe that difficulty in forming close, lasting relationships with their peers represents a fundamental failure. And, in some ways, they are right. That makes it all the more important that parents engage in their relationship-building process, rather than back away from it. We can help them gain the insights and skills they need to be successful in forging—and keeping—friendships. Not being able to do so, for both boys and girls *with* both boys and girls, undermines healthy development.

Popularity among peers is so important to teens, because it affects their overall emotional, even physical, well-being. That is a powerful motivation for young people to make choices they previously would have quickly ruled out; it's all in the interest of having friends. As 14-year-old

Chase, a self-assured, articulate 8th-grader with mussed-up blond hair and an easy smile, explains, "When you first start middle school, your instinct is to be popular, to be liked, and to do almost anything other kids are doing." But with his parents' help, Chase resisted those temptations, even girls offering oral sex for money. He's confident in himself and his decision-making, and describes a close relationship with his parents and their ability to communicate about most anything. He says that parents of teens should, "Talk to them a lot more often and tell them you'll back them up and support them."

Most of us can remember the urgency, anxiety, and purpose with which we pursued peer relationships during middle (or junior high) school and high school. It's not much different today. And it's not always easy. Teens, particularly younger ones, have a remarkable capacity to tease, taunt, harass, and exclude those they deem less deserving of respect or friendship. A visit to any school lunchroom reveals a veritable laboratory of social anxieties and status.

What is important to remember is the degree to which our teen can be influenced by what she sees other kids her age, and older kids in her school, doing. Cindy is a friendly, personable 11th-grader, who describes herself as interesting, fun, exciting, and outgoing. Enrolled in a large, urban New England high school, she knows well the smorgasbord of behaviors engaged in by her classmates. And, to her credit, she even seems aware of some of the dangers. "I've seen so many of my friends go down the drain," she says. "I don't think it's worth it." Nevertheless, Cindy herself is an occasional drug user, admitting to smoking pot since freshman year. Cindy also says she's a big drinker—mostly Smirnoff Ice and beer—a habit that also began in the 9th grade. According to Cindy, her parents are fairly hands-off. They'd prefer she not drink, but "really don't care." When it comes to sex, her parents don't talk about it at all . . . despite the fact that she and her boyfriend regularly share a bed in their home. In truth, Cindy has no idea of her parents' values and real expectations of her. And they probably have no idea of how relevant sex, drugs, and drinking have become in her life. Or why she might be engaged in these behaviors at all.

When I ask teens why they are drinking, or using drugs, or having sex, or driving like crazy people, they almost always shrug and say, "Because it's fun." I dig a little deeper, "Yeah, but why else . . . there's plenty of other ways to have fun, right?"

"Well, yeah . . . " is often the reply. And then the truth slowly reveals itself.

Dressed in tan cargo shorts, a blue Old Navy T-shirt, and flip-flops, Robbie appeared for his interview tanned, relaxed, only too happy to share his recent experience with stress and its aftermath. The pressure he feels from his parents to do well in school, the academic difficulties that continue, and the trouble he's had making friends formed, for him, a "perfect storm" of stress and anxiety, leading him to alcohol for relief. For Robbie, drinking began in 8th grade. Most weekends include vodka, Malibu Mixers, and sometimes beer. But, as Robbie puts it, "Beer does-n't get you wasted fast enough." Robbie describes his drinking as the "only escape from the shit in my life: school, grades, and parents."

Perhaps not surprisingly, teens who don't feel good about themselves, about school, about their relationships with family, friends, or influential adults in their lives often do what adults do: self-medicate. Robbie is reacting to the stress in his life and his own feelings of inadequacy by compensating through alcohol. Numbness trumps reality. And alcohol is an escape, a way around the pain.

For many teens, relentless feelings of stress are a part of the pain they feel. Gone are the days of freewheeling independence during non-school hours. Society is not as safe a place as it once was—and fewer parents are around in the afternoons to keep a watchful eye on their children. The result: Teens are spending more and more time in structured extracurricu-lar activities. While there are certainly benefits to the adult guidance and supervision that come hand-in-hand with these types of activities, the more commitments a teen has, the more likely it is that pressure will mount.

In December of 2004, I was interviewed by Andy Gammill, a reporter for the *Indianapolis Star Tribune*, about the relatively new explosion of after-school clubs and activities. Gammill cited a recent "Public Agenda" survey, in which 62 percent of middle and high school students said they participate in school clubs or extracurricular activities, in addition to sports. While these activities provide important outlets for socialization and development of individual interests and skills (indeed, SADD encourages a host of activities, such as service-learning projects, meant to involve young people in constructive alternatives), over-involvement only adds to the demands of daily schoolwork, household chores, or jobs. Teens can quickly find themselves in over their heads.

Throughout adolescence, teens increasingly internalize a work ethic pushed on them by parents or teachers. And sometimes they go too far in creating unrealistic demands for themselves. This means that teens may require help to prioritize their time and ideas of how to incorporate pressure "release valves" into their schedules. Making time for family, play, and unstructured exercise, as opposed to just organized team sports, is just as important for teens as it is for younger children. Teens don't always receive as much encouragement to pursue leisure activities as they do to pursue academics or structured athletics. But such leisure activities help teens find balance and avoid the pitfalls of too much, too fast, too soon.

As we have seen in previous chapters, parents are well-advised to protect their teens from the sorts of inordinate, unhealthy stresses that may leave them anxious and depressed. The goal, however, should not be to remove all stress from the lives of children. That would be impossible. And, in reality, it wouldn't even be desirable, both because some level of stress helps us to function optimally in certain situations and also because stress can be normal and predictable. Instead, we should seek to monitor the sources and extent of the stress. I'll discuss this in more detail later in this chapter.

Also, like adults, teens juggle many variables when making decisions about personal behavior. But, unlike adults, teens' "consideration set" is remarkably malleable and their thought process fast and fluid. In other words, the things that influence their decision-making are constantly—and rapidly—changing, as they have yet to settle on an identity that, in adulthood, will steer them toward choices consistent with whom they believe they are. Without those guidelines in place, the factors they weigh in making decisions change in number and proportion, depending on their age and the choices they are facing. A 12-year-old, for example, might decide to experiment with drugs to fit in with friends who are doing so (I call this an external goal), while a 17-year-old is more likely to do so in order to feel good (an internal goal). Identifying those determining factors can help parents help teens plan detours around trouble.

Not knowing the many antecedents of decision-making and the environment in which those decisions occur reduces a parent's ability to help their teen confidently cross the stage toward healthy adulthood. As we've discussed, it's difficult to keep up with changing times, attitudes, and influences. Plus, the very teens we are trying to nurture and protect don't always make matters easy for concerned parents. Information about what leads kids to do certain things is helpful in our search for answers to the eternal, nagging questions: *Why did they do that? What were they thinking? Were they thinking at all?*

For generations, parents have scratched their heads in bewilderment at some of the decisions boys and girls make. The difference today is that we actually do know a whole lot more about their reasons.

The Difference Between Boys and Girls

Adolescence imposes many demands on young people. New cognitive and physical capabilities coincide with increasing academic and social requirements. It is a confusing, strenuous period, made more so by a culture that conveys different, and often conflicting, expectations for boys and girls. During this time of transition, age-old, gender-based stereotypes promoted by our society in books, magazines, movies, and television take on new life, shaping the perceptions and behavior of teens, while limiting their opportunities to fully explore their intellectual, physical, social, and emotional capacities.

For sure, there are biological differences between men and women when it comes to behavior, many of which are linked to surges of hormones in early infancy and again during puberty. In her book *The Female Brain*, neuropsychiatrist Louann Brizendine details those changes and reminds us of variances in brain structure and circuitry that make girls girls and boys boys. For example, Brizendine notes that, on average, women are better than men at observing and expressing emotions. No surprise there. Men, on the other hand, have more brain space set aside for sexual drive, action, and aggression. Sound familiar?

All that having been said, there is truth to the adage that children become who, or what, we tell them they are. Even in the twenty-first century, adults often send teens the wrong messages about what we expect their attitudes and behaviors to be. Nowhere are those messages more damaging than in the areas of emotionality and sexuality. And boys and girls receive vastly different, but equally damaging, messages.

We'll start with boys. Boys are conditioned, and presumed to be, emotionally tougher than girls. As a result, they are too often missing out on important conversations with caring adults, particularly men, about their emotions and what to do with them. It may also be the case that the adult male role models in their life do not easily exhibit or share their own emotions, making it even harder for boys to do so. That lack of communication and modeling leaves boys reluctant and ill-prepared to identify and articulate the emotional elements in their lives. Instead, they may just fall back on the stereotypical male popularized in our culture, even if it doesn't always match the true nature of boys. That can leave them feeling short-changed in their understanding of who they really are and disconnected from the people they love most.

In *Raising Cain*, Dan Kindlon and Michael Thompson point out that, whatever the role of biology in the expression of emotion, boys are very different from girls and much of that difference is likely "amplified" by our broader culture, which encourages emotional development for girls and discourages it for boys. They say, "Boys yearn for emotional connection, but they are allowed very little practice at it. They've had few lessons in learning to 'read' others, to pick up on emotional cues through conversation, facial expression, or subtle body language."

Discussing his relationship with his parents, 19-year-old Will tells me, "I don't discuss my feelings very much, or emotions. I don't know if I get it from them. They've always been very loving and caring, but not in a typical way. I know they love me, but they don't say it much."

Parents, Kindlon and Thompson argue, have a particularly strong influence on a boy's willingness to become emotionally literate. Indeed, we can all convey to boys—through encouragement and example—that it is important to learn the language of feelings, to identify those feelings, and to share them. In other words, to connect with others through emotional expression (love, anger, jealousy, for example) and receptiveness. While Kindlon and Thompson acknowledge that a relationship between a father and son may appear wholly different than a mother's relationship with her son or daughter in terms of the level of exploration and sharing of feelings, or the degree of affection expressed, they may not necessarily be "less emotional." Nevertheless, they say, "We believe that in general it is better not to leave important feelings unexpressed and that words are often the clearest and most unequivocal way to do this."

Yet, somehow, our society has come to confuse emotion and affection with sexuality. While it is undeniable that we live in a world where children, and the adults who care for them, must be vigilant against people who may do them harm, our children are at the same time unwitting victims of evolving social norms that equate expressions of emotion and appropriate touch ("good touch") with questionable intentions. Teenage boys, given a developmental predisposition to wonder about their own sexuality, are particularly vulnerable to missing out on much-needed attention and affection (giving and receiving), fearing that it might "make them gay," or at least to appear to be so.

Kindlon and Thompson talk about the emotional mis-education of boys, a phenomenon that contributes to a "culture of cruelty" and does little to nurture their emotional lives. Without encouragement from parents to explore, understand, and explain their feelings—about themselves and others—or to develop compassion, sensitivity, and warmth toward others, boys suffer in silence. The disconnectedness of boys— and the sadness and anger it spawns—leaves them longing for meaningful dialogue and makes them particularly susceptible to destructive decisions. When there's no healthy outlet for emotion, it comes out in other ways, like drinking or violence.

Real Boys and Real Boys Voices author William Pollack says, "Boys long to talk about the things that are hurting them—their harassment from other boys, their troubled relationships with their fathers, their embarrassment around girls, and confusion about sex, their disconnection from and love for their parents, the violence that haunts them at school and on the street, their constant fear that they might not be as masculine as other boys."

Recognizing the widespread neglect of boys, and their high rates of school dropout, adjudication, and drug and alcohol abuse, First Lady Laura Bush said in an interview with *Parade* magazine, "There are life skills that we teach girls but don't teach boys. We've raised them to be totally self-reliant, starting really too early. They need the nurturing all humans need."

Laura Bush is, of course, exactly right. Like girls, boys need and want nurturing, attention, and affection. Those important ingredients of humanity help anchor them against the robust tide of adolescence, reaffirm their place in the world, and give them the emotional energy they need to successfully tackle this most difficult of life's transitions.

And what about girls? Girls in our society are expected and encouraged to dwell in the world of feelings, but too often are left without adequate recognition and support for their logical, non-emotional intellectual capabilities—whereas boys have traditionally been celebrated for their academic and athletic accomplishments. The good news is that the gap appears to be closing. The bad news is that it comes with an additional set of burdens or expectations for girls that may account, in part, for their increasing use and abuse of substances like alcohol.

Additionally, and quixotically, girls are encouraged to learn the language of emotion, but then discouraged to apply it to themselves. Their job is to care for others even at their own expense. This sublimation leaves girls stuck with the burden of understanding the genesis of their own emotionality, but unable to act upon it lest they be viewed as selfish. "Take care of others, not you," is the message many girls receive. Mary Pipher writes in *Reviving Ophelia*, "Girls are uncomfortable identifying and stating their needs, especially with boys and adults. They worry about not being nice or appearing selfish." That presents dangers for growing girls, both psychologically and physically, as the emotional difficulties (internalized problems such as anxiety and depression) manifest themselves externally in the form of substance abuse, truancy, sexual promiscuity, cutting behaviors, eating disorders, and more.

During adolescence, especially, it is critical that girls be encouraged to recognize, act on, and accept the emotional fuel that comes with genuine, supportive, affectionate (and appropriate) attention from important adults in their lives. Doing so validates self-worth and platforms the very nurturing behavior others have come to expect of girls. When they allow themselves to be nurtured, they can better nurture others.

Pipher points out that at puberty, girls face enormous pressure from our society to abandon their "true self" in the interest of adopting a "false self" more consistent with the expectations of others than those they hold for themselves. "This is when girls learn to be nice, rather than honest," says Pipher, identifying four likely responses for girls: conform, withdraw, be depressed, or get angry. None of those options seems an ideal existence for girls struggling to find their place, and to make good decisions, in the rough-and-tumble world of adolescence.

For both boys and girls, at the most basic level, the Sense of Self informs and directs outward behavior. In other words, how a teen feels about himself plays a significant role in the decisions he makes. A teen who feels good about himself is less likely to make poor choices about alcohol, drugs, and sexual behavior. Not so much because he's having a good day as opposed to a bad one, but rather because he feels some sense of accomplishment in rising to the developmental challenges that face him without resorting to risky behavior to feel more grown up, more independent, or more in control. Each of these relates to his Sense of Self—one of a number of predictors about alcohol and drug use, for example.

Unlike self-concept (a fairly objective description of oneself, such as "I am short") or self-esteem (a more subjective evaluation of that description, such as "being short is bad"), Sense of Self—as I have defined it in my research—is a more global concept that captures a teen's assessment of her own progress in meeting the three developmental tasks we have discussed: successfully establishing an identity, achieving an appropriate degree of independence from her parents, and developing meaningful relationships with her peers. These successes boost a teen's Sense of Self, leading to more positive feelings about her place in the world, her family, and her peer group. High Sense of Self teens tend to describe themselves as smart, successful, responsible, and confident.

Fourteen-year-old Christopher, a Florida 8th-grader, tells me that he is "energetic, smart, kind, and easy to get along with." He also rates himself on the high end of a scale measuring such traits as happiness, optimism, success, and resiliency. Thirteen-year-old Tonya also describes herself as happy, capable, and successful, and says, "I have a nice personality and people like being around me."

Those are important considerations when it comes to decision-making. The data make clear that high Sense of Self teens feel better, make better decisions, and enjoy better interpersonal relationships than do their low Sense of Self peers. They are also more likely to avoid alcohol and drug use; more resistant to pressure from peers to drink, use drugs, or have sex; and more inclined to feel positively about their relationships with their parents.

On the other hand, low Sense of Self teens are more likely to use alcohol; more likely to use drugs to escape from or forget about problems; more likely to have friends who use drugs; more likely to cite boredom and depression as reasons to have sex and to associate it with negative emotional outcomes such as depression or loss of self-respect; and more likely to feel strongly that it is OK to drive after drinking or using drugs.

What You Can Do

This information offers parents some clues as to how they can move their teen toward a positive Sense of Self simply by helping him master the developmental tasks of the day. Just as Mom and Dad were there to witness his first steps, first swim, and first school day, a teen needs them to be around to lend support as he navigates the sometimes treacherous waters that lie between childhood and adulthood—brimming with opportunities to engage in behaviors they might object to. Parents—and other important mentors—can help their teen by supporting a wide sampling of interests, activities, and age-appropriate behaviors; encouraging separation from the family and age-appropriate independence in decision-making; and teaching peer-to-peer social skills and facilitating (positive) peer relationships.

Such parental intervention can go a long way toward helping kids stay away from trouble. More than half of teens whose parents provide a strong level of guidance say they avoid alcohol (53 percent) and sexual activity (52 percent), as compared with those whose parents do not (19 percent and 27 percent, respectively). Two-thirds (67 percent) of those teens say they avoid drugs.

Decision Factors

There are, of course, a myriad of factors that influence a teen's Sense of Self, and she performs an elaborate analysis in determining the pros and cons of any particular decision. According to my research, these decisions are influenced by mental states, personal goals, potential outcomes, and significant people.

Being aware of them gives parents a leg up in influencing them. And that needs to be done ahead of time, because when the moment of decision arrives, mom and dad or other significant adults are unlikely to be around. They're not at the parties on Friday and Saturday night, or riding around in the car after school, or down in the basement sitting around with teens in love. The best parents can do is to try to "set the table" with as many tools of positive persuasion as possible and hope, that on balance, those tools outnumber others that drive decisions toward high-risk behaviors.

Mental States

Emotional well-being has long been identified as a factor in decision-making by adults. Only recently has it been given its due in the choices made by teens. It wasn't all that long ago that the fields of psychiatry and psychology finally identified, or acknowledged, childhood depression, for example.

As we have seen, depression clearly plays an important role in the decisions of many adolescents—they say it themselves. So, too, do other mental states, including boredom, curiosity, and stress. Each has been closely associated with the behavior patterns of teens.

A study by the National Center of Addiction and Substance Abuse (CASA) at Columbia University concluded that high-stress teens are twice as likely as low-stress teens to smoke, drink, get drunk, and use illegal drugs. As 15-year-old Donny from Washington state tells me, "Some people are mad or hurt inside so they'll drink to get rid of it."

In many ways, it's a vicious cycle. Overworked, overscheduled, and overtired teens too often seek relief from stress and depression in alcohol, drugs, and sex. That

Like depression, stress appears to be a particularly strong trigger for substance use among teens. Teens in grades 9 through 12, in fact, list stress as the number-one reason to drink. And teens in grades 7 through 12 rank stress as the third-most-likely reason to use drugs.

self-medication, in turn, may actually leave them feeling worse, making it less likely they will enjoy the types of relationships with parents that can help them find sensible solutions to the challenges inherent in their quickly changing lives.

Breaking that cycle requires putting in place sturdy building blocks of communication. Regular parent-teen dialogue can be an effective antidote for trouble, helping to ameliorate unnecessary stress and remedy feelings of inadequacy and insecurity. Simply by asking, "How are you feeling?" parents can open dialogue about their child's mental state, making more likely the early identification, and thus treatment, of depression.

Mental states should not be ignored, and this is especially the case as teens mature. Ninth- through 12th-graders are more likely to cite mental states as reasons to drink and use drugs than are younger teens (although an alarming number of 6th-graders cite depression in their decisions to use drugs). Older teens are also more likely than younger teens to report that mental states play a role in their decisions to be sexually active.

Trey, who we met earlier in Chapter Two, is 15, just starting his sophomore year in high school. His bright, broad smile and long, straight red hair are the first things you notice about him. Suddenly tall, Trey appears to be fitting well into his new body—but not so well into his new boarding school. Friendly and easy to get along with, Trey does not lack for friends, but he has no energy or motivation to spend time with them. He is depressed. He misses being home, misses his family, and misses the kids he grew up with. When he feels particularly badly, Trey holes up in his room. Sometimes he cries, sometimes he drinks. Sometimes he does both. Away from his parents, he's making these choices alone—and without the input of adults he so values.

Trey represents a common trend among youth who medicate themselves with alcohol and drugs to feel better and to relieve stress. His story underscores the importance of monitoring teens for signs of emotional turmoil—whether they are close by our side or far away. If we can't check in on them, we need to make sure other concerned adults can, because what is often brushed off as typical adolescent moodiness may in fact signal deeper, more intractable problems.

Personal Goals

Personal goals can lead to both healthy and unhealthy choices on the part of teens. A personal goal to excel in academics makes certain behaviors (e.g., smoking weed before school) less likely. On the other hand, a goal of fitting in might propel a teen to drink when those around him are. For example, the personal goal of "feeling popular" is a leading cause of alcohol use among 6th to 8th-grade teens. "To fit in and belong" is the number-one reason those same teens give for engaging in sexual behavior.

Parents should take the time to inquire—and learn—about the personal goals of their teen. It is important to know what is important to them and to what extent they will go to satisfy those needs. Using an earlier example, if we know that Katherine places an extremely high value on being popular and she believes all the popular kids drink alcohol, we would rightly be concerned. Tempering Katherine's commitment to be "popular" with a more-realistic goal of "having friends" might lead her to different types of social events or activities to make that goal achievable. Believe it or not, parents influence the types of personal goals their children set and the relative ability or inability of their teen to meet them.

Teens need our help to set realistic goals for achievement, lest they suffer from the type of anxiety, frustration, and failure that can lead to destructive decision-making. Remember Adam from Missouri who was thinking of committing suicide in part because of his inability to meet the academic standards his parents set for him and which he eventually made his own.

Young people will also benefit from guidance in establishing goals that, in some ways, preclude certain high-risk behaviors. This means helping them to distinguish between what Carl Rogers refers to as the "ideal" self (idealized) and "real" self (actual) and also between what *Reviving Ophelia* author Mary Pipher meant when she wrote about the "true" self (real) and "false" self (conforming).

Many opportunities exist for parents to point out examples of teens and adults who fail to achieve their goals, or jeopardize that which has already been achieved, by making poor choices. These real-life examples, often involving alcohol, drugs, and impaired driving, are powerful motivators for teens with a clear idea of who they are and where they are going, like a girl from Massachusetts who says, "Drinking can ruin your future. You can't go to the college you want to and you can be marked for the rest of your life."

As you might suspect, teens need help to establish the types of personal goals that dissuade them from making poor choices! And this is another area in which parents can play a powerful role. I know one family that sets common and individual goals each year, reviewing them from time to time with one another to make sure they are on track, as kids, as parents, and as a family.

Parents, every year, or better yet, every six months, perhaps at the beginning of the fall and spring semesters, can sit down with their kids and list the goals for that season. Write them down. Paste them on their bulletin board. Review their achievements toward the goals. This is not for the purpose of adding stress. The purpose is to keep them focused on the straight path. If they have goals, they are less likely to get distracted by other destructive behavior. And the goals don't have to be about achieving certain grades; they can involve a volunteer project, art lessons, musical endeavors, etc. In particular, look for opportunities to help teens take positive risks that, as the *Teens Today* research points out, make negative risk-taking less likely!

Again, linking personal behavior to personal (and family) goals can be an incredibly effective tool in helping kids to stay safe. Talking about this approach, another teen suggests, "Kids may not know what can happen. Maybe educate them about what it is and what it does . . . why it's so bad. Our parents will just say, 'Don't do it,' but they don't say why." And another teen points out that showing the "real-life" situations and "what actually happens" are the most effective examples. "Don't censor anything; we should know what's really going to happen," he says.

Many Avoiders, like some of the ones we met earlier, say that drinking, drug use, and indiscriminate sexual activity is "just not who I am," reflecting both a strong, positive Sense of Self and, likely, a set of personal goals with which negative behaviors may be incompatible. We need to reinforce the positive choices they are making!

Potential Outcomes

Another decision factor teens weigh in making choices is the potential outcome of certain behaviors. Will I get caught? What will my parents say? Will it make it less likely that I will achieve what I want to achieve? Each of these questions is an important calculation in the real-life game of "Risk."

Adults have a responsibility to educate teens about the potential outcomes of risky behavior. The more information they have, the better. Teens need to understand the physical, social, and emotional consequences of drinking alcohol, using drugs, or engaging in early sexual activity. They also need to understand how undermining parental trust can erode our relationships, how police records can impact college or career choices, and how personal behavior can lead to a loss of self-respect, happiness, and fulfillment.

Equally important is setting and enforcing consequences for misbehavior. Many teens do not believe they will get caught (for example, only 23 percent of teens cite fear of getting caught as a reason not to drink, and only 18 percent list it as a reason not to use drugs) or that they will truly be held accountable for their actions if they are caught—we saw the effect on Tim in Chapter Three. Clear boundaries, communicated expectations, and enforced consequences each positively affects the choices teens will make, by helping them understand the potential outcomes. A Colorado teen says, "If I had my cell phone taken away, I would die. One night last year, I snuck out to my driveway and got caught. I was grounded for a month. No phone, no computer, no TV. It was the most horrible month of my life. I swore I would never do anything bad again."

Too often parents are reluctant to follow through with consequences when their children misbehave. Still others seek to impinge upon the ability of others, such as school officials or even law enforcement, to properly and appropriately administer discipline. Neither scenario affords teens the opportunity to learn from experience or to connect the dots between behavior and consequence. Remember the parents in Chapter Two who convinced a judge to issue an injunction against a school-imposed punishment that would have banned their daughter from competing in a track meet because she was caught at an underage drinking party.

In many instances, adults do teens a terrible disservice by denying them the chance to learn real-life lessons from the choices they make. Such was the case with many families following that homecoming dance in Scarsdale, New York. According to *The New York Times*, some parents contacted the principal to request immunity for their offspring, lest a more-than-generous consequence (a three-day suspension) dampen the enthusiasm of a college admissions counselor. One family even sent the housekeeper to pick up a teen in trouble, showing that the issue of underage drinking was of little importance or concern to them.

Teaching accountability is important. If kids want the right and the freedom to make their own choices, they need to be held responsible when they violate the rules, let alone the law.

As with many areas of teen life, there is no formula for what represents an effective consequence—or punishment—for any given teen. A good place to start in establishing meaningful outcomes for behavior is to focus on what is important to your teen. For example, some parents tell me that their son or daughter "cannot survive" without access to the Internet to e-mail their friends on an almost-constant basis. Voila! Denying that privilege can quickly grab their attention so that they don't even think about violating the same rule again. Other parents revoke driving privileges (even though this may cause some inconvenience for them), subjecting their child to not only limited mobility but, perhaps more significantly, the embarrassment of being dropped off in front of school by mom! It may very well be the case that he can't think of anything worse.

Whatever punishments you believe will be most effective, we serve our kids well by making sure they know ahead of time what the consequences will be for any given behavior. Advance notification makes infractions of family rules less likely and our kids' ultimate reaction to punishment more predictable. Of course, some parents face the prospect of a teen refusing to comply with whatever punishment has been applied, say, a grounding or limited access to the television. This makes advance rule and punishment setting all the more critical. If parents and teens can agree ahead of time what consequences are reasonable and fair, we stand a better chance that they will be adhered to if they need to be put in place.

Significant People

Last but not least, in making decisions, teens weigh the input, advice, expectations, and values of the people they view as important in their lives.

As we know, parents are the number-one reason that teens avoid destructive behaviors. And while friends are the number-one reason they don't, they can also be incredibly powerful forces in promoting healthy, as opposed to unhealthy, behaviors among their peers. That's the primary goal of SADD—to empower young people to help their friends make good decisions!

Siblings are important as well. Older teens seem to hold particular sway in the decisions of their younger brothers and sisters. As one teen put it, "My older brother would kill me if I drink. He wouldn't stand for that, and I am influenced by him."

Conversely, the responsibility of setting a good example for younger siblings can play a role in dictating behavior.

Both dynamics are important for parents to understand. Armed with that information, they can reinforce to older teens the importance of their relationship with younger brothers or sisters and impress upon

Young people rank "setting an example" for brothers and sisters as one of the most commonly held reasons they choose not to drink or use drugs.

them the value of role-modeling and constructive dialogue. Eighteen-year-old Matt, who we met in Chapter Two, steered clear of alcohol and drugs throughout high school in no small part because his older sister Maya, whom he admires immensely, did the same. Maya was vocal about her decisions, and the example she set for Matt was quite clear.

Other adults, such as teachers, counselors, and coaches, also have an important role to play in guiding the behavior of teens. They serve as an alternative sounding board against which teens can toss their ideas about identity, independence, and relationships with peers. They are also key conveyers of value systems consistent with healthy lifestyles. Indeed, when you stop and think about it, our children spend as much time with these "influencers" as just about anyone else. What they say and what they do are powerful motivators in the behavior of teens.

Parents should recognize that children naturally seek out guidance, affirmation, and support from other adults during their adolescence. Supporting rather than discouraging that effort is important. So, too, is steering young people toward responsible role models who can provide teens with other tangible examples of how to live life responsibly and productively. These mentors also influence a teen's Sense of Self and increase the probability that they will take the types of positive risks that make negative risk-taking less likely.

Short Circuit

Sixteen-year-old Phil, a sophomore from Baltimore, had long ago made his decision about sex: nothing intimate until after high school and only in a committed relationship. He's comfortable with that, feels it's right for him, and won't be persuaded otherwise. That is until his classmate Pauline asks him if he'd like to have oral sex. Seems she's introduced some 15 other boys to the activity. Initially, he agrees before thinking better of it and declining, saying, "I'm not ready for that." Tough choice. Close call.

Was Phil's temporary change of heart simply a typical adolescent response to the onslaught of hormones raging through his body? Or did it reflect something deeper, more mysterious, and harder to quantify and explain?

In truth, such decision-making is complicated, influenced by the decision factors just discussed (mental states, personal goals, potential outcomes, and significant people), but also by body chemistry and brain function, both things that are changing at an extraordinary rate during adolescence. And while Phil's ultimate decision was a positive one, some kids are not so self-aware.

How many times have you opened the morning paper or watched the evening news and puzzled over reports of dangerous—even horrific—adolescent behavior involving alcohol, drugs, sex, violence, or driving? The epidemic proportions of risky teen and pre-teen behavior provide salacious and frequent content for broad dissemination by the news media, leaving in its wake more questions than answers. Examples are not hard to find.

- **Sarasota, Florida:** Influenced by the movie *Jackass*, three trespassing teens leap from the top of a condominium building, aiming for the pool. Two make it. One hits the side, fracturing both legs and an arm and cracking his pelvis.

- **Hilton Head, South Carolina:** Two teens are arrested after they show up to use the pool at a hotel where they had robbed three people 15 hours before.

- **Red Lion, Pennsylvania:** Brandishing his stepfather's 44-caliber Magnum, an 8th-grade boy stands up in his school's cafeteria and shoots the principal in the chest, killing him. He then uses a 22-caliber weapon to kill himself.

- **Macon, Georgia:** Three boys, ages 13 and 14, are charged with aggravated cruelty to animals after they burn a dog alive.

- **Godfrey, Illinois:** A teenager is jailed after being accused of stealing 500 lottery tickets from the store where he works.
- **Prineville, Oregon:** Two teens are arrested for shooting up a sheriff's department sign, reading, "Training Exercise Ahead."

These incidents form just the tip of an iceberg that has been composed by forces we have yet to fully comprehend. Nevertheless, we're making progress. Information is emerging about some serious neurological rewiring that takes place during adolescence. In her book *The Primal Teen*, Barbara Strauch illuminates startling advances in science that may help to explain teen behavior heretofore chalked up simply to immaturity. She says, "The brain is working constantly, and one of the tasks it works at is to inhibit itself from a variety of actions. As the brain develops—in children and, science is now learning, in teenagers—it is this very inhibition machinery that is being fine-tuned."

It is reasonable to conclude that if inhibition is compromised, or not yet fully realized, poor choices related to drinking, drugs, sex, and violence might be more likely among teens than among adults whose cognitive development is more advanced. Strauch asks, "And what can we expect of adolescents if that inhibition machinery, the prefrontal cortex, is not yet fully tuned?" Probably some of the behaviors I just mentioned. Conversely, Strauch ponders, "Looked at another way, could a more mature and finely tuned prefrontal cortex explain a newfound ability to resist that need to buy the first clothes you see or impulsively blow up in anger at a parent? Can we now say that such fundamental shifts in behavior are likely linked to actual developmental and structural changes in the architecture of the teenage brain?" The answer appears to be, "Yes."

Recent research at UCLA's Lab of Neuro Imaging suggests that, during adolescence, boys and girls undergo significant brain changes that affect such functions as self-control, emotional regulation, organization, and planning. And, of course, these are but a few of the many elements of adolescent life that drive us crazy! *Why can't Bobby be more responsible? Why is Maureen not responding to my arched eyebrow and look of disgust? Why is Katie so moody these days? And why can't Brooke ever seem to get his homework finished and turned in on time?* Obvious questions for harried adults interested in eliciting the best from the kids they care about. After all, we see their potential, right?! Why can't they just be all they're capable of being?

The clues lie in a dramatic and seemingly predictable transformation in the brain during adolescence and early adulthood. A radical "pruning" of gray matter literally reorganizes cognitive functioning, preparing the brain to handle the highest order of functioning in adulthood, according to UCLA's research. In tandem with studies performed at the National Institute of Mental Health and at McLean Hospital in Massachusetts, this information offers some important insights into why teens act the way they do, and provides clues as to how we can help them develop the self-control they need for effective planning and decision-making. This may be true especially when it comes to the potentially life-altering choices we've been discussing throughout this book—and when done in conjunction with an understanding of the Decision Factors just discussed and the Decision Points we'll see later in this chapter.

The new research challenges traditional thinking that brain development is complete by age 8 or 10, positing instead that massive changes are still taking place well into our twenties. Knowing that adolescence introduces significant restructuring of the brain helps to explain some quixotic adolescent behaviors by linking them to a natural, even predictable, neurochemical process. (It also suggests that the introduction into that neurochemical process of alcohol and other drugs may pose even greater risks than previously thought, perhaps permanently changing the way brains route and process information.) Of course, this does not mean that teens are scientifically destined to make poor choices. If that were the case, we could just close up shop and save hundreds of millions of dollars on research, education, and prevention.

It may be the case, however, that allocation of those dollars might be divided differently to achieve the best-possible results. For example, Temple University psychologist Laurence Steinberg argues that new brain research such as I've just outlined suggests that society-based strategies, such as raising the price of cigarettes and more vigorously enforcing laws on underage drinking, may be more effective than trying to raise adolescent awareness or alter adolescent perceptions through education. In advancing this case, Steinberg says, "More than 90 percent of all American high school students have had sex, drug, and driver education programs in their schools, yet large proportions of them still have unsafe sex, binge-drink, smoke cigarettes, and drive recklessly."

Either way, the data may mean that teens are even more predisposed to risky behavior than we might have believed. Why? Because that massive reorganization at puberty seems to impact the area of the brain, the prefrontal cortex, that is responsible for, among other things, the exhibiting of judgment. And judgment shades choices. If we know that teens are, to some degree, biologically handicapped to exercise appropriate judgment, especially in group situations where social stimulation makes negative risk-taking more likely, we are better able to know when our help in weighing options and anticipating outcomes is most needed. Understanding the antecedents of choices, be they biological, chemical, or social, underscores the value of adult involvement in teen decision-making and best-positions us to short-circuit destructive teen behavior . . . or at least to try our hand at persuasion.

A calm, clear voice of reason—gently guiding dialogue about the choices at hand—can go a long way toward slowing down speeding synapses and encouraging a thoughtful consideration of the risks attached to taking that drink, smoking that joint, getting into the backseat of that car, bullying that classmate, or acting on suicidal thoughts. One 8th-grade boy states it this way, "If someone you really loved and cared about sat down and talked with you—and really opened up—they can make you stop."

On occasion, the substitution of adult judgment for adolescent enterprise may be necessary to countermand a decision deemed too dangerous to allow. For example, when Kathy wants to drive eight hours round-trip to New York with six friends for a concert at Madison Square Garden, or when Geoffrey wants to attend a largely unsupervised co-ed sleepover at his girlfriend's house because "everyone else is allowed to go."

Indeed, while it is important to systematically loosen the leash, allowing young people to make independent choices and learn from the results, there are clearly times when we need to intercede. Health and safety supersede independence and self-sufficiency. Teens cannot yet be left all on their own to make all their own critical choices. The stakes are too high, and the potential outcomes too permanent for us to simply look the other way and hope they make the right decisions. Collaboration works best—in other words, teaming with our child to explore, explain, consider, and plan behavior. Even so, there may be times when we have to intercede and adopt a more authoritarian role as parents and caregivers.

As we have seen, it is incredibly important to help young people come to sensible solutions to life's challenges by defining the potential short-term and long-term consequences of behaviors—consequences their still-evolving brains may not yet fully embrace or even slow down long enough to notice. This can be particularly true when the behavior includes alcohol and other drugs. After all, the flip side of the effects of neurological development on teen behavior is the effect of teen behavior on neurological development. It's not too hard to imagine the impact of substance use and abuse, not to mention scores of other unhealthy experiences, on a transforming cerebral cortex where new pathways for the transmittal of information are being forged.

While that impact may be hard to see, there are other more immediate, and more identifiable, ramifications of substance use. Alcohol and drug use have been repeatedly linked to increased rates of automobile crash deaths, risky sexual behavior, sexual assaults, depression, suicide, and declining school performance. The transparency of these outcomes makes them easier to understand and address. But the serious, perhaps permanent, outcomes related to future cognitive functioning may be just as consequential.

Try as we might, we will never successfully transform teen thoughts and actions into those that mirror our own. Nature has a different plan (something Strauch calls "crazy by design"). The best we can do is to drill deeper into the adolescent brain and psyche, seeking to understand what drives their decisions and what influencers can be brought to bear to keep them safe and alive.

Decision Points

While knowing the "whats" and "whys" of adolescent behavior can go a long way toward helping teens stay safe, it is just as important to know the "whens." *Teens Today* has defined a set of Decision Points—that is, when first-time experimentation with certain behaviors is most likely to take place. The data reveal significant spikes in destructive behaviors at predictable times. This helps us plan when to undertake discussions with our kids about the physical, social, emotional, and legal risks associated with underage drinking, other drug use, early and intimate sexual behavior, and distracted or impaired driving—as well as some of the other behaviors (bullying, hazing, or cutting) we have been talking about.

"Jump the shark," a recently popularized term that refers to forecasting the failure of everything from sitcoms to politicians, has roots dating back—believe it or not—to an episode of the '70s TV mega-hit *Happy Days*. It seems the Fonz vaulted over one such predatory fish while waterskiing—a spectacle deemed to be so preposterous even to loyal fans of the show that it ushered in the beginning of an irreversible slide into syndication, at least according to jumptheshark.com pioneer and *When Good Things Go Bad* author Jon Hein. Inextricably linked to a moment in time when a bad decision tests the limits of good, the same catchy concept might very well predict—if not preempt—destructive behavior by young people.

As we've seen in previous chapters, negative risk-taking tends to increase throughout adolescence. This trend presents an inherent problem—an inverse correlation of parental persuasion. The younger teens are, the more likely they are to listen to the views and directions of their parents. Yet the behaviors their parents find most troublesome don't often appear until later in adolescence, when their opinions hold more limited sway. But by discussing certain issues before they are likely to become relevant, parents lay the groundwork for good decision-making by well-prepared teens.

"Early and often" remains an important catch phrase in educating young people about healthy choices—before they "jump the shark." Now more so than ever. As we discussed in Chapter One, it is important to understand the environment in which our teens live as well as the unfortunate decisions some of them are inclined to make. Not knowing reduces a parents' ability to help their teen confidently move toward healthy adulthood. In light of the facts of their fast-changing children and the almost-daily introduction of new people and new issues into their children's lives, it is difficult for parents to know *when* to worry about *what*. Of course, every teen is different. Each one comes with his or her own personality, family history, crew of influential friends and "advisors," and level of tolerance for risk and appetite for reward. Thus, it's no surprise that there are many different motivations behind the choices that any young person makes.

Knowing when certain behaviors generally first occur helps create a road map for us to follow, identifying important intersections along the way where choices are likely to be presented and decisions are likely to be made.

Why are teens making these decisions at these times? For a variety of reasons, including to "look cool" (drinking in 7th grade), to "anger my parents" (drug use in 9th grade), and because "everyone else is doing it" (sexual behavior in 11th grade). Armed with this knowledge, parents can work effectively toward closing the reality gap. Stephanie's mom had no

A thorough examination of the behavioral trends of middle school and high school students reveals some interesting information. For example, drinking increases significantly between 6th and 7th grades, drug use increases significantly between 8th and 9th grades, and sexual activity increases significantly between 10th and 11th grades.

idea about her sexual relationship with Craig, but when she found out, her bond with her daughter grew closer, because they were now compelled to discuss personal decision-making about a sensitive subject in an open, honest, and mutually respectful way.

Of course, there are many reasons teens choose to engage in, or not engage in, negative risk-taking behavior. For example, when we look at decisions by middle and high school students to drink alcohol, 62 percent say they drink to have fun, 39 percent say it is to forget or escape a problem, 34 percent say it is because of curiosity, 33 percent say it is to fit in with other kids, and 27 percent say it is just to take a risk or because they feel stressed. Alarmingly, almost 1 in 6 teens (17 percent) reports drinking because he or she is depressed.

But just as important is to understand why young people choose not to drink. The highest number of teens (39 percent) say it is to please their parents. Thirty-two percent say it is because they are afraid of getting caught, and 30 percent say it is to set a good example for their brothers or sisters. More than 1 in 4 teens say they don't drink because they don't want to lose control (29 percent), because it will impact on their academic performance (28 percent), and because it is illegal (27 percent). Other factors teens weigh in deciding not to use alcohol include the fact that they plan on driving (25 percent), worry about its impact on their athletic performance (24 percent), and, encouragingly, to fit in with friends who don't drink (15 percent). (Interestingly, parents tend to overrate their teens' legal concerns and undervalue their teens' fear of getting caught.) The antecedents of these choices can be used by parents to steer conversations toward the outcomes our children either seek or fear, thus maximizing the impact of what they shared. After all, these are *their* reasons and rationales, not ours!

Teens' Reasons for Drinking or Using Drugs

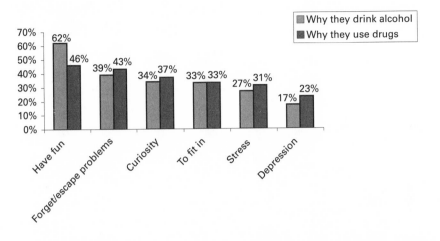

As you might expect, decisions regarding drug use follow similar routes. Teens site having fun (46 percent), to forget or escape problems (43 percent), curiosity (37 percent), to fit in with friends (33 percent), stress and depression (31 and 23 percent, respectively), and boredom (22 percent) as reasons for using other drugs.

As is the case with not drinking alcohol, pleasing parents is an important consideration for teens declining drugs (40 percent). Other salient motivators for Avoiders of drug use include illegality (42 percent), fear of injury to themselves or others (32 percent), impact on academics (32 percent), and athletic performance (25 percent), and to set an example for brothers and sisters (30 percent).

When it comes to sexual intercourse and other sexual behavior, more than half of teens say they have intercourse to become closer to their girlfriend or boyfriend (65 percent), because it's fun (56 percent), or to please their boyfriend or girlfriend (54 percent). More than one-in-three do so to satisfy their curiosity, and almost one-quarter (22 percent) have intercourse because they feel pressure to do so. Fourteen percent say they have sex to feel grown up.

On the flip side of the intercourse-decision coin, more than half of teens cite a fear of pregnancy or sexually transmitted disease (57 percent and 54 percent, respectively) as the principal reason they choose not to have sex. Forty percent feel they are too young, and more than a quarter (28 percent) abstain in order to please their parents. Other factors include not being in a relationship or in love (23 percent), wanting to set

Teens' Reasons for Having Sex

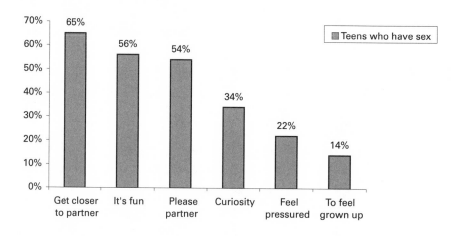

Teens' Reasons for Abstaining From Sex

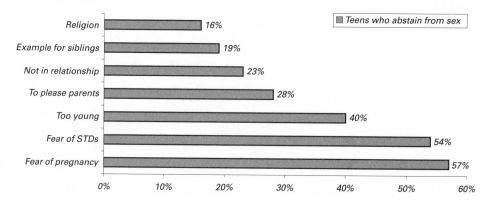

a good example for siblings (19 percent), or that it's against their religious beliefs (16 percent). Similar motives drive decisions about other sexual behaviors as well, such as genital touching or oral sex.

What You Can Do

This treasure trove of information provided by teens themselves opens all kinds of avenues to embark on a discourse about decision-making. Understanding common motivations for different choices, to some degree, circumvents the necessity of asking too many questions, which often drives teens crazy. Rather, it allows us to demonstrate an appreciation for the difficult nature of these decisions. It also permits us to seek feedback from our teen, furthering the likelihood of constructive dialogue, back and forth, about attitudes, values, expectations, risks, and rewards.

—I know a lot of kids your age feel that having sex is the best way to feel closer to their boyfriend, but I sometimes wonder if it's the best way.

—Do you think a lot of kids drink because they aren't feeling so good about how they're doing in school or at home?

These are better conversation starters than *Don't you think it's ridiculous that kids your age are having sex?* or, *Those kids who are drinking are going to be in big trouble if they get caught.*

In these instances, we are simply grilling our kids for answers, or hammering them over the head with our opinions. With patience, we can learn to use effective communication skills, but we also have to be willing to practice. However, once the dialogue is flowing, we are better positioned to help our teens plan, strategize, and problem-solve. We can hear about their experiences, understand their perspectives, evaluate their attitudes, and help them formulate the answers they *want* to give. It also provides us with a window on their motivations: *to look cool, to feel grown up, to fit in, to make friends, to rebel!* Not different at all from our own reasons for doing things when we were teens.

We can prepare our kids for making difficult decisions by formulating a plan *together*, as opposed to just responding and reacting in the heat of the moment. Because teens often don't think ahead, they may make important—perhaps life-altering—decisions impulsively and without full exploration of the potential consequences of their actions. When I talk with teens about decision-making, I find it helpful to pose hypothetical situations and have them think through how they will respond. For example, to a 10th-grader: "What if your friend asks you to sneak out to meet some boys in the park?" Or to an 8th-grader: "What if someone pulls out a joint on the walk home from school?" Helping teens plot the "what ifs" arms them with the confidence they need to live up to our expectations. Many teens who have managed to avoid poor choices tell me their parents help them to strategize responses to potential questions.

Here are some examples of the types of answers young people can fall back on in tough situations:

- "My parents would ground me for the rest of my life if I got caught sneaking out!"
- "The doctor says smoking weed will make my asthma worse."
- "I'm on medication that will make me sick if I mix it with alcohol."
- "No thanks, I already had sex five times today."

Like a football player practicing a fumble drill or a firefighter practicing a rescue, teens who think through and role-play responses to tough situations are more likely to do what they want to do than to make a split-second error in judgment due to peer pressure. A 17-year-old who had been suspended for smoking marijuana puzzled over the choice he made when offered the joint. "I've never done anything like this before and I seriously don't know why I did it," he told me. Knowing what decisions they *want* to make is clearly not enough. They need practice to say no in an almost instinctual way.

The principal of a Massachusetts high school advises parents to "be willing to be the fall guy when kids don't have the strength to refuse on their own." She also recommends "helping kids develop the skills to allow them to be themselves by walking through decision-making models where kids can examine the consequences for each of their decisions."

Some argue that teens already know the risks and may, in fact, overestimate them. According to a December, 2007, story in *The New York Times*, a study by researchers at the University of California, San Francisco, revealed that teens are more prone to exaggerate risks than are parents, suggesting that focusing on an actual risk may make poor choices more likely. As one mom said, "I remember hearing from my high school son that the stats were in his favor, so don't bother with the gloom-and-doom arguments." Nevertheless, young people may not always ascribe those risks to themselves, much like parents who know that a majority of high school seniors drink alcohol, but choose to believe that their senior son or daughter does not. In addition, even if teens overestimate risk it doesn't mean they aren't also overestimating reward. We need to help them accurately weigh all of the factors involved in decision-making.

Some families establish "bail-out" strategies, putting in place procedures that make it easy for teens to extricate themselves from environments that become uncomfortable while not "losing face" or becoming embarrassed about not wanting to participate in destructive behavior. I remember one family's bail-out plan: "If other kids start drinking or using drugs, call home and ask how grandma's surgery went. We'll pick you up around the corner."

Of course, Decision Points reflect only the averages—times when young people are *most likely* to start drinking, using drugs, or having sex. We need to prepare ourselves for the possibility that such behavior might start earlier (or later) and be ready to act. If we find some of *our* prescription medications in *his* backpack for example, it's time to talk, no matter what age he is.

Parents approach me all the time after lectures or workshops voicing the same complaint and expressing the same bewilderment: "We used to talk about everything. Now it seems we talk about nothing. It's just a series of arguments about homework, chores, and curfews." Teens are often just as frustrated. In St. Louis, 15-year-old Matt told me, "I try to talk to my parents, but we end up arguing and the conversation just falls apart."

Because of this "conversational clogging" during our child's adolescence, we need to be careful about what topics we raise in conversation. Not everything warrants serious discussion, especially when disagreements, however politely expressed, may result. We need to pick our battles carefully and not waste precious "talk time" arguing about things that, in the long run, don't count for much. I often witness parents and teens spending hours bickering with each other over trivial things, such as when they'll get a haircut or how long it will take them to complete their English paper.

We should constantly ask ourselves, "Is this really important?" If in doubt, leave it out. At least for the time being. When it is important, spend some time thinking about how best to approach your teen, what messages you want to convey, and how best to make your points.

Jay Heinrichs, author of *Thank You For Arguing: What Aristotle, Lincoln, and Homer Simpson Can Teach Us About the Art of Persuasion*, offered some intriguing tips on persuading, or winning an argument with, a teen that I found in a *US Airways Magazine* on a recent trip to New York. Here are just a few:

- Don't Try to Win on Points—Persuasion entails making another person change his mood, come around to your way of thinking, or do something—which in the case of a Teenager might involve things like cleaning her room or turning the stereo down.
- Character Counts—Even With a Teenager—If your kids are willing to listen to you because they find you trustworthy and likeable, they're much more likely to do what you want.
- Demonstrate Your Virtue—That means showing belief in your teenager's values (e.g., personal freedom, coolness, the environment).
- Practice Disinterest—One way to make an audience believe in your objectivity is to seem reluctant to deal with something you're

really eager to prove. Make it sound as if you reached your opinion only after confronting overwhelming evidence.

- Know Their Language—Teens use jargon and slang to distance themselves from the older generation and solidify their group identity. Words can bring us together or tear us apart. Learn the ones that will be uniters.
- Irony Is Like Oxygen—You can use irony to sugercoat the message you're giving to your teenager.

Whatever your techniques, establishing and communicating expectations for our teens' behavior—as well as explaining the rationale behind them—opens the door to time-sensitive dialogue about the choices they face and the decisions they make. Once that door is open, there are a host of ways that we can work collaboratively to fully explore the different possible outcomes of any particular behaviors.

Positive Risk-Taking

Risk-taking has become synonymous with adolescence. Or perhaps it is that adolescence has become synonymous with risk-taking. Either way, it is now common for parents and, by extension, their teens to believe that there exists some developmental death-wish that prompts behaviors more suitable to movies like *Jackass* (as we saw earlier) than to real life. As a result of this belief, many adults view drinking, for example, as a normal and developmentally appropriate risk, and thus we become desensitized to its true destructive force.

In her book *The Culture of Adolescent Risk-Taking*, Cynthia Lightfoot speaks to common efforts to parse risk by behavior. For example, she says, "Experimenting with alcohol and marijuana is typical of American youth, whereas crack addiction occurs less often and carries more serious consequences. We are dealing in the first case with behaviors that are considered normative, exploratory, or transitional to adult status and functioning, whereas the second case is an example of behaviors that are clearly health compromising, destructive, and pathogenic." Viewing alcohol and marijuana use as normal, inevitable, even productive steps on the path toward adulthood enables poor decision-making and sends exactly the wrong message to young people. And this very sense of normalcy plays into common depictions of teen life in the twenty-first century: media images repeated across television, computer, iPod, and movie screens thousands of times a day. Such repetition further cements a perception of the acceptability of behavior that is often illegal and self-destructive.

Knowing that the earlier one starts consuming alcohol, the greater the risk of encountering alcohol-related problems later in life; or that experiments with rats suggest that alcohol use during adolescence may permanently change the processing of information; or that drug use is closely associated with violence, and depression should make us think long and hard about how we define risk-taking and which risks should be accepted as socially and developmentally appropriate. Of course, part of the problem is that, as adults, we know from our own youthful experiences that risks become more thrilling during adolescence. And that fact makes taking them more likely. But, risks need not be dangerous to be alluring.

I find it fascinating that adults have been conditioned to believe that "risk" means "bad," while kids have not. In fact, a majority of young people (52 percent) believe that risk-taking refers to positive activities.

In truth, there are bad risks and good risks. Negative risks and positive risks. Risks that thwart healthy development and leave children susceptible to physical, emotional, social, and legal harm, and risks that actually promote well-being, satisfaction, and achievement. After all, it is quite conceivable that whatever sense of maturity, independence, or social status a young person might find in getting drunk, they might also find in starting their own Web development business!

It is really helpful to be able to sort out positive from negative risk-taking, because teens who seek out positive risks (Risk Seekers) are 20 percent more likely than teens who do not take positive risks (Risk Avoiders) to avoid alcohol and other drugs, and 42 percent more likely to avoid drinking because of concerns about academic performance.

Risk Seekers are also more likely than Risk Avoiders to describe themselves as responsible, confident, successful, and optimistic. They report they often feel happy and are more likely to consider potential negative outcomes of destructive behaviors, such as being more likely to think they will get hurt, more likely to think they will get caught, and more likely to think they will be held accountable. Risk Takers are also less likely to suffer from boredom and depression. Why? Because they are engaged and challenged in meaningful ways. Adults who help to channel the energies of their risk-taking teens into positive activities, such as trying out for an athletic team or volunteering for community service, are more likely to have kids who make good choices.

Another important thing to remember is that there is no "one size fits all" when it comes to positive risk-taking. What constitutes a risk for one child may be old hat for another. For example, for a shy "homebody," volunteering for that community-service project may be a big step, initially

How Teens Feel About Themselves

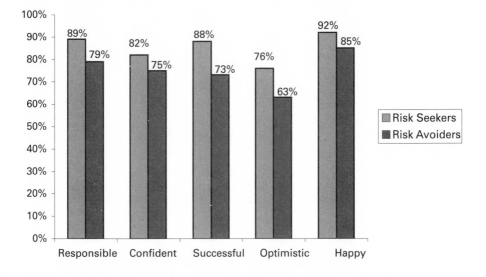

Risk Types and Consideration of Negative Outcomes

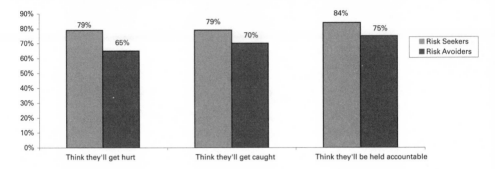

causing anxiety and avoidance behavior, but ultimately resulting in positive feelings, good will, and self-worth. On the other hand, a more outgoing teen may easily perform community service without feeling any reticence or nervousness at all. Other teens may have no problem with trying out for the soccer team because they played the sport at younger ages, while some may be trying it for the first time, thus making it a more-risky enterprise. It is important that parents help their child evaluate which activities truly represent a reach beyond his or her comfort zone and then encourage them to participate in those activities.

In my research, I have found that the positive risks teens talk about can be lumped into three broad categories:

1. Life Risks
Life risks fall into three subcategories: social risks, such as joining a school club or a musical group; emotional risks, such as asking someone out on a date or sharing some personal feelings with a friend; and physical risks, such as taking up snowboarding or rock climbing.

2. School Risks
These include academic risks, such as taking an advanced-placement course; athletic risks, such as trying out for the field hockey team; and extracurricular risks, perhaps running for the student council.

3. Community Risks

Community risks include volunteering for community service, such as helping the elderly or homeless; mentoring younger children; and leading by starting a business or charity, for example.

Again, what constitutes a real, reasonable risk will differ from child to child.

There are a number of things parents can do to help children take positive risks, such as modeling inclusive social behavior (inviting a single parent to join a group of couples going to dinner, for example), identifying and discussing emotional reactions to issues or events, encouraging focus on academics and consideration of higher-level courses, supporting club or activity membership or athletic participation, and involving family and friends in community-service projects (such as volunteering together to serve food to the homeless at Thanksgiving).

In these ways, teens may begin to internalize the value inherent in "pushing the envelope" in positive, healthy directions, while satisfying their natural curiosity about, and propensity for, testing their own limits in a safe way.

Understanding the many and varied forces that guide personal development and influence decision-making and risk-taking, both good and bad, helps us to help our kids steer clear of trouble and instead make choices that promote healthy advancement toward becoming who they want to be. As the mom of 16-year-old Seth puts it, "My number-one priority is raising him to be a happy, healthy, intelligent, honest, and compassionate man to send out into the world." A pretty-good goal if you ask me, and one that will be greatly facilitated by her appreciation of the developmental dilemmas and tasks that Seth faces, what her role is (and can be) in encouraging him to move toward independence and personal responsibility in decision-making, knowing when to back off and where to barge in, teaching him to pinpoint and share his feelings, helping him to develop meaningful peer relationships, and pointing him toward the type of positive risk-taking that will make poor choices less likely.

Five

Conspiracy of Silence

There's not much that frightens me about public speaking. But presenting to some six thousand New Jersey high school students assembled at an outdoor amphitheater, home to many a summer concert, to hear a succession of talks on a variety of "teen topics" was a whole other venue for me. My speech focused on impaired driving. It wasn't the size of the crowd that I found daunting, or even the fact that most of the kids, having just finished lunch, seemed restless and practically bursting with adolescent energy—no doubt wishing to be freed from this day-long parade of speakers. The source of my anxiety was on stage, "warming up the crowd" for my presentation. I was peeking through a slit in the heavy, black curtain at the back of the enormous stage, and ascertaining that this crowd is already thoroughly warmed. They were red-hot, in fact.

The man on stage appeared to be one-part comedian and two-parts acrobat, given his fast, agile movement across the vast open stage. I could feel the beads of sweat forming just below my hairline. This guy was making me nervous! I didn't want this large crowd of teens more fired up than they already were.

"Before I go," he screamed into his microphone, "I just want to say that New Jersey is cool!" And six thousand teens lifted from their seats in unison to applaud.

"You guys are cool!" he continued, further inciting a near-riot, as high fives are shared all around.

"Bruce Springsteen is cool!" he intoned, as anticipation mounted.

"And Stephen Wallace is cool!"—my cue to emerge on stage. As I passed through the curtain and walked toward the microphone, I'm struck by the complete silence. Thousands of high school students were looking at me, and each other, mouthing, "Who the heck is Stephen Wallace?"

As I found out that day, silence can be deafening. Especially when the source of that silence is a generally excitable teenager (or, in my case, about six thousand of them). It's the kind of silence that causes plenty of parents to wonder: "What ever happened to that chatty little kid whose tumbling discourse after school would include stories of just about *everything*?"

For years, SADD presentations like the one I am about to deliver have included a brief role-play to dramatize the changes in communication that typically occur between child and parent over time.

Here's how it works: I start by choosing a student to join me on stage, usually what I call "a captain of the football team type kid," who is well known, easily recognized, and used to being front and center without being embarrassed or intimidated. Next, I have the audience try to picture him back in elementary school—what he might have looked like, what he would have been wearing, even what type of lunch pail his mom would have packed up for him on his first day of school. Next, I play out what happens when he comes home.

"He bounds off the bus and into the waiting arms of his mom," overeager to tell her about his day, I explain to them. Now, I continue the dialogue: "We had recess and nap time, and I even found the right bathroom . . . on the third try. And look, Mom, I drew some pictures!" We all know where those are going, right up on the refrigerator for everyone to see. And on through bedtime I go, each step highlighting the ease of communication and openness of discussion that marks child-parent communication at a young age.

As we move through middle school to 12th grade, the audience laughs at the changes. They know them all too well. Mom says, "How was school today?"

"Eh," comes the brief reply.

"What did you do?" she tries again.

"Nothin'."

"Do you have homework?"

"I did it."

Desperate for some tidbit of information, his mom tries another tack: "What did you have for lunch today, honey?" But the answer is not much more revealing than those that came before it.

"I don't know; it was brown."

The punch line is humorous, but it aptly drives home the point that our conversations with our kids are often not like they used to be—and are certainly not what they could be. As our children become teens, many changes are afoot, not least of which occur within the communication patterns that we established over time and on which we have come to rely as barometers of physical, psychological, social, and even spiritual well-being. Bereft of that accustomed feedback loop, parents easily lose touch with their teens, and that can make it increasingly difficult for them to make sense of their changing attitudes and interactions. And sometimes it seems like this happens in a blink of the eye!

The mother of 15-year-old Christian tells me, "There are so many kids I know who are outstanding: obedient, thoughtful, already contributing to society, conscious of the future, friendly, respectful, hardworking . . . You know, the kind of kids who win awards and people's hearts. Bob and I have tried to do everything 'right' to raise that kind of person, [but] suddenly, overnight, we found ourselves living with a stranger."

So often, parents like Christian's wake up to find a person of seemingly unknown origin living right in their own house. *What did we do wrong?* they want to know, and *What do we do now?*

The first answer is easy: nothing! The very developmental dilemmas outlined in the last chapter account for many of the changes. As our children wrestle with their own emerging identities, pull away from us in their quest for independence, and work to build a social-support network separate from the family, they often experience inner conflict that manifests itself in moodiness, belligerence, disrespect, and what we may consider unacceptable conduct. The stressors placed on both child and family while significant, are considered to be normal, or "normative"—meaning, they are predictable outcomes in the life-cycle of a family, not unlike children leaving for college or getting married, or the aging and ultimate deaths of grandparents. But knowing that a certain behavior is normal doesn't make it a joy to cope with. Especially when it marks dramatic changes—seemingly for the worse—in our relationships with our children.

In an article she wrote for the *Boston Globe* in January of 2006, columnist Beverly Beckham recounted the story of a boy and his dad, with whom she shared an airplane ride. The boy, just eight or nine years-old, clearly loved his dad, wanted to sit next to him, talked to him constantly, asked questions incessantly, and pointed at things out the window to make sure his dad saw them, too. Beckham wrote, "It's a short time in a lifetime that a boy adores his dad. Too soon, the boy will be wearing headphones and ignoring dad. Too soon, he will be too big to say, 'I want to sit next to you.' It's only for now that it's 'Dad, what do you think?'"

When the easy, natural communication between us and our child has been replaced with quiet discomfort, the gulf between parent and teen widens quickly. We can feel her slipping away, drifting further and further from our ship. Our natural instinct is to keep throwing a lifeline to try to reel her back in. But that's not always the best tactic. In fact, it may be time to let go a little–especially if old strategies are no longer working—and to develop new "rules of engagement" with teens who no longer embrace, and are unlikely to benefit from, past patterns of interaction. This is the "holding on while letting go" I referred to in Chapter Four.

Working hard to establish new strategies to stay connected with our teens pays off in happier, healthier lives, and leaves both parents and teens feeling better about their "new," more adult-like relationships. Teens may be able to take responsibility for their own bedtimes or when homework gets done, watching out for younger siblings, or using the car to run family errands. Similarly, they may now be confident enough to debate politics or economics with mom or dad—demonstrating the capacity to participate in a new level of communication, and perhaps signaling that they are better-prepared to make informed, independent, and healthy choices.

Teens reporting such open communication with their parents about issues such as drinking, drug use, and sex are significantly less likely to make poor choices than teens who say they do not have open communication. And it's interesting to note that teens who say they don't have good communication with their parents tend to say they wish that they did! Maybe more surprising is the fact that almost three-quarters of teens say they want their parents to offer opinions about personal behavior.

What You Can Do

So, how might these strategies to connect manifest themselves? According to SADD's partner, the Office of National Drug Control Policy (ONDCP), there are some simple steps you can take that will allow you to hold on and let go at the same time:

- set rules,
- know where your teen is and what he will be doing during unsupervised time,
- keep teens busy,
- talk to your teen,
- check on your teenager occasionally,
- establish a "core-values statement for your family,"
- get to know your teen's friends, and
- stay in touch with the adult supervisors in your child's life.

Now, these may seem obvious and even self-explanatory. Nevertheless, if followed, they will help you to keep track of your child's activities and to effectively communicate with her, while putting in place some parameters to help keep her safe. Let's take a closer look.

First, set rules. Let your teen know that drug and alcohol use is unacceptable and that the rule about this has been devised to protect her. Set limits with clear consequences for breaking them. Enforce those consequences for noncompliance, but at the same time, praise and reward good behavior.

Positive reinforcement (praise and reward) makes good behaviors more likely to recur, so it is a powerful motivator. "Hey, you did a great job staying at the speed limit, especially when everyone else seemed to be driving so fast," is an intrinsically rewarding statement that will increase the chances that he will drive safely the next time. While something tangible—like money—can be quite effective as well, mere words are powerful all on their own. Remember, our teens very much value what we think of them, and when they make us happy and we let them know it, they are more likely than not to continue to try to earn our praise. You can determine what works best within your family framework.

There is another kind of reinforcement that is helpful to know about. It's called "negative reinforcement." While many people think of this as punishment, it actually is not. As we will see, punishment makes bad behavior less likely to occur. Reinforcement, both positive and negative, makes good behavior more likely to occur.

Say your teen has broken curfew and you ground him for the following weekend. This is a form of punishment. When he talks openly and honestly with you about what he was doing the night he broke curfew, you might consider reducing the punishment to one day rather than two, thereby reinforcing his efforts to talk with you about what is really taking place in his world. In more clinical terms, we would call that *change* in his punishment (the grounding) a "removal of a negative stimulus," or negative reinforcement.

In theory, punishments make bad behaviors less likely to occur again. If Jenny is required to clean out the basement (a task she abhors) for talking back, or loses her driving privileges for sneaking vodka into the prom, she may not talk back or try to use alcohol again . . . or, at least, not for a while. As most any parent can tell you, there are limits to the effectiveness of punishments. Those proven to work best are ones that are certain—meaning kids can bank on them being imposed—and swift—

meaning they are applied in close proximity to a rule being broken or an expectation not being met. When punishments are neither certain nor swift, they quickly lose value.

Consider speeding tickets. How many people continue to speed even though they know it is against the law? The chances of getting caught and thus being punished are hit or miss, at best. And the imposing of a fine or points on a driver's license can be a long, drawn-out process. Both of these eventualities perpetuate speeding. If we knew for certain that a ticket would be issued every time we exceeded the speed limit and that we would have to pay the ticket immediately, we'd be less likely to speed again!

Discipline vs. Punishment

Like it or not, disciplining children is part of a parent's job. It's important to remember that discipline is not always the same thing as punishment. Just as a point of reference, Webster's defines discipline as "training that is expected to produce a specified character or pattern of behavior."

Discipline provides structure. And structure helps kids to feel safe and confident. Without structure, many children will "test limits," break rules, and engage in inappropriate behavior until structure is provided. Structure, in the form of rules, guidelines, and expectations, serves as a guide and helps children to pattern their behavior. In other words, it helps *them* to be structured!

A reasonable approach to discipline demonstrates that you care enough about your child to provide clear guidelines that will help her find her way to behaviors that are rewarded.

As we have seen throughout this book, expectations are an important determinant of a child's behavior. There is truth to the adage that children will live up (or down) to your expectations for them. Clarify your expectations early and stick to them.

As you already know, from time to time most children and teens will deviate from the rules and expectations you have established. They do this for many reasons, not the least of which is to see if you're paying attention!

There are basically two ways to handle a disciplinary situation: helpful and not helpful. Helpful approaches to discipline correct the situation without making your child feel threatened, incapable, or overly embarrassed. Helpful approaches also assist teens in correcting their behavior, while learning about themselves and how their behavior impacts others.

My experience has been that appropriate and effective punishments are usually those that have been decided on ahead of time (i.e., in the event of that, this will happen . . .), and those that have been determined to be reasonable (i.e., the punishment fits the crime), and safe (meaning no punishment should ever place a child or teen in physical or psychological jeopardy). Punishing children by beating or humiliating them is way out of bounds. So, too, is denying them attention or love over the long-term, because we let our anger get the best of us. While all of us may be become distraught by a teenager at one time or another, we are well advised to apply reasoned thought to our reactions, because otherwise we may precipitate an outcome that is far worse than the initial infraction.

Even in the best case, punishment has its limitations. It can produce the desired outcome right away but may not always translate into a lesson learned for the future, or to better self-understanding. Randall Grayson, a camp director and former member of the *Camping Magazine* Editorial Advisory Committee, suggests a process through which we can help young people understand the need behind their behavior: I am doing x because I want y—perhaps control, affection, love, self-esteem, or fun. We can then assist them in understanding their behavior by asking them some simple questions: *What happened? How did that make you feel? What did you want? What did you do to get it? How did that work? What other choices could you have made?*

> To be effective, discipline must be consistent.

Clear expectations and consistent responses to behavior make the environment more predictable. Predictability helps a child to better monitor and adjust her behavior (it also makes her less anxious because she knows what to expect). So, what does that tell us? When disciplinary situations arise—approach them judiciously! Our kids should know that our goal is to help them "make things right." Whatever the case, it is important that teens understand what the rules are and what the consequences will be for breaking them.

The second step in "holding on while letting go" is, **know where your teen is and what he will be doing during unsupervised time.**

Unsupervised teens are also more likely to engage in risky behaviors, such as under-age drinking, sexual activity, and cigarette smoking, than other teens. Thus, it is particularly important for us to keep on top of where our kids are and what they are doing during times when there is likely to be less adult supervision, such as after school, in the evening hours, and during the summer or holidays.

> Research shows that teens with unsupervised time are three times more likely to use marijuana or other drugs.

We all remember those radio ads from way back in our own childhoods: "It's ten o'clock . . . do you know where your children are?" It's still an important question, especially in this day and age when the dangers confronting teens have become more prolific. Cell phones, pagers, and PDA's all make it easier for us to be in touch with our teens and for them to be in touch with us. We should use these electronic tools to our advantage—keeping track, within reason, of where they are going and who they're spending time with.

However, sometimes technology can be used to thwart even our best efforts to keep track of wandering teens.

In Seattle, watching the end of a high school focus group, I'm listening to teens relate their stories of drinking and drugging to the moderator, a young woman who seems taken aback by their ability to conceal their actions from their parents.

"How do you get away with all of this stuff?" she asked as a wrap-up question. A girl about halfway down the table practically jumped out of her seat, hand-raised, ready to reveal her secret strategy.

"I'll tell you what we do," she offered excitedly. "We pick a girl on Friday afternoon who is not very popular so that we know she won't have any plans that night and ask her if we can tell our parents we're sleeping at her house. Then, when curfew time comes around, we call her, and she uses three-way calling to patch us through to our parents. That way, *her* number shows up on *their* caller ID so that they think we're where we're supposed to be!" I call this "duplicity in the technological age."

Schemes such as this one point out the importance of forming a parent "network" so that everybody knows what's going on. A quick call to the unpopular girl's parents to confirm their willingness to host a sleepover and that there will be adequate adult supervision would thwart plans like this.

It is also important to **keep teens busy**—especially between the hours of 3:00 p.m. to 6:00 p.m. and into the evening hours. If you can't be personally available to your teen during these times, get him signed up for after-school activities, such as a supervised educational program or a sports league. Research shows that teens who are involved in constructive, adult-supervised activities are less likely to use drugs than other teens.

As I discussed in Chapter Four, it is important that we help our kids maintain balance in their lives to avoid becoming overscheduled and overstressed, which in turn can actually make destructive choices more, rather than less, likely. So, while keeping kids busy is a good tactic in an overall strategy to discourage dangerous behaviors, it is one that has to be monitored carefully through constant contact and communication with our teens, checking in with friends' parents and asking for updates from teachers, coaches, and counselors. Remember, no single tactic is effective in keeping kids on the straight and narrow all by itself. Successful approaches require multiple, concurrent strategies designed not so much to make poor choices hard to make, but good choices easy to make.

Another helpful strategy is to **spend time together as a family regularly** and to be involved in your teen's life. Create a bond with your child by sharing special time with her. Some parents I know make sure that they participate in a child's favorite activity (such as travel, sailing, hiking, or going to the movies) with them from time to time. This builds up credit with your child so that when you have to set limits or enforce consequences, it's less stressful and less adversarial because your relationship will be more balanced overall.

Next up, **talk to your teen.** We'll cover this a lot more thoroughly in Chapter Nine, but here I mean something basic. While shopping or riding in the car, casually ask your teenager how things are going at school, about his friends, and what his plans are for the weekend. This may sound obvious, but a natural, casual approach such as this will often yield far more information than an interrogation: *What are you doing? Who are you hanging out with? Are they good kids? Are you getting into things you shouldn't be?*

My research confirms that regular dialogue during "normal" conversations is most effective in influencing behavior. Many parents tell me that long car rides are their favorite times to talk with their teens. "They're captive . . . they can't go anywhere, and they don't have to look at me," one mom explained. These types of conversations also help to close the reality gap by filling the void with information and input offered up by our teen.

It is helpful to **check on your teenager occasionally** to see that she is where she said she was going, and that she's with the people she said she'd be with. Understandably, some parents are reluctant to do this, fearing that such an act will be interpreted as a lack of trust or faith in their child. But, as we saw with Tim in Chapter Three, and the Seattle girl in the previous example, our teens may not always be where we think they are, or doing what they should be doing. Remember that Tim's night ended in jail.

When we help teens to decipher that our "checking in" is simply part of our job as parents to keep them safe, they will see our efforts not as a lack of trust but of a sign of caring—albeit an annoying one for some. Teens understand, but need reminders, that some of what we do that drives them crazy (such as calling a friend's parents before allowing an overnight) is done out of love and concern. A little later in this chapter, we'll see teens themselves offering similar advice for parents. A further note on the benefits of this approach: Young people can effectively use our attentiveness to explain away decisions to their friends. It gives them an "out" when they don't *want* to break our rules and violate our trust: "I can't go to Sharon's house, because I know my mom will be calling here soon to talk to your parents and see what we're up to."

One of my favorite recommendations from ONDCP is to **establish a "core-values statement"** for your family. Consider developing a family mission statement that reflects what you all believe about your responsibilities to one another, how and when you will communicate, and what the consequences will be for breaking family rules, such as always wear a seat belt, no drugs, and be sure to call if you're going to be late. This might be discussed and written up during a family meeting or over a weekend together. One family I know uses mealtimes to reinforce what they've all agreed to. The parents raise recent incidents at the boys' schools, commenting on who did what, asking questions about what their children think, and reaffirming their confidence that their boys will make different choices under similar circumstances.

> By checking in or checking up, we stand a better chance of being able to intervene *before* a mistake can be made.

Being given the chance to talk about what they stand for is particularly important for teens who receive pressure daily from external influencers on issues like drugs, sex, violence, and vandalism. They need to talk things out for themselves, to understand how they feel about the issues (this is also a great opportunity to reinforce their good intentions). If you don't provide a compass to guide your kids, the void will be filled by the strongest force—and that can be dangerous! They need to see their values in relation to yours. When they match up, young people feel more grounded and more confident about their ability to make good choices. After all, they want our approval and trust.

It might seem obvious, but it's so important that you **get to know your teen's friends (and their parents)** by inviting them over for dinner or talking with them at your teen's soccer game, dance rehearsal, or other activities. This will give you an important frame of reference that will help you to better understand your teen's social environment and the personalities, interests, and behaviors of their friends. It also sends a very important message that you care enough about him to want to spend time with his friends. Also, by getting to know his friends' parents, you can piece together a support network through which you can share—and learn—strategies as well as to achieve group-wide adult consensus on important parameters for all the kids in your teen's group, including curfews and driving rules. Knowing well the other people that inhabit your teen's world will supply you with loads of information that you can use to help her make good choices, even if, as one boy explained, that can be hard to do: "My parents don't know my friends' parents," he said. "Yeah, they knew them when we were younger, but stopped when I started having so many of them. Now, there are different classes of friends—school friends and out-of-school friends. Plus, we have cars now, so they don't know what's going on."

Finally, **stay in touch with the adult supervisors** in your child's life (teachers, coaches, employers, counselors) and have them inform you of any changes in your teen. This will help you to spot trouble and guide your conversations. Such an approach also builds a coalition of significant adults who share an interest in, and concern for, your teen and that can communicate among its members about his progress or their concerns for him. As the mother of a camper of mine likes to say, "Raising kids is a team sport!"

Everywhere Are Signs

Changes in mood, attitudes, sleeping habits, and hobbies, and also flair-ups in temper, are so common among teens. Given all this, how *can* you tell if your child is using drugs or alcohol, or might be suicidal, for example?

Start by looking for signs of real depression (discussed more thoroughly in Chapter Two), such as withdrawal, carelessness with grooming, or hostility. These are all strong indicators that something is not right in the world of your teen. Also ask yourself: *Is she doing well in school, getting along with friends, taking part in sports or other activities?* Other adults in your child's life should be able to help you assess this, if necessary.

Here is an easy-reference, general watch list for parents. The signs outlined may indicate alcohol and other drug use, but also deeper problems with depression, suicidal thoughts, and gang involvement. Be on the lookout for these signs:

- Changes in friends
- Negative changes in schoolwork, missed days of school, or declining grades
- Increased secrecy about possessions or activities
- Use of incense, room deodorant, or perfume to hide smoke or chemical odors
- Subtle changes in conversations with friends (e.g., more secretive, using "coded" language)
- Change in clothing choices, such as a new fascination with clothes that highlight drug use (e.g., a T-shirt with a marijuana leaf printed on the front)
- Increase in borrowing money
- Evidence of drug paraphernalia, such as pipes or rolling papers
- Evidence of the use of inhalant products (such as hairspray, nail polish, correction fluid, common household products) and, since these are such common items, rags and paper bags that may be used to administer the inhalant
- Bottles of eye drops that may be used to mask bloodshot eyes or dilated pupils
- Mouthwash or breath mints to cover up the smell of alcohol
- Prescription drugs missing from your medicine cabinet—especially narcotics and mood stabilizers

When such signs are present, it is important to act swiftly to prevent the injury or death of a child. But sometimes we aren't quite sure and may hold back, reluctant to make a scene or to fight with our child, especially if the "proof" doesn't seem clear enough. A good place to start your "investigation" is simply with a conversation, where you relate what you've seen and express that you are concerned. Something like, *"I've noticed that you seem sort of down lately and have been spending more time alone in your room."* Or, *"I'm concerned about you and am afraid that you might be experimenting with drugs."* Such openers can go a long way toward jump-starting dialogue about substance use. Similar strategies are effective in probing for depression, victimization from bullying or hazing, even sexual behavior.

Of course, there are situations where conversation may not yield the desired results. Teens may be too scared to talk openly about their alcohol use for fear of punishment; they may be so dependent on marijuana that they don't want to risk its confiscation or referral to a drug counselor; or they may be too embarrassed to admit they're being bullied or having sex. When we are unable to reach our kids, but suspect something is wrong and that they may be in jeopardy—particularly when problematic signs such as withdrawal, moodiness, or poor conduct are escalating—we need to consider alternative paths to intervention.

Teens themselves generally tell me that when a parent suspects their child might be in danger of some sort (taking drugs, for example), they have an obligation to do "whatever it takes" to reveal the truth and get them help, including steps that under other circumstances might be considered by a young person as an invasion of privacy: room or social-networking site searches, or drug testing.

The mom of Atlanta 10th-grader Justin was so alarmed by his sudden changes in behavior, both at home and as reported by his principal at school, that she figured out how to access his personal page on MySpace and discovered what was bothering him: He was being pressured to have sex he didn't feel ready for. She was able to effectively intervene (without disclosing her tactics) by talking to him about choices. Ultimately, Justin decided against meeting up with the girl.

On the flip side, as we will see shortly in the case of 16-year-old Jason, if we ignore the signs right in front of us—say, drug paraphernalia in her car, a condom in the pants he left in the hamper, or bruising on her arm—we place our kids at further risk.

An approach like drug testing might seem radical, but it is increasingly being used by some parents as a way to both detect drug and alcohol use, and to deter it before it begins.

It is worthwhile to consider under what circumstances you may want to take your child to the doctor and to ask him about screening your child for drugs and alcohol. This may involve your doctor just asking your child a few simple questions. Or it may involve something more invasive, such as a urine or blood screen.

What to Look for When It Comes to Alcohol and Other Drugs

Parents are rightly concerned about the prevalence of alcohol and drug use among youth, but often wonder, "How can I know? What should I be looking for?" The following are some signs of commonly used and abused substances organized by type for easy reference.

Alcohol: Odor on the breath. Intoxication/drunkenness. Difficulty focusing. Glazed appearance of the eyes. Uncharacteristically passive behavior or combative and argumentative behavior. Gradual decline in personal appearance and hygiene. Gradual development of difficulties, especially in school work or job performance. Absenteeism from school (particularly on Mondays). Unexplained bruises and accidents. Irritability. Flushed skin. Loss of memory (blackouts). Availability and consumption of alcohol becomes the focus of social activities. Changes in peer-group associations and friendships. Impaired interpersonal relationships (unexplainable termination of relationships with friends, and separation from close family members).

Stimulants—Cocaine/Crack/Methamphetamines: Extremely dilated pupils. Dry mouth and nose, bad breath, frequent lip-licking. Excessive activity, difficulty sitting still, lack of interest in food or sleep. Irritable, argumentative, nervous. Talkative, but conversation often lacks continuity; changes subjects rapidly. Runny nose, cold or chronic sinus/nasal problems, nosebleeds. Use or possession of paraphernalia such as small spoons, razor blades, mirror, little bottles of white powder, and plastic, glass, or metal straws.

Depressants: Symptoms of alcohol intoxication with no alcohol odor on breath. (Although remember that depressants are also frequently used with alcohol.) Lack of facial expression or animation. Flat affect. Limp appearance. Slurred speech. But note: There are few readily apparent symptoms; abuse may be better indicated by activities such as frequent visits to different physicians for prescriptions to treat "nervousness," "anxiety," "stress," etc.

Ecstasy: Confusion, blurred vision, rapid eye movement, chills or sweating, high body temperature, profuse sweating, dehydration, confusion, faintness, paranoia or severe anxiety, panic attacks, trancelike state, transfixing on sites and sounds, unconscious clenching of the jaw, grinding teeth, muscle tension, extreme affection. Depression, headaches, dizziness (from hangover after-affects), possession of pacifiers (used to stop jaw-clenching), lollipops, candy necklaces, mentholated vapor rub, vomiting.

Hallucinogens/LSD: Extremely dilated pupils. Warm skin, excessive perspiration, body odor. Distorted sense of sight, hearing, touch; distorted image of self and time perception. Mood and behavior changes, the extent depending on emotional state of the user and environmental conditions. Unpredictable flashback episodes even long after withdrawal (although these are rare).

Inhalants (cleaning fluids, deodorants, hair sprays, gasoline, propane, whipped-cream cans or felt-tip markers): Odor of the particular substance (say, gasoline) on breath and clothes. Runny nose. Watering eyes. Drowsiness or unconsciousness. Poor muscle control. Prefers group activity to being alone. Presence of bags or rags containing dry plastic cement or other solvent at home, in locker at school, or at work. Discarded whipped cream, spray paint, or hairspray cans. Solvents, aerosols, and glue can result in slurred speech, impaired coordination, nausea, vomiting, and slowed breathing. Brain damage, pains in the chest, muscles, and joints, heart trouble, severe depression, fatigue, loss of appetite, or bronchial spasms.

Marijuana: Rapid, loud talking and bursts of laughter in early stages of intoxication. Sleepy or dazed in the later stages. Forgetfulness in conversation. Inflammation in whites of eyes; pupils unlikely to be dilated. Odor similar to burnt rope on clothing or breath. Brown residue on fingers. Tendency to drive slowly—below speed limit. Distorted sense of time passage—tendency to overestimate time intervals. Use or possession of paraphernalia, including roach clips, packs of rolling papers, and pipes or bongs. Marijuana users are difficult to recognize, unless they are under the influence of the drug at the time of observation. Casual users may show no general symptoms. Marijuana does have a distinct odor and may be the same color as or a bit greener than tobacco.

Narcotics/Prescription Drugs—Heroin & Opium/Codeine & Oxycontin: Lethargy, drowsiness. Constricted pupils fail to respond to light. Redness and raw nostrils from inhaling heroin in powder form. Scars (tracks) on inner arms or other parts of body, from needle injections. Use or possession of paraphernalia, including syringes, bent spoons, bottle caps, eye droppers, rubber tubing, cotton, and needles. Slurred speech. In cases where an actual patient has received a prescription for pain, abuse of medication may be indicated by amounts and frequency taken.

PCP: Unpredictable behavior—mood may swing from passiveness to violence for no apparent reason. Symptoms of intoxication. Disorientation; agitation and violence if exposed to excessive sensory stimulation. Fear, terror. Rigid muscles. Strange gait. Deadened sensory perception (may experience severe injuries while appearing not to notice). Pupils may appear dilated. Mask-like facial appearance. Floating pupils, appear to follow a moving object. Comatose (unresponsive) if large amount consumed; eyes may be open or closed.

Remember that we also need to be keeping an eye out for the signs and symptoms of distress that might be leading our child down the path of substance use in the first place. And, of course, we need to always work hard to keep the lines of communication open.

Early and Often

Following a parent presentation at a private Massachusetts high school, Kari's parents approached me. "We think our daughter might be using drugs," they explained, but they seemed uncertain and confused about what to do. "Have you asked her?" I replied. They looked shocked, as though the thought of doing so had never occurred to them, or they feared they would somehow be trespassing beyond unspoken but firm boundaries.

"No," was their simple answer.

"Have you spoken to her about drug use and let her know of your expectations?" I persisted.

Glancing back and forth at each other, Kari's parents finally admitted proudly, "Yes, we talked to her back in 7th grade."

No, no, no! I wanted to scream! Instead, I calmly explained to Kari's parents that they must find time for *regular* communication about drugs and other concerning topics. You cannot talk about drugs—or sex, or drinking, or hazing—*one time only!* You have to keep it up, with ongoing dialogue that maintains open channels for information to flow through.

I say it over and over in the chapters of this book, and I say it again here: The most important measure in preventing substance use and abuse and other negative behaviors is maintaining a strong connection with your teen. Finding the time and tone to talk about the issues—again and again and again—will help you to anticipate, spot, and deal with trouble. Our friends from ONDCP offer some great advice for parents on what to do when we suspect our teen is experimenting with drugs . . . and when to do it. While these deal with substance use, they are similarly appropriate, and effective, in talking with teens about everything from sex to cutting to driving.

What You Can Do

Get Educated

First, learn as much as you can. Sign up for the anti-drug *Parenting Tips* newsletter, put out by ONDCP, or www.freevibe.com, for information and scientific evidence on drug and alcohol use by teens. Or, you can call the National Clearinghouse for Alcohol and Drug Information (NCADI) for free pamphlets and fact sheets. They'll even send it in a plain envelope if you wish. They can be reached at 1-800-788-2800; Spanish: 1-877-746-3764 (24 hours, seven days a week). Or visit their Web site at http://www.health.org.

Information on a fuller range of teen behavior, including bullying, sex, and suicide, can be found at www.sadd.org.

Have the Talk—Let Them Know You Know

The next thing to do is to sit down and talk with your child. Be sure to have the conversation when you are all calm and have plenty of time. This isn't an easy task—your feelings may range from anger to guilt that you have "failed" because your kid is using drugs, for example. This isn't true. By staying involved you can help her stop using and make choices that will make a positive difference in her life.

Wisdom from Our Teens

"Parents need to repeat the message. Telling someone at age nine not to drink or do drugs is not going to affect their behavior later on when the pressure starts. Repeating the message is more effective."

Be Specific About Your Concerns

Tell your child what you see and how you feel about it. Be specific about the things you have observed that cause concern. Make it known if you found drug paraphernalia (or empty bottles or cans). Explain exactly how his behavior or appearance (bloodshot eyes, different clothing) has changed and why that worries you. Tell him that drug and alcohol use is dangerous (and may lead to other risky behaviors, such as sex and violence) and it's your job to keep him away from things that put him in danger.

Remain Calm and Connect with Your Child

Have this discussion without getting mad or accusing your child of being stupid or bad or an embarrassment to the family. Be firm but loving with your tone and try not to get hooked into an argument. Knowing that kids are naturally private about their lives, try to find out what's going on. Do not to make the discussion an inquisition; simply try to connect with your teen and find out why he may be making bad choices. Find out if friends offered him drugs at a party or school. Did he try it just out of curiosity, or did he use marijuana or alcohol, for example, for some other reason? Your calm tone alone will be a signal to your child that you care, and that you are going to do your best to *help* him.

Here are some suggestions for what to tell your child:

- You LOVE him, and you are worried that he might be using drugs or alcohol.
- You KNOW that drugs may seem like the thing to do, but doing drugs can have serious consequences.
- It makes you FEEL worried and concerned about him when he does drugs.
- You are there to LISTEN to him.
- You WANT him to be a part of the solution.
- You will tell him what you WILL do to help him.

Finally, know that you will have this discussion many, many times. Talking to your kid about drugs and alcohol is not a one-time event!

Be Prepared. Practice What You'll Say

Be prepared for your teen to deny using drugs. Don't expect her to admit she has a problem. Your child will probably get angry and might try to change the subject. Maybe you'll be confronted with questions about what you did as a kid. If you are asked, it is best to be honest, and if you can, connect your use to negative consequences. Answering deceptively can cause you to lose credibility with your kids if they ever find out that you've lied to them. On the other hand, if you don't feel comfortable answering the question, you can talk about some specific people you know who have had negative things happen to them as a result of drug and alcohol use. However, if the time comes to talk about it, you can give short, honest answers like these.

"When I was a kid, I took drugs because some of my friends did. I wanted to in order to fit in. If I'd known then about the consequences and how they would affect my life, I never would have tried drugs. I'll do everything I can to help keep you away from them."

"I drank alcohol and smoked marijuana because I was bored and wanted to take some risks, but I soon found out that I couldn't control the risk—the loss of trust of my parents and friends. There are much better ways of challenging yourself than doing drugs."

Don't Make Excuses

Although it's natural for parents to make excuses for their child, you're not helping her if you make excuses when she misses school or family functions when you suspect something else is at play. Go back to the first two steps: get more information, and talk to your child.

Act Now

You can begin to more closely monitor your child's activities. Have a few conversations. Ask: Who? What? Where? When? Reflect with your child on why he is using drugs and try to understand the reasons why so that you can help solve the problem. When you get a better idea of the situation, then you can decide on the next steps to take. These could include setting new rules and consequences that are reasonable and enforceable—such as a new curfew, no cell phone or computer privileges for a period of time, or less time hanging out with friends or with *certain* friends. You may want to get them involved in pro-social activities that will keep them busy and help them meet new people.

Myths that Matter

As we have seen, regular conversations shrink the reality gap and help us identify trouble. It's as simple as that. So is the fact that in order to even recognize that discussion is necessary, we have to overcome five myths— or ways of thinking—that are commonly held by parents and children alike.

The Myth of Improbability: Here, the NIFTY syndrome we met in Chapter Two rears its ugly head, burying us in the false belief that it is always *other people's children* who are making poor choices. Remember, compared to what their parents say about them, high school teens are eight times more likely to say they drink alcohol, four times more likely to say they use drugs, and twice as likely to say they have had sex.

A surprising number of parents don't actually want to know what's going on with their teen. Out of sight, out of mind: "If I can't see the problem, it doesn't exist." Blissful ignorance. More than a few parents avoid asking the tough questions, because, quite frankly, they're not ready to deal with the answers. One mother likes to say, "If you don't want to know the answer, don't ask the question."

Let's face it, it's easy to avoid the truth when the stakes are high and the ones we love may be engaging in behavior we hate. Joe, a tall, olive-skinned 15-year-old sophomore of Italian-Cuban descent says, "I don't tell my parents a lot of stuff, and they don't really ask. Whatever they don't ask, they don't want to know." That avoidance cedes to teens a free ride toward self-destruction.

The Myth of Inevitability: Many parents don't want to know what's going on, because they have come to believe that they have little ability to control—or alter—what they view as typical teenage behavior. Indeed, more than half (53 percent) of parents agree that drinking is part of growing up, and that teens will drink no matter what. Approximately one-quarter (22 percent) of parents say they let their teens make their own decisions about drinking. And more than one-third (37 percent) allow their teens to make their own decisions regarding sex.

Alcohol, drugs, and sex—not to mention other destructive or potentially dangerous behaviors—need not be rites of passage. Yet many parents believe they are and so fail to establish and enforce ground rules that would actually steer their kids away from the so-called inevitable.

The myth of inevitability extends to young people, as well—it's called "social norming." If drinking is perceived as normal, then they want to do it, too. But my experience is that middle and high school students tend to wildly overestimate the number of their peers who are doing this or that. Many teens tell me that almost everyone drinks. And yet the fact is that there are a lot of kids who don't drink.

Remember, if 63 percent of high school students say they drink, that means that 37 percent don't. That's a pretty significant number that kids need to be made aware of. Otherwise, their misperceptions can result in a desire to conform to what they merely think is going on.

The Myth of Irrelevancy: As children reach adolescence, many parents believe they are no longer welcome in their kids' lives. But our kids *do* want to talk with us; they *do* want to know what we think; they *do* want to know of our expectations for their behavior; and they *do* want to be held accountable when they mess up. Teens want limits—and appreciate parents who are willing to set them. They need to know the boundaries within which they can test their budding identities and natural inclinations toward risk-taking. Without such boundaries, they will push until they find some. Teens whose parents convey their expectations, clearly and regularly, are more motivated to try to live up to those expectations and to avoid behaviors of which their parents disapprove.

The Myth of Invincibility: This reflects a commonly held view among young people: "I am young, and I am indestructible." The Myth of Invincibility is similar to David Elkind's construct of adolescent egocentrism and its "Personal Fable," which maintains that teens, because they believe everyone is watching them (Elkind calls this the "imaginary audience"), view themselves as so unique and special that they cannot be subject to harm. In *The Hurried Child*, Elkind says, "If everyone is watching you and is concerned with your behavior, then you must be something special, something unique upon this earth. The fable leads us to believe that other people will grow old and die but not us, other people may get sick but not us, and so on." He concludes that this Personal Fable explains a lot of adolescent risk-taking: "It will happen to somebody else, not me." (Although as intimate peer relationships take hold, teens begin to realize they may be more similar to peers than they previously thought, and the impact of the Personal Fable starts to diminish.)

Unlike the Personal Fable, The Myth of Invincibility reflects both inexperience with abstract thinking *and* a lack of exposure to the consequences of certain behaviors. That is something parents can act on by discussing the real-life outcomes of poor choices. They are easy to find.

Just as I was working on this chapter in June of 2007, the morning paper ran the story of four California teens killed on a beach trip just days before they were to graduate. Despite the fact that a drunk-driving awareness campaign had been conducted at their high school (including a mock memorial service), these teens apparently did not believe they were vulnerable and instead chose to race another vehicle at speeds up to 100 mph after passing a busload of classmates, waving beer cans out the windows.

Some time before this story, I sat in a Boston television studio with local teens, taping *The Road Ahead: Stay Safe at the Wheel,* a DVD for Liberty Mutual Group—a free resource about teen driving based in part on the HBO Family documentary, *Smashed: Toxic Tales of Teens and Alcohol,* which shows a succession of seriously injured teens being treated at the University of Maryland's R. Adams Cowley Shock Trauma Center in Baltimore. After viewing some clips, the kids seemed stunned.

"You just don't think it's going to happen to you" was a common refrain, accurately reflecting the Myth of Invincibility. One of the injured kids in the film corroborated this sentiment: "Everybody thinks they are invincible—nothing can happen to me—and you just make that one dumb mistake and then that's it, your life changes forever."

Catherine, a high school senior, learned this tough lesson early on.

"When I was a freshman, I received a hard reality check," she says. "There was a car accident and all four of the boys that were in it went to our school, and I was friends with all of them. Joshua was one of the boys who never got to walk away from their tragic mistake of drinking and driving."

The Myth of Immunity: Many young people have come to believe that they will not be held to account for misbehavior. Too often, they're correct. Because many times we "rescue" them, rather than letting them suffer the consequences of a poor decision. Time and again, I witness parents blame someone or something else (like school) for their child's actions. Doing so sends the clear message that kids are not responsible for their own decisions. It also deprives them of important lessons, taught with consequences that are relatively minor compared to the consequences they could suffer later in life for similar behavior.

Parents also tend to believe that the grunts and glares from our adolescents in response to questions about personal behavior mean, "You're way out of bounds now!" We let it go. And so we give them immunity for their bad behaviors, even in our own home.

The mother of 16-year-old Jason didn't pay much attention to the late-night phone calls from strangers, until she found a bag of marijuana in his shirt drawer—evidence of a lifestyle that ultimately led to a near-death overdose of alcohol, barbiturates, and hallucinogens. And yet, ironically, most teens say that if their parents came right out and asked them direct questions about behavior ("Are you and John having sex?" or "Did you drink at the party last night"), they would reply honestly. One teen told me that if his parents asked if he was drinking at the parties he attends, he would say, "yes." "And if they asked you to stop?" I inquired. "I'd stop," he said, looking at me as if I had two heads! Sometimes it's just that simple.

What Teens Have to Say

Teens themselves offer valuable recommendations as to what safeguards will be most effective in keeping them out of harm's way. And, after all, they're the experts. Their advice is pretty straightforward.

- **Initiate dialogue about decision-making.** Teens want to know what their parents and other significant adults think.
- **Set curfews.** Despite what your teens might say, most kids have them.
- **Stay up until teens return home.** Simple, but extraordinarily effective. A staggering 70 percent of teens say they would be less likely to drink alcohol if they knew their parents would be waiting up for them.
- **Limit overnights.** This is a tough one, but most kids say it would significantly reduce misbehavior. When teens know they don't need to go home, they are more likely to break the rules their parents have established for them.
- **Call other parents.** Coordinating expectations and supervision is vitally important to maintaining a safe and healthy social atmosphere. It can also provide some moral support for parents who are constantly (and incorrectly) told that they are "the only parents" with rules.
- **Ask teens to check in by phone throughout the evening.** Cell phones make this an easy task and can go a long way toward preventing, or addressing, problem situations.
- **Enforce consequences for breaking the rules.** Nearly three-quarters of teens say that punishment imposed by their parents is effective in convincing them not to repeat the offending behavior.

It's a challenging, difficult, evolving task to maintain vigilance—or even a healthy suspicion. But too many kids are dying from alcohol poisoning, drug overdoses, sexually transmitted diseases, suicide, and impaired, distracted, dangerous driving for us not to make the effort.

Six

Weapons of Mass Persuasion

"Hey, that was great!" exclaimed the young man standing in front of me, extending his hand for a congratulatory shake.

"I'm glad you liked the speech," I replied, pleased that my remarks to the student body at this Connecticut boarding school had been so well received. Or so I thought.

"Nah," he rifled back. "Not the speech. It was the way you loosened everybody up at the beginning. That was really funny."

He was referring to the fact that, upon my introduction and ascension of the steps to the side of the stage, I managed to trip and cartwheel my way to the podium, causing laughter to rain down all around me. *They thought I had done that on purpose!* I was vindicated of being a klutz by being validated as a comic!"

"Oh yeah," I said. "That was funny, huh?!"

It's not exactly a secret that young people often interpret what we do and what we say in ways that we not only don't mean but also in ways we might never suspect. As we discussed in Chapter Four, cognitive changes taking place during adolescence affect the way that teens receive information. Though we may think we are being clear with our words and about our intentions, teens may take away something wholly different from what we have presented or implied. Our arched eyebrow or icy stare may not even be noticed by our teen—even though we think it must have been—and this only furthers our frustration that she has not heeded our wishes. Sometimes by design and sometimes by chance, young people sort through input and information in ways that often surprise us.

If our teen has so much trouble discerning *our* messages, we can only speculate what they glean from other people, those they know and others—including fictional characters—they see in advertising, on

Indeed, while our teens are now able to think abstractly—a hallmark of something Swiss psychologist Jean Piaget referred to as formal operational thought—they can still be remarkably literal. Thus, clarity and repetition often prove quite useful in our conversations with teens: saying exactly what we mean and saying it again!

television, and at the movies. And that is a frightening idea.

In their increasingly diverse and electronic world, young people today receive countless messages that inform their perspectives on everything from body image to violence. Parents tell me all the time that they worry about what their kids see on television, on the movie screen, or on the Internet. *Does it matter? Is it harmful? Do they think that's real?* Tough questions to answer and certainly there is a divide and much debate as to how much sway media messages have over teen behavior. But there is enough statistical and anecdotal evidence to suggest that we are well-advised to keep a careful eye on what our children are exposed to.

Understandably, many parents often feel powerless to do much about media content. After all, how can we possibly keep up with everything our child might see or hear, especially with video and audio images on just about every conceivable gadget our child has access to?

Yet, as I have said, there is enough evidence of the potentially harmful effect of "adult" messages delivered regularly and repeatedly to young minds to warrant concern, especially at a time when our children are wrestling to establish internal controls in the face of seemingly endless external temptations. Scientific corroboration or not, many parents seem to feel that relentless exposure to violence, sex, and substance use is likely to influence how their teen perceives the world and, subsequently, how he establishes his own standards for what constitutes normative, acceptable behavior. Repetitive viewing of violent behavior or demeaning acts may result in a "numbing" effect, leaving kids jaded and indifferent to the damaging effects on others.

A case in point occurred in December, 2007, when a seven-year-old Colorado girl was allegedly beaten to death by her 16-year-old half-sister and her 17-year-old boyfriend. They were imitating the Mortal Kombat video game—kicking, karate-chopping, and body-slamming the victim into unconsciousness.

Parents aren't the only ones concerned. In April of 2007, the Federal Trade Commission (FTC) issued a report to Congress on the status of self-regulation of violent content in entertainment targeting children and teens. In the report, the FTC cast doubt on the effectiveness of allowing the movie, music, and videogame industries to police themselves, pointing out that while each generally adheres to their own voluntary standards with respect to labeling and ratings, some R-rated movies, M-rated videogames, and explicit-content on television and Web sites continue to be both marketed to young audiences and easily accessed by kids even if meant for adults.

As a part of the report, the FTC details results from its ongoing "mystery shop," where unaccompanied children attempt to purchase R-rated movie tickets or DVDs, explicit-content-labeled music, and M-rated electronic games. While there is some encouraging news with regard to the electronic game industry (in 2000, 85 percent of children were able to make a purchase, as compared to 42 percent in 2006), the review of progress with respect to the successful purchase of theater tickets and music points to significant problems (46 percent vs. 39 percent, and 85 percent vs. 76 percent, respectively). When it comes to purchasing R-rated movies on DVD, almost three-quarters of the children (71 percent) were successful. The same number of children was able to buy unrated DVDs.

The ease with which children and teens can gain access to content meant for more mature audiences points to the dilemma many parents face. Clearly, they cannot be all places at all times, and, despite the rules they may have established with their children, many kids will seek out the "forbidden fruit" in an atmosphere that has few age controls.

Here, too, this natural proclivity for limit-testing in adolescence requires supervision when it comes to the subject of what Jim or Sue chooses to watch or listen to. Media promotion involving alcohol, drugs, and sex, leaves many young adults susceptible to self-defeating thoughts (and actions). Maybe *I* should be doing that! How come life doesn't seem so good for *me?*

In his book *The New Brain: How the Modern Age Is Rewiring Your Mind*, Dr. Richard Restak, a neurologist and neuropsychiatrist at George Washington University Medical Center, points out that digital content affects brain stimulation, leaving some kids at risk for psychological harm and feelings of unhappiness and vulnerability. He says that while each person may react somewhat differently, new research reveals how exposure to violent content, for example, can activate the prefrontal cortex, establish new circuitry, and leave individuals susceptible to distress when such images reoccur. Restak states that more than one thousand studies support the conclusion that when children watch violent media, they become more aggressive and that simply by limiting their exposure to violent content, we can reduce such aggression by as much as 25 percent.

In truth, our kids are being bombarded by media messages that have a "norming" effect with respect to inappropriate and often-illegal behavior. While each of us is influenced by what we view as common and acceptable, this is especially true during adolescence, when the almost-innate drive to "go along to get along" platforms such developmental prerogatives as independence, identity formation, and socialization. Media images that portray violence as effective, drinking as routine, other drug use as only marginally deviant, and sex as casual and unimportant, create a false sense of acceptability in the minds of those already predisposed to test limits and take risks.

Dr. Susan Villani, a Johns Hopkins University psychiatrist, published a sweeping survey of 10 years of research on media violence, sex, and risky behavior. She concluded that what children watch can directly influence their actions and suggests that, while it has been difficult to establish more than an anecdotal link between televised sex and violence and actual behavior, depictions of risky behavior in the media have been associated with increases in sexual activity, drinking, smoking, and drug use among children. In many ways, Villani's work only confirms the suspicion many parents have that at least some of what their child or teen is watching on TV is corrosive to the values and behaviors they try to model.

Television

As an undergraduate communications major in the early eighties, I spent a year researching and writing about the effects of media, specifically television, on children. What I found won't surprise you: Exposure to seemingly endless violence, indiscriminate sex, and questionable values often leaves kids facing a distinct dichotomy between what they are taught by parents and caring adults and the actions of "role models" on television. And the studies I looked at back then were based on television programming that seems pretty mild by today's standards.

Deployment of these most powerful weapons of mass persuasion propels youth down a dangerous path of indulgence, overgrown with the underbrush of self-deceit that obscures the longer-term physical, social, and emotional ramifications of what may, for a moment at least, seem like a good idea. Much as we suffer from a reality gap, so do our children when they fail to understand the very real risks associated with underage drinking, other drug use, sexual behavior, and dangerous driving—relying for information on images that instill the message that such choices merely represent milestones along the developmental highway.

In 2006, the Federal Communications Commission began an aggressive crackdown on indecency in television and on radio shows, levying hefty fines on broadcasters who air racy language or images.

Former FCC commissioner and University of Virginia law professor Glen Robinson says that advocacy groups have successfully moved this issue into the spotlight, enlisting many Americans who care about "family values" to join in the effort to rid television of objectionable material that may be seen by children and teens by speaking out about their concerns of its effects on perceptions and behaviors. In this regard, perhaps some progress is being made in protecting children from content that could be harmful—whether in the short term or later on.

One such advocacy group, the Parents Television Council, encourages consumers to file complaints with the Federal Communications Commission, saying, "The default setting for broadcast television used to be family-oriented, while those desiring edgier, more-explicit fare were free to seek it out. Today's prime-time television programming has become almost uniformly unsuitable for families, and often directly hostile to their values, making it very difficult for parents to shield their children and seek out alternative entertainment."

For sure, many adults dispute the connection between what teens see on television and their decisions about behavior. But the teens themselves say something different. According to Teens, Sex, and TV, a survey conducted by the Henry J. Kaiser Family Foundation and *US News & World Report*, 72 percent of 15- to 17-year-olds believe that sexual content on TV influences the behavior of kids their age, with 22 percent reporting it influences their own behavior. As 18-year-old Robert tells me, "If you watch television, you just assume everyone is having sex." Added 15-year-old Steve, "Television, movies, and music add to the pressure of wanting to have sex. They portray how men should be masculine and hook-up with women."

Another area of increasing concern when it comes to television has to do not only with the shows our teens are watching but also what they are seeing in commercials. A *Boston Globe* story, titled "Violent TV ads leave parents wincing," outlines the very real concern of adults who, even when they monitor the television programming their children watch, are virtually helpless in controlling the ads that often appear during commercial breaks. In the story, parents cite ads for such films as *Disturbia* and *Hannibal Rising* and for shows such as *Desperate Housewives*, as imposing on otherwise family-friendly content they want to share with their children. As *Time* magazine writer Richard Corliss says in an article on the subject, "Now the violence comes to you, child, in advertising on your TV, computer, or bus shelter." But, thus far, the issue of program content as opposed to advertising content has dominated the debate among regulators. In that regard, new technology—such as services like TiVo—can once again help parents by allowing them to screen-out, or in this case, pass-by, objectionable material.

When it comes to teens' favorite television programs, many of them are paired with alcohol advertising. For example, since 2001, alcohol ads have appeared every year on 13 or more of the 15 programs most popular with teens ages 12 to 17. Throughout 2005, alcohol companies placed more than 1,300 ads on 14 of the 15 programs most popular with teen audiences, including *Lost*, *Desperate Housewives*, *Monday Night Football*, and *CSI*, at a cost of nearly $38 million. Why? Some answers might be found by following the money trail. According to a 2001 article published by the American Medical Association, the short-term cash value of underage drinking to the alcohol industry was $22 billion in that year alone—15.5 percent of total consumer expenditures for alcohol!

> When you contrast that exposure with positive messaging, the story gets more alarming. For example, over a three-year period, young people were 96 times more likely to see a product ad for alcohol than an alcohol industry ad about underage drinking. And they were 43 times more likely to see a product ad than an alcohol company ad about drunk driving.

Another group, the Center on Alcohol Marketing and Youth, raises awareness about what our kids are being exposed to when it comes to the issue of alcohol use and abuse. They maintain that alcohol advertising, and youth exposure to it, has increased dramatically during this decade and that those ads hold powerful appeal to young audiences. According to the center, everyone is seeing more alcohol ads on television. From 2001 to 2005, the exposure of youth ages 12 to 20 to those ads increased by 41 percent, compared to a 39 percent increase in exposure to young adults ages 21 to 34, and a 48 percent increase in adult exposure. They also point out that teens ages 12 to 19 ranked ads for Bud Light number one, and Budweiser number four, when asked to choose their favorite television commercial in a spring 2005 study.

What do these alcohol product ads look like, and why are they so appealing? Many of the ads feature animals popular with young audiences, including some you probably remember, such as the talking Budweiser lizards and the Spuds MacKenzie dog. Other ads trade on masculinity (Miller Lite's "Nectar of the Guys"), sexuality (an ad for Bud Lite shows a woman straddling and kissing a man with text reading, "Get it started"), music (Coors Light's, "Mountain Jam"), and athleticism (Heineken's "It's Game Day" and Miller Lite's, "The Sweet Smell of Success").

Still others market sweet, soda-like products, such as Mike's Hard Lemonade, Smirnoff Ice, and Skyy Blue, in colors and packaging alluring to youth. According to the Center for Science in the Public Interest (CSPI), almost half of teens (41 percent) have tried a new breed of sweet-tasting, colorfully packaged alcoholic beverage. In 2007, the Center urged a nationwide recall of an alcoholic energy drink from Anheuser-Busch called "Spykes," maintaining the product was meant to appeal to young people. According to CSPI, Spykes came in colorful, two-ounce bottles with child-friendly flavors like Spicy Mango, Hot Melons, Spicy Lime, and Hot Chocolate. The drinks cost $3 or less, contain 12 percent alcohol by volume, and are fortified with caffeine, guarana, and ginseng, further increasing their youthful appeal.

The town of West Bridgewater, Massachusetts, acted quickly to ban these products, fearing their sale to children. "I'm quite frankly disgusted with Anheuser-Busch for their lack of corporate responsibility in this case," Matthew Albanese, chairman of the West Bridgewater selectmen, told WHDH-TV in Boston. "Every year, communities such as West Bridgewater spend thousands of dollars . . . educating our children on the dangers of alcohol abuse." Ultimately, the brewer pulled the product from store shelves across the country.

The federal Substance Abuse and Mental Health Services Administration (SAMHSA) also acknowledges that television commercials influence the habits of youth, from poor nutrition (perhaps resulting in obesity) to aggressive behavior (such as fighting). And, while we may not be able to control everything our child sees on television, we can monitor what they are watching, limit how much time they watch it, talk about what it depicts, and discuss the real-life consequences of some of the choices shown.

As a former Massachusetts state-government official heavily involved in both economic development efforts and regulatory issues, I understand and very much appreciate the role that advertising plays in our economy. Brewers, manufacturers, and service providers have a right to market what they sell. But, they also have a responsibility to children. It is easy to point fingers and assign blame. It is more difficult to discern the intent of marketing strategies we are not privy to, even if some seem pretty obvious. Nevertheless, common sense dictates rethinking the proliferation of advertising content that adversely affects the attitudes and behaviors of young people.

Indeed, much of what teens do mirrors what they see and hear in the popular media. Smoking, drinking, drugs, sex, and violence portrayed in songs, sitcoms, and movies indelibly mark young minds. Family hour doesn't seem so family-oriented anymore!

Even televised sporting events (and their attendant commercials) are filled with messages that proclaim that drinking and sex are the keys to happiness . . . and are no big deal. Take Super Bowl XXXVIII's now-infamous halftime show. The obscene lyrics, choreography, and nudity in Janet Jackson and Justin Timberlake's performance inspired outrage among countless fans and families who thought they were watching a youth-friendly sporting event meant to celebrate hard work, teamwork, sacrifice, and reward. What they got instead was a debasing, simulated act of sexual assault that may have effectively countered unparalleled advances in the education of young people (especially boys) about important gender issues, not the least of which is respect for sexual, physical, and psychological boundaries. That this scene was played over and over in television newscasts about the event only added to its impact.

In 2004, Rebecca Collins of the RAND Corporation, and a number of her colleagues, released a study of 12- to 17-year-olds regarding their television viewing habits and sexual activity. They found that teens who watch sex on TV are more likely to become sexually active sooner—and concluded that teens with the highest levels of such exposure were nearly twice as likely to have started having sexual intercourse during the year in between when the surveys were administered as were those who watched shows with the least sexual content.

More evidence of the effects of exposure to sexually laden content can be found in a study conducted as part of a five-year project funded by the National Institute of Child Health and Human Development and housed in the School of Journalism and Mass Communication at the University of North Carolina at Chapel Hill. It found that teenagers between the ages of 12 and 14 who use media with high sexual content are more than twice as likely to have had sexual intercourse by the time they are sixteen than teens who do not. "Teens are defaulting to entertainment media for sexual information because they aren't getting this information in other places," said Dr. Jane D. Brown, James L. Knight Professor in UNC's School of Journalism and Mass Communication and the principal investigator of the study. "Unfortunately, the media aren't the best sex educators. The media tend to leave out the crucial three C's: commitment, contraception, and consequences." Meaning what we've been saying here all along: Talk to your kids about the full range of issues that comes with being sexually active, including the possible physical, emotional, social, and legal consequences.

Parents can help by commenting on what they see, probing for what their teen sees, and talking about the context and possible consequences of such behavior in "real life." Doing this creates an opportunity to establish, or reaffirm, our expectations for teens and what will happen if they break the rules. Significantly, Brown and her colleagues found that one of the strongest protective factors against early sexual behavior was clear parental communication about sex. Talking with young people about what they see on television is enormously helpful both in terms of keeping up with what they watch and also by imbuing their thought process with our own perspectives, based on personal experience or the experiences of others we have known or heard about.

Better yet, watching television with our teens gives us opportunities to teach "media literacy"—prompting them to think critically about what they see and what impact it might have on their perceptions, attitudes, and behaviors. SAMHSA promotes media literacy, claiming it can help youth recognize and understand messages—actual or "between the lines"—delivered in music lyrics, promoted on clothing and jewelry, illustrated in advertisements, and portrayed on TV or in movies. "Media literacy helps children build resiliency skills, come to understand that all messages are constructed deliberately, and develop the ability to identify and resist messages that support the use of illegal drugs, tobacco, or alcohol." SAMHSA recommends engaging kids in a structured, in-depth discussion that encourages them to become good, discerning consumers of what they see on television, in the movies, and on their computer screen (and what they hear in music) by asking five critical questions.

- **Step 1—Reality:** Media messages represent someone's reality. What is the message maker's point of view?
- **Step 2—Interpretation:** People interpret media messages differently. How does the message make you feel?
- **Step 3—Construction:** Each media message is a collection of words, images, and sounds. What special words, images, and sounds are used to create the message?
- **Step 4—Purpose:** Each media message has an author and a purpose. Who created the message and why?
- **Step 5—Form:** Media messages come in different forms. How is this message delivered (magazines, television, radio, newspapers, etc.)?

These conversations are important because, in short, content equals consequence. And, sadly, there's no shortage of content. A study conducted at the University of California, Santa Barbara, found that two-thirds of all television shows (64 percent) have some sexual content, including 1 in 3 (32 percent) with sexual behaviors; that 1 in 7 shows (14 percent) now includes sexual intercourse; and that in the top 20 shows among teen viewers, 8 in 10 episodes include some sexual content (83 percent), including 1 in 5 (20 percent) with sexual intercourse.

Other studies have fueled debate about whether children should be watching television at all. The American Academy of Pediatrics points out that while television can be educational, it may teach some things we don't want our kids to learn. And, as we have seen, these lessons often come in the form of shows and commercials that depict violence, alcohol and drug use, and sexual behavior. The academy addresses particular areas of concern, including the amount of time our kids spend in front of the flickering screen: Children in the United States watch about four hours of TV every day. Watching movies on tape or DVD and playing video games only add to time spent in front of the TV screen. It may be tempting to use television, movies, and video games to keep your child busy, but he needs to spend as much time exploring and learning as possible. Playing, reading, and spending time with friends and family are much healthier than sitting in front of a TV.

Of course, television is not the evil empire and, obviously, it is very much a part of everyday life, here in America and elsewhere in the world. Our kids are exposed to its content whether we like it or not. So, we best serve them by seeking out and accentuating its positive influences—providing educational programming covering everything from history to health to hard work and sacrifice, for example—while screening-out the images and messages that may be harmful to impressionable minds.

Movies

On a recent trip to Isla Mujeres, Mexico, I passed through Cancun, a place I had not visited before. On the trip from the airport to the ferry, I couldn't help but recall a movie I had read about a few years earlier. *The Real Cancun*, a spring-break run-amok documentary from New Line Cinema, had an envelope-pushing reality-television feel. For almost two hours, it followed a battalion of fresh-faced college kids romping through this Mexican party-playground filled with endless opportunities for self-destructive behavior. Dubbed the "16 party animals who put the 'can' in Cancun," these uninhibited "cast members" were on a mission of sorts—to "drink, flirt, fight, and canoodle"— seemingly oblivious to the potential consequences of their quest, not to mention any collateral damage they might inflict on others along the way. More recently, *Girls Gone Wild* evoked similar themes and strategies, influencing young minds and creating an undercurrent of expectations for spring break.

That exploitive and exploited conduct by teens and young adults passes for entertainment says a lot about, well . . . entertainment. That it is spun as reality perpetuates the social norming of dangerous, even aberrant, behavior, making such choices more likely among kids because they seem commonplace. Reflecting the environment and expectations that such movies likely help spawn, Cale, a 16-year-old academic, athletic, and extracurricular standout at a suburban Seattle high school says, "Next Thursday I am headed to Mexico. While I can't wait for the trip, while I'm on it, I'll probably have some tough times related to drugs and alcohol." Cale says that the whole group, "is going to be perpetually drunk" while they're there.

Young people like Cale face such choices more often than we may think. For now, he's decided that he owes it to his teammates to abstain. But what about next time? And what about all those other kids he talks about? He and they are making decisions—at least in part—within a context that has been created for them through television, movies, and the Internet.

Eighteen-year-old Robert says he was determined to have sex before college because, as he puts it, "If you watch movies like *American Pie*, you just figure that's what you're supposed to do." Adds Phil, a 16-year-old 10th-grader from Missouri, "Any movie that speaks on sex and substance abuse and driving glorifies negligent habits."

While some of the *Cancun* cast publicly professed personal and parental pride at their participation, one can't help but wonder how they will feel in the cold, hard, sober light of maturity, knowing that their alcohol-influenced indiscretions have been digitally captured for all, including maybe someday their kids or potential employers, to see.

Also alarming are reports of "ratings creep," a push by filmmakers for PG-13 ratings, which are more commercially viable than R-ratings, and for R-ratings as opposed to NC-17-ratings for films with extreme content. Why the concern? A Federal Trade Commission report found that 80 percent of the R-rated films it studied were marketed to children under the age of 17. In addition, its test of theaters' enforcement of access to R-rated films found that unaccompanied children ages 13 to 16 were able to purchase tickets to R-rated films 46 percent of the time.

At summer camp, we restrict access to R-rated movies to campers under the age of 17. Yet, a surprising number of parents call, e-mail, or write me to convey their blanket permission for their underage children to watch whatever it is they wish to watch. Unfortunately, the messages these kids often receive from content meant for older people skip the part about the potential drawbacks and risks of certain behaviors.

As with television, when it comes to movies, we need to take care to sort through both the good and the bad, recognizing the valuable resource that movies represent in exposing children to the wider culture, to creativity, and to the power of storytelling.

Social Networking Sites

Television and movies (not to mention songs and video games) aren't the only problem in media promotion of unhealthy or risky behavior. The

Internet and, perhaps especially, the proliferation of social networking sites and streaming videos, have set off alarm bells for parents and educators about our kids' exposure to inappropriate content and the opportunity for misguided interaction with friends and strangers alike.

Parents everywhere no doubt cringed at the story about the 16-year-old Michigan girl who recently flew to the Middle East without her parents' knowledge or consent (she told them she was going to Canada with a friend) to see a 25-year-old man she met on the social-networking site MySpace.com. While made more salacious by time (she was gone five days) and distance (Jordan), the story mirrored many others of its kind, highlighting the dangers lurking in the shadows of the online world. She was detained by U.S. officials and sent back home, according to the Federal Bureau of Investigation (FBI). But not all teens escape harm.

Free to all comers, forums, such as MySpace, Facebook, Xanga, and Friendster, provide easy access to anyone searching for e-mail addresses, cell phone numbers, or details about body type, sexual preferences, and alcoholic beverages of choice. And the information flow doesn't stop there. A *Dateline NBC* investigation of teen pages found scenes of binge drinking, apparent drug use, and sex acts.

Law enforcement officials are so concerned about social-networking sites that at least two states, Connecticut and Massachusetts, have investigated the link between these sites and incidents of sexual assault. But they're not going it alone. By 2006, the FBI had opened dozens of cases nationwide regarding activity on the sites and had received more than 500 complaints:

- A 33-year-old Alabama man was alleged to have met a 14-year-old girl from New Jersey on one site and later abused her in Florida.
- A 13-year-old girl from Georgia whose online profile said she was 29, was allegedly abused by a 30-year-old South Carolina man.
- An 11-year-old girl was allegedly fondled in her Connecticut home—while her parents slept—by a man she'd met through an online network and let into her home.

In its recent report, the FTC, for the first time ever, tracked trends in marketing on social-networking sites and video-hosting sites such as YouTube, finding that few postings contain prominent ratings information, even though they reach a large audience under the age of 17, the result being that many children are being exposed to content on the Internet that would make most parents uneasy.

But, child predators and lax industry policing are just part of the Internet puzzle. Young people themselves often use the Internet to taunt, criticize, harass, intimidate, and gang up on each other. Like traditional bullying, cyber-bullying leaves many kids feeling unsafe, humiliated, angry . . . and perhaps looking for revenge.

Essex County, Massachusetts, District Attorney Jonathan W. Blodgett told the *Boston Globe*, "We've seen an increase in assault crimes involving young people as a result of the computer. They go on and 'instant-message,' threatening each other, and it becomes assault the next day."

Still other teens surf porn sites online. According to *Teens Today*, more than 1 in 4 middle and high school students (26 percent) say they have used the Internet to view sexually explicit content. Of those teens, 30 percent said doing so makes it more likely that they will engage in sexual behaviors. Randy, at 17, says he looks at porn sites every day.

What You Can Do

So, what can parents do to keep their child safe? Wiredsafety.org offers some tips:

- Convey to your child that personal information is personal, and shouldn't be shared on the Internet.
- Make sure your child doesn't spend all of his or her time on the computer.
- Keep the computer in a family room, kitchen or living room, not in your child's bedroom (knowing you are watching, kids are less

likely to put themselves in risky situations and you can oversee what's going on).

- Learn enough about computers so that you can enjoy them together with your kids; watch your children when they're online and see where they go.
- Communicate with your child about online risks so that they will feel comfortable coming to you with questions.
- Keep kids out of chat rooms unless they are monitored.
- Discuss these rules, get your children to agree to adhere to them, and post them near the computer as a reminder.
- Help them find a balance between computing and other activities.
- Remember to monitor their compliance with these rules, especially when it comes to the amount of time your children spend on the computer.
- Get to know their "online friends" just as you get to know all of their other friends; and warn them that people may not be what they seem to be (predators often pose as children to gain our children's trust).

There are also a number of parental controls on computers that can limit young people's exposure to mature content. But parents can't be the only ones on the lookout. Just as in real life, young people have a responsibility to protect themselves in the online world. i-SAFE America outlines for youth "The 4 Rs" of Internet safety that you can share with your teen:

1. Recognize techniques used by online predators to deceive.
2. Refuse requests for personal information.
3. Respond assertively if you are ever in an uncomfortable position online. Exit the program, turn off the computer, tell a trusted friend, or call the police.
4. Report any suspicious or dangerous contact that makes you feel uncomfortable.

i-SAFE also advises teens to take these precautions:

- Protect your identifying information (name, sex, age, address, school, teams)—it takes only a little information for a predator to identify you.
- Create a username and online profile that is generic and anonymous.
- Know how to exit an inappropriate Web site.
- Guard your pictures—you never know who may be looking at them.
- Keep in mind that chat room "friends" are not always who they say they are.

Certainly, the advent of the Internet—and more recently of social-networking sites—has brought with it new opportunities for the meaningful exchange of ideas and dialogue, better connecting young people to the wider world beyond their front door. In that way, the Internet offers young people far more freedom to explore their interests and share them with others than many of us had growing up. When done responsibly, surfing the Net can be profoundly educational. Yet, even for parents immersed in this relatively new technology, it can be difficult to fully appreciate the far corners to which their kids can travel with the click of a mouse. Some of those corners are potentially dangerous ones. Much as we would try to protect our children from crime on the streets in an unfamiliar city, so too must we seek to protect them from the fastest, most dangerous lanes on the information superhighway.

It's important to stress that the media can also play a role in discouraging inappropriate behavior by teens. For example, in 2002 and 2003, respectively, SADD presented Lifetime Achievement Awards to television producers Arnold Shapiro and Allison Grodner (*Teen Files, Flipped*) and Bill Cosby for their portrayals of the consequences of teen behavior. As with many things, too often we focus only on the problems, but will likely benefit also from highlighting the positive—in this case, hopefully encouraging other producers to follow suit and create programming that promotes healthy youth development and decision-making.

Seven

What They Learn from Us

In his book *Kick Me: Adventures in Adolescence*, author Paul Feig notes, "Childhood is built on bad decision-making. In fact, if it weren't for all the bad decisions we were constantly carrying out as kids, there's a good chance that none of us would have figured out all the things we weren't going to do when we became adults."

While there may be validity to Feig's appeal that experience is the best teacher, I suggest an antithetical idea: that children learn best from those who truly understand how they think, learn, and grow, and then use that knowledge to help them make good decisions that will fuel their individual development and ultimate success in adulthood. Parents and other significant adults in a young person's life are just the people to do so.

Now there are, of course, volumes of literature, including Judith Rich Harris' popular book *The Nurture Assumption*, highlighting the influential role of peers—as opposed to adults—in a teen's life. Indeed, in the normal course of development, teens become less reliant on, and influenced by, parents. But too often we mistakenly believe it's only the peer group that matters at this stage.

In fact, nothing could be further from the truth. Our role remains vitally important, if somewhat altered. As we have discussed, it is during our child's adolescence that each of us "renegotiates" our roles, learning new patterns of interaction. If we fail to adapt to the changes in our teen we risk becoming less relevant. But if we recognize change for what it is (healthy developmental progress as discussed in Chapter Four) and implement new strategies for communicating with and guiding our teen, we can continue to play a meaningful role in her growth and decision-making.

Not as I Do

Although frequent, open dialogue with our children is vitally important, much of what we communicate to them is done nonverbally. In other words, what we *do* is just as powerful as what we say. Parents constantly transmit unspoken messages about personal integrity and responsibility, and so we need to be certain that our messages—both what we put across and how we do it—resonate with respect for oneself, respect for the family, and respect for the rules.

> "Live so that when your children think of fairness and integrity, they think of you."
>
> —author H. Jackson Brown, Jr.

Unfortunately, much of what parents say (or don't say) on the topic of disturbing teen behaviors like drinking, drug use, and sex, mirrors the attitudes and actions of adult behavior our kids too frequently witness—such as adults getting drunk at sporting events, getting high at concerts, or just trying to "get" sex in the movies. In such a climate, there can be little regard for respect and responsibility.

On November 30, 2004, members of the Danvers High School (Massachusetts) cheerleading squad showed up for a playoff game against nearby Walpole High School drunk and allegedly unable to perform. When confronted by adults, the girls unleashed a barrage of obscenities. The co-captains, both 17-years-old, were arrested and charged with disorderly conduct. Such alcohol-imbued antics provide important insights not only into the world of too many of today's teens, but also the adults who influence them by modeling poor, inappropriate, and dangerous behavior at sporting events of their own.

Indeed, responsibility for underage drinking, to take just one issue, lies not just with teens, but also with the adults who guide them. Influential adults who exhibit inappropriate alcohol-related behavior set a compelling, and easily replicable, example for teens to follow. They also undermine important education, prevention, and enforcement efforts on the part of concerned parents, students, teachers, and police officers, and reinforce the message that they not only will tolerate underage drinking, but enable it, as well.

Also, a startling number of adults demonstrate disinterest in holding teens accountable for personal behavior, perhaps fearing they will have to contend with angry children or the lasting effects of a suspension, expulsion, or arrest. Others figure drinking is just part of growing up—the Myth of Inevitability that we talked about earlier. Not making teens responsible for violating rules perpetuates the perception that adult America is not really all that serious about curtailing underage drinking, say, and does little to prepare teens for the far less forgiving world that lies ahead when they are adults. By letting teens off the hook with few, if any, consequences for underage drinking, we teach them that "it's really not that big of a deal."

I was addressing this very issue to parents and students in Washington state. The gymnasium was hot and everyone had been sitting a long time. But their interest hadn't waned. Having answered a succession of questions about teens and alcohol, I was inspired to climb up on my proverbial soapbox and challenge our more traditional approaches to reprimanding kids for underage drinking.

"If we are serious about tackling this problem," I said, "we've all got to be on the same page. It's not just about the kids. It's not just about the parents. It's not just about the cops. It's not just about the teachers or the media or the alcoholic beverages industry. It is about all of us!"

Part of being on the same page means holding teens responsible for breaking the law. When we let them go with a "slap on the wrist," such as a phone call and a ride home, or a $25 ticket, we are doing precisely the wrong thing.

"I was thinking on the plane ride here," I continued, certain I was about to spark controversy, "suppose we automatically revoked drivers licenses?" The adults were nodding approval and, surprisingly, the kids were, too!

One blurts out, "That's what should happen!"

Wow. Not a stir of controversy to be found.

High-profile incidents of alcohol-fueled behavior detail a clear, and disturbing, precedent for young people to follow. Television viewers, for example, watched the long-awaited championship celebration of the Boston Red Sox, complete with the chugging, crumpling, and throwing of beer cans . . . then recoiled in horror at similar behavior taking place by teens just on the other side of (or, in some cases, on top of) Fenway Park's fabled "Green Monster." The subsequent assertion by the Red Sox's first baseman that the champs had downed shots of Jack Daniel's just prior to the start of the historic games was a further destructive revelation for young people already confronting difficult decisions about personal responsibility—making behaviors like dangerously climbing on top of the wall seem just fine.

Destructive messages come from other places, as well. From professional sports, to Hollywood, to politics, the last decade has ushered in a new wave of poor precedents on which young people too often base their own decision-making. It seems obvious that this exposure, combined with conflicting—and sometimes shifting—messages from adults and schools about values and personal responsibility often leaves kids confused as to what exactly they are supposed to do and who exactly they are supposed to be. And this occurs just as their struggle for identity becomes of paramount importance.

What is the message when popular rappers preach hate and intolerance, or gun each other down on the streets of our cities? What is the message when sports and television stars check in and out of rehab like shoppers spinning through the revolving door at Macy's? What is the message when on the national Take Your Daughters to Work Day, a Wisconsin mother (and lawyer) advised a class of 7th-grade girls to, "Sleep around all you want . . . just don't get married."? And what is the message when speakers at a Colorado high school encourage students to enjoy themselves as they experimented with sex and drugs?

In the face of such examples of adult behavior, responsible parents and other caring adults need to be the ones who help young people make sense of the gap between what they see and hear in their real world and the values that are taught and modeled at home. Adults are invested with tremendous power to influence children. It's important not to squander those opportunities amidst a causal and careless approach to role modeling or communicating.

When influential adults drink to excess in front of teens, make light of casual drug use, or refer to sexual behavior in ways that make it sound unimportant or inconsequential, they send a resounding message that will linger long after it's been delivered.

Most of us seek to use our influence in positive, productive ways. But there are some strongly negative means by which adults actually push teens toward drinking, drug use, impaired driving, early sexual behavior, and violence by unwittingly sending the wrong messages to young people.

"Have you been sneaking into the woods to drink beer?" asked the adult relative of one of my teen campers with a knowing look, a wink, and a smile. I cringed. The answer is no, fortunately. But a message has been sent by the way the question was posed: "It's OK if you do." Even expected. Consider, too, the message of a high school lacrosse coach to his players in the wake of allegations of rape leveled at a handful of Duke University lacrosse players. It was relayed to me by a 15-year-old team member: "You're lacrosse players, so I know you're going to party. Just don't do anything stupid." A better message would have been one that pointed out risks associated with alcohol and communicated the expectation that underage drinking by members of this lacrosse team would not be tolerated.

In another example of adults sending kids the wrong message, 16-year-old Billy tells me, "Up to about three weeks ago, I would say I considered myself to be a pothead. I started smoking weed when I was 13. My parents were aware and were complete hypocrites because of their own actions, back then and even now." Apparently, Billy's parents were upset by his drug use, despite his implication that they were marijuana users themselves.

Understandably, young people are particularly sensitive to double standards—parents' saying one thing and then doing another—and frequently complain about hypocritical behavior on the part of the adults in their lives.

"If they can do it, why can't we?" is a common refrain from teens who view inconsistencies as opportunities to justify their own behavior. Even some defensible demarcations between adult and teen behavior (alcohol consumption, for example) can be suspect in the eyes of an adolescent wrestling to set internal standards for appropriate and inappropriate behavior. Remember what 17-year-old Jack said: "Parents need to look at themselves and see what kind of example they are setting." A Massachusetts teen says parents should think about their own drinking behaviors, adding, "Some will say, 'Don't drink,' but then you'll see them drinking. Or they'll say, 'Don't drink and drive,' but then they're going to the bar and drinking with their buddies. My dad has a beer once a year. He says, 'Don't drink,' and I don't feel the need to."

Another teen adds, "I've watched grown-ups at parties get so drunk that it's embarrassing. I look at them and say, 'Oh my God, I never want to do that in my whole life.' But I'm not sure if I influence myself or I get influenced by looking at other people being drunk."

As adults, we need to be sure that the messages we are sending about alcohol and drug use, driving, sexual behavior, and violence are consistent and clear, not diverse and filled with nuances. If we don't want our teen drinking, we need to say, "I do not want you using alcohol under any scenario, in any situation." Clear. Unambiguous. Any confusion may be mistaken for, or at least taken as, consent by teens looking for excuses to break the rules. Remember that the research shows that teens who are allowed to drink at home, even just on special occasions like a birthday or New Year's Eve, are more likely to be drinking at other times as well.

Mentoring

As the parent-child relationship is transformed during adolescence, it is more important than ever that we model appropriate decision-making by our own actions. When we use our seat belts, enjoy ourselves at a party or sporting event without using alcohol, avoid using illegal drugs, talk about sexual behavior as something positive in the context of mature, committed relationships, point out that violence is an unacceptable way to solve problems or resolve conflict, and speak regularly about our feelings (such as joy, sadness, excitement, and depression), we send powerful messages about what we think is right for our teen. In this way, we can begin to shift the paradigm from "manager" to "mentor." This offers us a new dynamic with which to shape our interactions with our teens, and the outcomes they affect.

Studies of formalized mentoring—such as the kind found in "Big Brothers Big Sisters" programs—show that there is significant value in such relationships, and universally point to the positive outcomes they engender. According to "Mentoring Programs and Youth Development: A Synthesis," a report of the Edna McConnell Clark Foundation, an organization committed to improving the lives of people from low-income communities, "Warm and close relationships with caring adults, supervision, and positive role models are the common resources and investments—or 'inputs'—that mentoring interventions contribute to youth development."

And a study by Child Trends, a nonprofit, nonpartisan research organization providing social-science research to those who serve children and youth, "Mentoring: A Promising Strategy for Youth Development," assesses the effects of mentoring in three areas: educational achievement, health and safety, and social/emotional development. It finds that adults can have a profound influence on youth safety and development across a broad cross-section of outcomes. For example, youth participating in mentoring relationships experience positive academic returns. These include better attendance, a better chance of going on to higher education, and better attitudes toward school.

Commenting on the study, Child Trends president and co-author of the brief, Kristin A. Moore, Ph.D., said, "Our review highlights the positive effect that caring adults can have in a young person's life. It's important to note, however, that these mentor/mentored relationships need to be consistent and committed. Mentoring relationships can actually do more harm than good if they are short-lived or sporadic." Among the findings:

- Youth participating in mentoring programs had fewer unexcused absences from school than did similar youth not participating in these programs.
- Youth in mentoring programs were less likely to initiate drug use.
- Youth who were mentored had significantly more positive attitudes toward school and the future.

There's other great news in findings that informal or "natural" mentoring is just as important as formalized mentoring—because our time with our children and teens offers ample opportunities to teach and model good decision-making and resistance skills. Daily life provides a plethora of "teachable" moments during which we can impart our values and expectations and talk to our kids about choices and consequences. What we say when a car passes us on a narrow roadway traveling well above the speed limit; how we explain a story on the news about the arrest of a parent for providing alcohol to children; or how we react to our teen's assertion that two kids in her 7th-grade class are "hooking-up" after school, reveals a lot about what we think and what expectations we hold for our child.

Parents have two unique roles to play when it comes to the mentoring of their children. The first may be the more obvious: Make good choices yourself! Parents rate number one among adults who teens consider influential role models. This may come as a surprise to many parents who feel marginalized in their efforts to stay involved in the lives of their growing children. Nevertheless, the data makes clear that parents hold the principal place of power when it comes to influencing the choices their children make.

The second important role that parents play is providing opportunities for their children to be mentored by *other adults* who can contribute positively to their personal development. This doesn't mean *in place* of parents, but rather in addition to them! Relatives, neighbors, teachers, coaches, and counselors are all people that teens identify as mentors or role models in their lives. And each has the potential to positively shape our teen's perceptions and behavior. The America's Promise Alliance, a multi-sector collaborative interested in promoting the well-being of children and youth, speaks about the importance of support and guidance from caring adults in both formal and informal relationships. They call such adults the "cornerstone" of development and say, "Parents come first. But children also need to experience the support from caring adults in all areas of their lives." Sadly, they report that one-third of teens and 20 percent of younger children lack quality relationships with their parents and that more than 40 percent of young people ages 8 to 21 say they want more adults in their lives to whom they can turn for help.

While promoting positive relationships with other adults in their families, communities, and schools may seem an obvious path, parents are becoming more and more reluctant to share their children with the broader adult world, perhaps out of fear for their well-being. While this fear may be grounded in a reality—there are myriad recent examples of young people harmed by adults, such as teachers, coaches, members of the clergy, aunts, uncles, and next-door neighbors—this concern should not prevent parents from seeking out mentors for their children who may become important adults in their lives.

Adolescents need, and very much want, consistent exposure to caring, supportive adults. And with good reason. The "Child Trends" report I talked about earlier in this chapter concludes that adults other than parents provide important emotional support, advice, and guidance, while also helping to build self-esteem and self-control.

While parents are wise to be careful, there are some simple steps they can take to be sure their children remain safe, and they are very similar to the guidelines for keeping teens away from drugs and alcohol: stay involved;

Reality Gap

Would Not Having a Mentor Negatively Affect You?

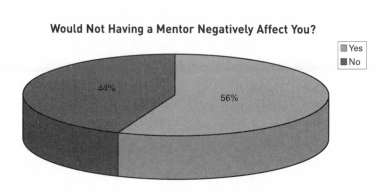

Legend: Yes, No

44%   56%

Do Your Parents Discourage You from Mentoring Activities?

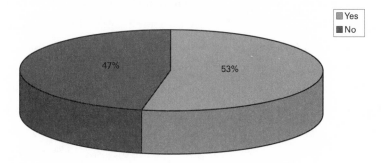

Legend: Yes, No

47%   53%

Chief Reason Your Parents Discourage You from Mentoring Activities

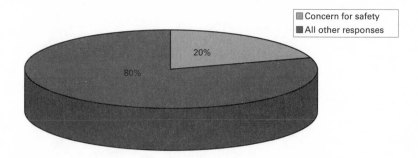

Legend: Concern for safety, All other responses

20%   80%

know who your teen is spending time with, where she is going, and what she is doing; get to know your teen's mentors—working together will benefit your teen and give you a better sense of his safety; and encourage your teen's involvement in organizations that conduct employee or volunteer screenings and/or criminal- and sexual-offender background checks.

The research tells us that teens who identify at least one influential, "natural" mentor in their lives—a person like a teacher or a coach, who is not assigned by a formal mentoring program—report that they have a higher Sense of Self and are more likely to take risks that affect their lives positively. For example, 46 percent of teens with a mentor report a high Sense of Self versus only 25 percent of teens without one. According to the study, 35 percent of teens with no mentor have a low Sense of Self (versus 12 percent of mentored teens).

You'll recall from Chapter Four that *Teens Today* identifies Sense of Self as teens' self-evaluation on their progress in three key developmental areas: identity formation, independence, and peer relationships. High Sense of Self teens feel more positive about their own identity, growing independence, and relationships with peers than do teens with a low Sense of Self. Again, they are also more likely to avoid alcohol and drug use. Teens struggling with those developmental areas, on the other hand,

Mentors and Sense of Self

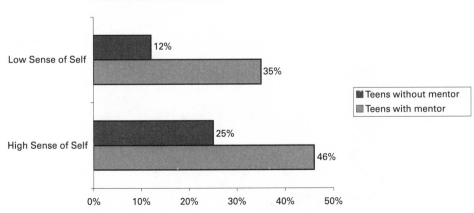

are more likely to drink, to use drugs such as Ecstasy and cocaine, and to cite boredom and depression as reasons to have sex. They also note a greater susceptibility to peer pressure when making choices.

Teens with mentors are significantly more likely than those without mentors to also report frequently feeling happy (94 percent versus 86 percent) and less likely to report regularly feeling depressed (24 percent versus 31 percent) or bored (66 percent versus 75 percent). They are significantly more likely than teens without mentors to challenge themselves by taking positive risks (38 percent versus 28 percent), such as joining an athletic team or volunteering to perform community service. Conversely, teens with no mentors are significantly more likely to shy away from positive risk-taking than are their mentored peers (51 percent versus 31 percent). And, as we have seen, young people who take positive risks are 20 percent more likely than teens who do not to avoid alcohol and other drugs, and 42 percent more likely to avoid drinking because of their concerns about academic performance. Many of these teens are also more inclined to delay intimate sexual behavior.

The data also reveal that the breadth and depth of mentoring—the number of mentors teens have or the range of topics teens can discuss with a mentor—significantly influences decisions teens make around

Mentors and How Teens Feel About Themselves

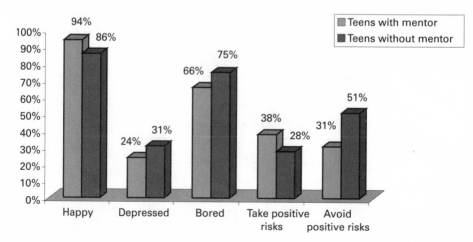

drinking, drug use, and sex. Teens who report high levels of mentoring—those who can talk with a variety of people about a wide range of topics—are more likely than those who report low levels of mentoring to be Avoiders of alcohol, other drugs, and early sexual behavior (69 percent versus 64 percent). And, among those teens who have reported using alcohol or marijuana, those with high levels of mentoring said initiation of such behavior was significantly later than teens with no or low levels of mentoring. They are also less likely than "low-mentored" teens to have driven a car under the influence of alcohol (13 percent versus 26 percent).

This new research demonstrates that adults who make an extra effort to connect with teenagers can have a profound impact in guiding them. So, we owe it to our kids to help them find the organizations or activities through which they may gain exposure to such positive role models and influencers. Young people describe the important mentors in their lives as trustworthy, caring, understanding, respectful, helpful, dependable, fun, compassionate, and responsible. They also cite being a good listener and offering good advice as important characteristics of mentors.

These good people help teens build new areas of competence and feelings of self-worth by offering validation from an "outside" source that he is capable and loveable. Young people likely already know how their parents feel about them, and many believe their parents "have to" love them, or to at least say that they do. On the other hand, when it comes to another adult mentor, there are no guarantees of acceptance, interest, or warmth. When those are forthcoming, a teen sees himself through another set of eyes, which offer a positive perspective that is similar to the one held by his parents.

Rites of Passage

Another valuable gift parents and mentors can bestow is the recognition and celebration of important transitions, or rites of passage. We remember to celebrate even small milestones with very little children, but inexplicably fail to do so for some of our teens.

Indeed, for years, sociologists, anthropologists, and psychologists have mourned the loss of traditions marking important adolescent rites of passage. In earlier American culture, movement toward adulthood was accompanied by more ritualistic, meaningful celebrations of transition to independence and responsibility to the family and community. These often included joining Dad in work (farming, for example, or the family store) for boys, and learning homemaking (such as cooking and sewing) for girls.

Without a reasonable recognition of milestones—puberty, school change, birthdays, receiving a driver's license, purchasing that first car, graduating from high school, and dating a first boyfriend or girlfriend—many young people seek alternative routes to "maturity," including all the negative behaviors we've been discussing in this book.

Teens Today reveals that high school students whose parents pay the least attention to significant transition periods are more likely than teens whose parents pay the most attention to engage in high-risk behaviors. Teen drivers who report high levels of parental attention, for example, are significantly more likely than those who report low levels of parental attention to say they never speed (45 percent to 14 percent). Additionally, the data suggests that these teens are more likely to wear seat belts while driving and are less likely to drive while impaired or to ride in a car with an impaired driver.

Teens who receive the least attention also seem more prone to depression and are more than twice as likely to report daily stress. So anxious are teens to say, "Hey, look at me! I'm growing up, I'm more responsible, I'm pretty much an adult now," that if we don't hear them, they are likely to try to get our attention in other ways. Even if it is negative attention that results.

Kids today often experience a shorter childhood—ushered out by a typically younger onset of puberty—and an extended adolescence, ushered in by an increasingly protective culture and elongated academic preparation. Many struggle through this vast, vague period of human development, and it is during this time, more than ever before, that young people seek initiations that demonstrate their movement toward adulthood. Yet, sadly, half of high school teens say that their mom and dad miss the boat when it comes to recognizing or celebrating what they consider to be meaningful life events during their adolescence. When we forget to note that moving from middle school to high school is a big deal for Kathy or that making the JV football team is a milestone for James, we let them down, appearing uninterested, or at least uninvolved, in what are important steps toward maturity.

By recognizing key adolescent transitions, we can aid teens in building bridges between who they were, who they are, and who they are becoming. In turn, those connections help teens with their search for identity, meaning, and purpose, all the while preparing them to be productive, giving members of their families, schools, communities, and society. Just as important, rites of passage can link generations through tangible representations of physical, and sometimes subtle, social and emotional change. Passing down family traditions related to change and advancement emphasizes commonalities with our children, and thus fosters intimacy. Sometimes a simple gesture, like the handing down of a silver pocket watch that started with great-grandfather to grandfather, and continued from grandfather to father, and now extends from father to son, can be enormously effective in signaling recognition of growth and maturity. Many girls find that recognition in a mother's acknowledgment of her physical changes, such as breast development and her first period.

Interestingly, middle school students report significantly higher levels of parental attention to what they consider to be important passages than do high school students. This trend signifies that we often assume young people are more mature and more independent than they really are or are ready to be. This imposes a pseudo-maturity on young people that manifests itself in an ever-pervasive pressure to act like grownups and leads even the most caring of adults to doubt the necessity of giving their full attention to growing teens.

So it's not surprising that middle school teens whose parents communicate about and recognize or celebrate important transitions benefit greatly as well. For example, they are significantly more likely than other teens to report they have an extremely close relationship with their parents (69 percent vs. 22 percent); say they have excellent communication with their parents (55 percent vs. 12 percent); say their parents talk to them about their concerns associated with drinking (95 percent vs. 80 percent), drinking and driving (89 percent vs. 66 percent), using marijuana and driving (79 percent vs. 46 percent), illegally using prescription drugs (83 percent vs. 51 percent), and using other drugs (92 percent vs. 72 percent); to indicate they are influenced by parents not to drink (96 percent vs. 73 percent) or use drugs (98 percent vs. 74 percent); to report being honest with their parents about what they are doing and with whom they are spending time (96 percent vs. 84 percent); and to feel happy every day or almost every day (83 percent vs. 55 percent).

In order to begin incorporating rites of passage into the structure of the family, we need to be sensitive to the possibilities. Important transitions in adolescence can be a one-time thing, such as some of those previously mentioned—a first date, first job, or first driver's license—or the gradual progression toward maturity, including physical, social, and emotional change (puberty, expanding one's group of friends, becoming more open and affectionate with siblings or parents). Figuring out which transitions

Highly Nurtured Middle-School Teens and Parents

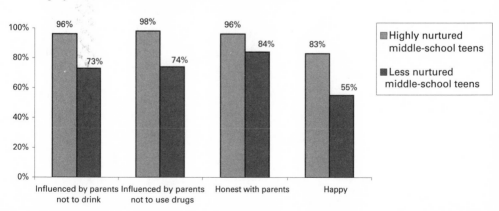

216

are most important to your teen is a critical first step in helping him or her move to adulthood. Much like the positive risk-taking discussed earlier, what "counts" for one teen may not matter much to another teen. For example, some teens tell me that graduating from middle school was no big deal, while others see it as an important step in growing up.

I remember the story of a friend who described her disappointment in her parents' reaction to the first paycheck she brought home.

"I was so proud to show it to them," she said. "They just grabbed it and said, 'That's going into your college fund.'" She saw that check as a metaphor—tangible evidence of maturity, and a big leap toward adulthood. Her parents viewed it as a practical means to help fund her college education.

Fifteen-year-old Kevin describes his important milestones as "getting a defined vision of who I am, having my first real girlfriend, being exposed to drinking, and making my own decisions."

Here are some things for parents and mentors to keep in mind:

- Tune in to the things that seem important in his daily life, such as friends, sports, and grades.
- Notice how she spends her days so that you can flag changes.
- Ask how he feels about different transitions.
- Note how she talks about transitions with friends.
- Talk about important transitions in your own adolescence.
- Watch for signs of happiness, joy, stress, anxiety, or depression surrounding change. This way, you can be sure to celebrate those events your teen feels good about, rather than transitions that make her feel awkward.

Once we know how Bobby or Jill feels about impending change, we can discuss how we might celebrate this important life event. It could be a party, it could be a dinner out, it could just be a special trip to a ball game with Dad or to the mall with Mom. Sending the message that you are dialed in to your teen as he takes significant steps along the path to adulthood is an important way to say, "I love you, I care about you, and I hear you!" Teens look for signals that they are making real progress toward becoming adults and care very much what you think about them, even if they don't always show it. Here is what you can do: Talk regularly—and casually (teens hate "the big talk")—about the transitions you see her tackling (e.g., taking responsibility for making dinner or helping her younger brother with his homework) and recognize these transitions through small gifts, privileges, words, or deeds. It's not so much what you do, but rather that you do it in the first place!

Again, teens want to know that we know—that we've noticed what to them is a big step or an important change. Extending his curfew because he built that dollhouse for his little sister, or granting her use of the car on weekends to get to her job instead of insisting that she always walk or ask for a ride from us can be simple but meaningful gestures. Kevin's parents prepared him for transition to high school by "talking about how it would be different, and how to deal with it." And they celebrated with what he called a "big dinner."

"I felt good about that," Kevin says.

Other mentors can play a similarly influential role in promoting and recognizing advancement toward maturity. But, as we discussed earlier, parents need to be open to allowing or arranging for those relationships to develop. We can also help by pointing him toward structured, goal-oriented activities that have recognition and appreciation built into them, and by identifying extracurricular opportunities that will promote her development through the progression of skills or contributions. Some organizations, such as service-learning clubs, summer camps, and Boy Scouts and Girl Scouts, have embedded rites of passage that will encourage her to invest time and effort toward advancement.

When training summer camp counselors and future child-care workers, I often say that while we will all make mistakes when working with kids, the single biggest mistake we can make is to underestimate how important we are to them and the degree to which our words and actions can have lasting, and profound, consequences. The same holds true for Mom and Dad.

Eight

Breaking Down Barriers

At 16, Billy, the depressed musician I had met in Denver a year and a half earlier, was looking just as disheveled as the last time we spoke. He was wearing more jewelry than before, but seemed less edgy, easily flopping down in the swivel chair to the right of my desk at the research facility. He seemed more at ease, less jumpy, more optimistic. He's a whole different kid from the suicidal boy I met over a year ago.

"I'm confident," he says, "happy and secure with who I am." Looking back on his depression, he offers, "I think it was all about my mom, you know, how to cope with her not letting me grow up." He goes on to describe his mother's hovering and smothering, what he perceived as over-involvement in his life, making the already difficult task of separation all the more daunting.

Billy's descriptions of his mother's vigilance are in synch with what many kids today call "helicopter parents," a new breed of caregivers who hover over their adolescent children, hyper-involving themselves in the lives of young people who are more in need of independence than nurturing. Remember, the teenage years are a time for letting go, for both teens and parents, to the extent that is reasonable and age-appropriate. As we have seen, letting go is different from giving up. It is a slow, steady progression of withdrawing not love, affection, attention, or expectations, but rather a continued shift of responsibility in decision-making from "ours" to "theirs."

Giving teens practice with decision-making about non-life-threatening issues is a worthwhile strategy to pursue in preparing them to make choices that have greater consequence later. Typically, we allow more independence in decision-making as children grow older. This seems to be the case particularly when the demands of their transition to adolescence and desire for autonomy and independence begin to prevail, testing our previously established patterns of interaction and rule-setting.

During adolescence, decision-making can be divided in three ways: decisions that teens make for themselves, decisions teens and parents make together, and decisions parents make for their teens. Creating a chart that can be regularly updated as teens mature gives both parent and child a starting point for critical conversations about expectations, behavior, responsibility, and accountability. It also recognizes a teen's growing independence and his role as a partner in, not a bystander to, the decision-making that affects him.

Such a chart might look like this:

Decisions	Yours (Teen)	Ours (Parents and Teens)	Mine (Parent)
Hairstyle	X		
Dress	X		
Curfew		X	
Homework		X	
Peer Group		X	
Car privileges		X	
Drinking			X
Drug use			X
Sexual behavior		X	

Over time, families should see a migration of decisions from "mine" (Parent) to "ours" (Parent and Teen) to "theirs" (Teen), reflecting a young person's healthy, incremental movement toward independence and a parent's healthy progress toward letting go. Seventeen-year-old Felicia says, "My parents set restrictions and guidelines for me, but as long as I am not doing something that is harmful, they pretty much let me do whatever I want. I think parents should let their kids have enough freedom to discover things for themselves."

When we fail to adapt to our child's growing need for independence by insisting on "control," we deprive them of much-needed opportunities to try out their decision-making capabilities and ease into young adulthood. This approach will negatively affect them now (these kids may appear nervous or stressed, depressed, or may have difficulty making meaningful connections with peers), and later on (they may have difficulty making reasonable decisions because the decisions have always been made for them).

While it's difficult to measure how many parents might be considered helicopter parents, some recent surveys of college administrators, students, and their parents offer some interesting information. For example, based on her analysis of a series of interviews she conducted with college officials, Patricia Somers, an associate professor of education at the University of Texas–Austin, estimates that the majority of parents of college students—some 60 to 70 percent—are involved in helicoptering behavior. And the newest edition of *Millennials Go to College*, by authors Neil Howe and William Strauss, reveals that "Gen X parents" tend to be more protective and involved with their kids than boomers, with significantly more than half (63 percent) saying they began planning for their kids' college education in elementary school or earlier. The book includes new data from surveys of 1,000 college parents and 500 college students conducted in the fall of 2006.

Fearing for their children's safety in a post-9/11 world and, facilitated by technology, an increasing number of parents are keeping their kids on a tight electronic leash. This has led many educators to question how many opportunities contemporary teens are being given to differentiate themselves from Mom and Dad and succeed in establishing a healthy, stable identity of their own. Some institutions, such as schools and summer camps, are even helping the helicoptering along, posting daily pictures and live video feeds online so that parents can see first-hand what their children are doing.

Talk with most any camp director about this practice, and you'll find the results have been a mixed bag. Parents are happier because they feel they have a closer connection to their child's life at camp, but administrators may find they're spending more time responding to unfounded parental concerns and demands: "My son seems to be walking a half-step behind the other boys in the picture; is he being ostracized?" or "She looks a little thin. I want you to make sure she is eating OK."

The media has recently highlighted the recriminations coming from frustrated school administrators and directed at parents who insist on jumping in to try to solve their children's problems, rather than giving them the time and space to learn how to solve them for themselves.

Some colleges now conduct parent—as well as student—orientations to explain where the boundaries are. "Don't call us, we'll call you," is often the message to parents from exasperated deans who may be asked to intercede in a roommate conflict or to speak with a professor about a grade (I have experienced this myself at the college where I teach). In such situations, parents are "fixing" things, rather than giving their children the opportunity, and the incentive, to figure out how to do it on their own, or at least to seek out help from others in their current environment when they need it.

With this dilemma in mind—and recognizing the anxiety that many parents feel when their child heads away from home—I worked with my colleagues at camp to develop some barometers for determining whether a child had had a successful summer experience. While these pertain specifically to children at camp, similar gauges might be used by parents to tell how their kids are doing at home . . . and whether they, as parents, are appropriately loosening the reins on rules, decision-making, and the resolution of problems or conflicts.

- **Independence**—A child uses the many community resources available to ask for help and support when experiencing difficulties.
- **Self-Reliance**—A child makes positive choices and accepts responsibility for personal behavior.
- **Self-confidence**—A child expresses confidence in his/her ability to succeed educationally and socially.
- **Exploration**—A child embraces opportunities to try new things, make new friends, and contribute positively to the community as a whole.
- **Respect**—A child contributes positively to the community as a whole, demonstrating respect for oneself, others, and the institution.

Looking for ways to regularly determine whether we are finding balance in our approach to parenting helps us to calibrate the level of nurturing and independence we are giving to our children at any given point in time.

Paradoxically, criticism of parents for helicoptering comes on the heels of studies that suggest parents are not paying enough attention to their teens, thus spawning an epidemic of destructive behavior. What's a confused parent to believe?

There is no question that as young people turn the corner from childhood to adolescence, they have innate needs for independence. It fuels an important developmental quest for personal identity, and a peer group with which to assimilate. But it does not require an emotional abandonment by parents—the polar opposite of helicoptering—that can accompany the teenage years. So, for parents, it's once again all about finding and maintaining the balance between holding on and letting go. It can be hard to know where the right line is, but surely any issues involving physical and psychological health require our involvement.

Holding on, letting go—letting go, holding on. It's a tough choice and one that's hard to make, not only because of the conflicting messages we get from experts and the media (and, as we'll see in a moment, even from teens themselves), but because there are few absolutes. The boundaries of parenting are often unclear and the lines between helpful and not-so-helpful approaches are fuzzy. One approach parents can take is to go back to the chart we looked at earlier and ask themselves: *Are things moving in the right direction (e.g., toward independence), moving in the wrong direction (e.g., away from independence), or staying the same?*

Another way to think about this concept is to apply the healthy movement toward independence and adulthood to a continuum of control and freedom. As our children grow and move through their adolescence, we should be preparing them for freedom but also to be ever-mindful of the responsibilities that freedom brings, such as making reasonable, safe, and legal choices. Below we can see what that continuum looks like, as we give up control and teens move toward freedom.

Control —————————————————————————— **Freedom**

Finally, refer to our guideposts from camp. Is your teen becoming more
- independent?
- self-reliant?
- self-confident?
- exploratory?
- respectful?

The age-old standard of giving kids roots to ground them and wings to fly applies today more than ever! We need to be judicious about the degree to which we micromanage our growing teens' lives—despite the temptations offered by technology that make over-involvement so much easier. As the English poet Henry Blake said, "He who binds to himself a joy does the winged life destroy; but he who kisses the joy as it flies lives in eternity's sun rise."

While we don't want to "bind" our teen to us throughout his adolescence, we need to remain alert to the fact that teens still require significant time and attention from their parents. Unfortunately, adolescence is exactly the time when Mom and Dad are most likely to leave their teen on his own to make decisions about things like drinking, drugs, and sex.

> Almost one-quarter (22 percent) of parents leave it up to their children to decide whether to drink or not.

As they progress through their teenage years, young people benefit from our continued input when faced with choices about destructive or potentially destructive behaviors. But, absent the type of daily interaction, communication, and monitoring they used to take for granted, teens often feel cast aside. Their independence now becomes a struggle.

As much as adults send mixed messages to teens about behaviors such as underage drinking and sex, teens return the favor—sending confusing signals of their own as to whether or not they want, and value, parental involvement in their life. There are sophisticated social and societal mores that lead teens to at least attempt a cursory rejection of parental support. This happens because young people often equate becoming independent with becoming separate—not yet grasping the nuances of relationships that are at once close and independent. But when kids push away, caring parents need to push back, lest they be pushed out. That would mean that both sides lose out on maintaining a meaningful connection.

"I don't want you involved in my life" is the message many teens intentionally, or inadvertently, send. But odd as it may seem, that's not necessarily what they want. What they want is support, affirmation, and guidance. Teens know better than most adults the slippery slope they must traverse to get where they want to go. And, like it or not, they know they need help to keep from falling.

Surprising? Not really. In my teen discussion groups, young people often say, "Parents should talk to us more." Even if they don't always act like it, rolling their eyes in disgust, or responding to a conversation opener with an "Oh, Mom!" we shouldn't be deterred. Sixteen-year-old Paul responds to his mother's innocuous inquiries about his friends with a look of frustration that she's even attempting to talk to him, answering with an overly affirmative, "Mom! I *don't* know!"

Often, parents feel pushed aside in favor of a newly minted peer group. Almost overnight it seems that our teens no longer want to spend time with us, preferring the company of friends to the company of Mom or Dad. Those family dinners and vacations become harder to plan—and if they do take place, they often include one or more friends so that "I have someone to talk to and hang out with." Like they can't talk to or hang out with us!

Over time, we come to believe our influence has waned and that our opinions and counsel don't hold a candle to those of our child's friends. It is true that the peer group plays an increasingly important role in our child's life as he nears and enters adolescence. But in failing to fully appreciate the many ways in which they can continue to connect with their child, parents abandon their authority and thus their ability to help their teen stay away from trouble.

In reality, parents continue to be a vital part of a teen's everyday existence, even if at times he may act otherwise. Not hovering, or helicoptering, but involved. Not investigating, but gently guiding dialogue that offers up the possibility of shaping perceptions, conveying expectations, and influencing behavior.

All of my years of research point to one solid, unavoidable conclusion: Communication makes a difference. When tackled in the right way, at the right time, and with the right follow-through, it is an incredibly effective weapon against poor decision-making by our children. We just need to find the right tools to help us establish and maintain good rapport with our young people.

Family Communication Tips

So, how can family members assure good communication? Through genuine respect for each other's positions and by making a concerted effort to develop conversational skills.

SADD and its research partner Liberty Mutual offer some suggestions on how to start, even before there are any "issues" to discuss.

- **Praise your kids for doing the little things that can so easily be taken for granted.** Be positive and build a strong foundation with your children by regularly acknowledging and praising them for their accomplishments. Let your kids know that you love them unconditionally so that they will be less likely to hide things from you. Let them know that you may get angry at certain behaviors, but you will always love them, no matter what they do. And when your child does tell you something unpleasant, try not to overreact.

- **Make an extra effort to understand your teens' world.** Give your teens your undivided attention when they want to talk to you. They need to know that you're there for them 100 percent. Meet their friends and include them in family or household activities whenever possible. Sit and listen to one of your child's favorite pieces of music with him, and ask what he likes about it. Tell your child about a particular piece of music from your teen years that had strong significance for you.

- **Always remember the importance of reasoning.** Show your teens that you respect and trust them. Ask for her opinion on important matters from time to time. By showing your teens your trust, you are creating a mutually respectful relationship. Don't just say "no" or disagree with your teens without thinking about the message you're sending them. Try to teach your teens to meet you halfway. And always be prepared to give a valid reason for your answer to show your teens that you may disapprove or disagree out of concern for them.

- **Remind your children that you love them and care about their safety.** Find ways to reassure your teens that you have their best interests at heart, even when you're not around. Think of new ways of communicating with them. Give them something of yours to hold on to when you are away, or write them a cheerful, non-helicoptering e-mail from work every day, talking about what you're doing or maybe what you plan to do when you get home. Don't discredit your teens' need for you, despite what their actions may indicate. Reinforce your commitment by proving to them that you will always be there for them—through good and bad times. And don't ever give up.

- **Set a good example—your kids will do as you do.** If you expect your teen to always wear a seat belt, you should be vigilant about buckling up. Don't drive home from a party after you've been drinking. Don't speed or disobey traffic rules and then expect your teen to be more law-abiding than you. You can't enforce the rules unless you follow them yourself. Kids are sensitive to double standards. Make yourself a role model that your kids can look up to, learn from, and respect.

By following these guidelines, you will have laid the groundwork for thoughtful, productive conversations when it comes time to actually talk about serious issues like underage drinking, violence, or sex.

Here are some more tips from SADD:

- **Talk with your kids early and often about tough topics.** Make sure your kids know where you stand on important issues from their earliest days. Elementary school is not too early to start emphasizing traffic safety, the dangers of alcohol and drugs, and the importance of standing up for what you think is right. Keep discussion of difficult issues in your regular conversation with your kids. Don't wait for a crisis to talk about issues such as drinking, drug use, peer pressure, and other risky situations that kids face every day. And remember that it is never too late to start talking! Use discussion of an event at school or in the newspaper to open a dialogue about the topic, and listen to your child's thoughts and feelings.

- **Teach your kids to listen by listening to what they have to say.** Good communication is not about "winning" the argument. Good communication is about listening to the other person, understanding his or her point of view, and trying to reach a solution acceptable to both parties. By listening to your kids, you are setting the right example that will teach them to listen, too.

- **Read between the lines.** Your children may find it hard at times to say what's on their mind. Keep an eye out for nonverbal communication. People often express their views without ever speaking a word. Perhaps your child might surprise you by doing a nice favor without being asked after an argument or misunderstanding. These unspoken gestures can be a means to reach out to you or acknowledge your point of view.

- **Lighten up—take time out if you need to.** Unkind words can be so hurtful, even if you don't mean for them to come across that way. Bring humor to the discussion whenever you can. Try something fun, like role-playing, with your kids so that you both can understand each other's position, instead of shouting at one another. For example, parents can assume the role of the teen calling from a party where drinking was taking place, and the teen can play the parents responding to the teen's call. Seeing each other's perspective is an important tool to help build communication. Teens may be surprised at how well their parents remember their own teenage years, and parents may be surprised to hear how they sound to their teen!

- **Be prepared to let some things go, and take advantage of opportunities to make a positive point.** Avoid the trap of policing every little thing—in other words, helicoptering. Too easily you and your teen will end up on opposing sides, arguing all the time. Sometimes you have to bite your tongue and let some smaller things go. Be cautious about nagging, or your teen will soon tune you out. Place value on your own words, and try to determine appropriate opportunities to get your point across when your teen is open to listening. If you have something important to say, look for a time when your teen is mellow and open, perhaps at the end of the day, or when you have shared a good time. Then choose your words thoughtfully, make your point, and then sit back and be prepared to listen.

- **Respect your children—try to work together as partners.** Encourage your teens to talk more about their feelings or expand on what they're saying. Don't treat your teens as if they are too young to know or understand. Teens today are forced to deal with many adult issues, so show them that you recognize these issues and provide them with the support and guidance they need to realize their goals. Be an ally to your teens, not another obstacle.

Knowing *when* to talk (for example, when they are open and receptive and you are calm, and also prior to Decision Points, when they are likely on the cusp of making the decision) is a great start to the successful parenting of teenagers. And practicing communication skills will help promote effective dialogue between you and your teen. Still, the question of content remains: *What do I say?*

While there is no fail-safe recipe that outlines the perfect, measured ingredients for successful conversations, we serve everyone best by remaining focused on the risks associated with certain choices (such as alcohol and drug use and intimate sexual behavior) and steering clear of more emotionally charged debate about the motivation behind them. That can come later. For example, when the time is right, we might probe the rationale behind behaviors by asking, "Tim, why is it that so many kids seem to want to drink at prom?" or "Mary, do you think girls feel they need to be sexually active to have a boyfriend?"

Teens instinctively understand and secretly appreciate our concern for their health and safety. When we avoid moralizing about their behavior and remain fixed instead on the dangers posed by certain choices (as well as such consequences as social embarrassment), our words are more likely to be met by receptive ears on the other side of the dinner table. ("We've all seen tragic consequences when teens decide to drink," rather than "Smart teens don't drink alcohol.")

As we discussed earlier, there are five key risks that permeate underage drinking, drug use, and early, intimate sexual behavior: physical, emotional, social, developmental, and legal. By imbuing our conversations with concrete, real-life examples of these hazards, we can help our teens to truly understand the breadth and depth of the problems associated with certain choices.

Talking about Alcohol

While the likelihood of teens engaging in risky behaviors tends to increase over time, there are specific moments when talking with teens might very well dissuade them from trying those behaviors in the first place. If your child is in the 6th grade, this is the time for you to begin—or continue—to have conversations about alcohol. This is the common age for first initiation, and that means it's time to talk in order to prevent a bad decision.

Don't yell and don't threaten. Just explain . . . and listen. And remember that there's no magic bullet, no right or wrong thing to say, only some important ground to cover, such as the many dangers that go hand-in-hand with underage drinking: dependency, potential decline in schoolwork, disrupted relationships, and a higher risk of depression and sexual assault. If one approach doesn't work with your child, try another. If that doesn't pan out either, take a break and set your sights on a "do over" at some later date, when your teen is more receptive. Much as Goldilocks sampled every bear's porridge until she found one that was just right for her, we often have to try, and try again, until we find just the right tone and pitch to reach our kids. We need to find our "voice," and also listen for theirs. Our only failure as parents comes from not trying in the first place.

Here are some examples of various openers parents can use in approaching their kids about alcohol, which you may want to try using your own language, in your own way. As you will see, each of them is brief and non-confrontational. Many utilize "I" statements as opposed to "you" statements, which often sound accusatory. Some ask questions, drawing teens into the conversation and thereby making communication a two-way street.

- *I guess a lot of kids are starting to think about trying alcohol, and I want to let you know that there are some pretty big risks associated with drinking. Right now your brain is undergoing a lot of changes, sort of reorganizing itself, getting rid of cells it doesn't need and adding ones it does. Alcohol can actually affect that reordering and cause permanent changes in how you will learn and remember things in the future.*

- *Alcohol, like tobacco, is addictive, meaning once you start using, it may be hard to stop. And that can cause some big problems later in life, such as trouble getting or keeping a job. Can you imagine showing up for work drunk? Or sneaking off at lunchtime to get a drink? There are a lot of people so dependent on alcohol that they do those things and end up losing their job.*

- *I have read that a lot of kids use alcohol to feel better about themselves or some situation in their life, only to find out that it actually makes them feel worse. For example, some kids drink because they feel sad or depressed, but then find it only makes them sadder or more depressed. Do you know any kids like that?*

- *I can remember from when I was a teen that alcohol can cause a lot of kids to do things they later wish they hadn't, such as being mean to a friend, throwing up on a friend in the car, or even having sex with someone. I'll bet you have heard of kids doing things under the influence of alcohol that they later regret.*

- *For many teens, drinking interferes with important goals they have set for themselves, such as getting good grades or performing well in sports. Do you think there are kids at your school who aren't doing as well as they'd like because they're drinking?*

When we ask questions in a calm, gentle, loving way, teens will almost always tell us everything we need to know. We just need to be ready to hear it, and ready to respond calmly, rationally, and consistently.

Talking about Drugs

Talking about drugs with children and teens is often easier for parents than talking about alcohol. The points seem clearer, more obvious, and less controversial. This phenomenon largely reflects the common connotation of drugs in our society (bad) as opposed to that of alcohol (fun). The danger is that the distinction may lead us to believe that our kids already know the pitfalls associated with using marijuana, prescription or harder drugs, such as cocaine or heroin. But that is not necessarily the case. Remember that first initiation of drug use can happen early and that, according to the *Teens Today* research, there is a significant jump in drug use between the 8th and 9th grades. Similar data from the National Center on Addiction and Substance Abuse at Columbia University (CASA) echoes that trend: Compared to 13-year-olds, 14-year-olds are four times more likely to be offered prescription drugs, three times more likely to be offered marijuana or Ecstasy, and twice as likely to be offered cocaine. So, discussions with our teens about transitioning from middle school to high school should include dialogue about drugs and the risks they pose.

- Parents and other significant adults can best help young adults navigate the difficult path of decision-making by engaging them in meaningful dialogue about the role of drugs in our society and their very real impact on the individual. Teens themselves say their parents are influential in the decisions that they make about using drugs! That's good news.

- Also good news is that almost three-quarters of teens (74.3 percent) are already predisposed to view drug use as harmful, so we can begin the conversation by pointing that out and asking our teen what his thoughts are about drugs and what choices he believes are right for him. It is helpful to remind teens of the many ways in which using drugs can cause health problems and thus interfere with the personal goals (one of the Decision Factors previously discussed) they may have set for themselves, such as getting high grades so that they can attend a good college or excelling in sports to earn a scholarship.

Concerns about the effects of drugs on academic and athletic performance are common reasons that young people give for not using them (31 percent and 26 percent, respectively). Again, there is a predisposition on the part of many teens to stay away from drugs, and reinforcing their concerns about the effect drug use might have on their grades or athletic performance can be an enormously effective deterrent. There are some other consequences that are worth pointing out as well, such as the possibility of not being able to get or hold a job that might be needed to earn money for college or a new car, or the impact of an arrest record on a potential college admission.

Of course, communicating what we expect of them when it comes to decision-making about drugs is critical. Almost all teens (97 percent) say that it is important to them to live up to their parents' expectations regarding drug use. Unfortunately, more than one-in-four teens (31 percent) say their parents don't tell them what those expectations are!

As is the case with discussing underage drinking among our children, we best start conversations in a non-confrontational manner, talking about our own perspectives and gently probing for theirs.

- *I have heard that a lot of kids start using drugs when they get to high school. Have you heard that, too?*
- *What decisions do you think you will make about using drugs?*
- *I remember thinking that smoking marijuana was probably not a big deal, but then saw how some of my classmates just got stoned all the time, became dependent, and pretty much ruined their grades and long-term plans.*

- *You might know kids who use drugs, like marijuana or their parents' prescription drugs, to feel better about themselves. I think a lot of adults do the same thing.*
- *What do you think the fallout would be if a kid got arrested for possession of marijuana or cocaine?*

Almost half of teens (41 percent) report that their parents know about their drug use and about one-quarter (22 percent) say that their parents do not try to dissuade them from drugs. Like underage drinking, perhaps many parents see drug use—or at least experimentation with drugs—as inevitable, a part of growing up, and something that their teen will do no matter what. Yet, it is clear that parents who communicate effectively with their teen about drug use are more likely than not to influence the choices they will definitely be facing.

Talking about Sex

Young people today are hitting puberty sooner, are exposed to sexual stimuli more frequently, and seem to be engaging in intimate behavior earlier than ever before. And that means that the significant adults in their lives have an important role to play in helping them figure out what lies between puberty and full-fledged sexual intimacy. That is a role many teens say they'd welcome.

Often, teens tell me they are uncertain if they are ready for intimacy, yet feel compelled to become sexually active because of their perceptions that "everybody else" is doing it, that it's the only way to keep a girlfriend or boyfriend, or to prove their masculinity or femininity. The social-norming of early sexual behavior is combined with a reluctance on the part of many adults to raise issues of sexuality and sexual activity—and that leaves kids alone, or with just peers, to make important choices about what they do with their bodies, hearts, and minds.

No doubt talking with teens about sex is tough—likely because of our own anxiety about raising what for far too long has been considered "taboo." Even when we do talk to young people about sex, we tend to talk in generalities.

"Wait until you are ready." "Protect yourself against getting pregnant." "Use condoms to prevent STDs." Sometimes we even wrap our questions in supposition, as if we are hoping we won't really have to talk about much. "You know about sex, right?" Or, "I'm sure the class you took in school told you about how to use birth control." Neither of these approaches is particularly helpful to young people trying to decide what they want to do and when. Rather, kids benefit from forums for open, honest discussion about emerging sexuality and sexual decision-making. It occupies a lot of their thoughts, and likely much of the give-and-take with their friends. Sixteen-year-old Carl says, "It's pretty common for kids to ask each other how far they've gone." For sure, kids are going to gain some of their perspective and glean some of the guidance they receive from their peers. But, is that the only perspective and guidance we want them to have? Probably not! And that makes it all the more important that we learn how to begin and continue the dialogue about sex prior to and throughout our child's adolescence.

Here are some talking points that may help get the ball rolling in discussing sex with pre-teens and teens:

- *There are a lot of changes going on right now, socially, emotionally, and physically. When puberty starts, it seems like everything is different— from how we interact with our friends, to how we feel about our parents, to what's happening to our bodies.*
- *Many teens wonder about their sexuality . . . Am I straight? Why do I look at the other boys in the showers? Why am I attracted to some of the other girls I hang out with? Those are all normal questions and feelings.*
- *You might also start wondering what to do with sexual feelings and when you should become sexually active. What do you think is right for you?*
- *Sometimes young people can feel pressured to engage in sexual behavior they may not really want. Do you know someone who has had to deal with this?*

- *You're in charge of your body and what you choose to do with it! Whatever decisions you make, they should be ones you want to make, not ones someone else thinks you should make! Nobody gets to control our bodies.*
- *There can be a lot at stake when it comes to sex—one decision can have lasting consequences. What do you think some of those consequences are, good or bad?*
- *There is usually an emotional element attached to sexual activity that doesn't disappear just because we may want it to. A lot of kids think they can just have sex or do something sexually intimate (like having oral sex) for fun and not have any feelings associated with it. That's not usually the case.*
- *Many young people (and probably older people, as well) confuse sexuality with sex. Sexuality is an important part of identity formation and helps us learn "who we are."*
- *Learning about our sexuality doesn't mean having to have sex; it just means figuring out whether we are straight, gay, bi-sexual, bi-curious, or something else.*
- *It is important to think through the "whens" and "whys" before engaging in sexual behavior. What do you think that means?*
- *Young people receive a lot of messages through music, television, and movies, that sexual behavior is the norm and expected. Can you think of some examples?*
- *Maybe you and I, together, can best judge when you feel you are old enough and mature enough to become sexually active.*

As you might guess, these are just some of the many talking points you might use to begin discussing the issue with your teen. Each parent, each family, needs to examine their own value and belief systems to guide the types of conversations they want to have, the type of information they want to impart, and what expectations for behavior they want to communicate. The most important thing is to have the conversation, early and often, so that kids know what's coming up in terms of what they can expect of their own physical, social, and emotional development, and what types of decisions they will likely face.

Talking about Driving

When it comes to driving, like most everything else, young people want to know where the boundaries are. They know the risks and often have first-hand accounts of friends or relatives who have been injured or killed in automobile crashes. They want to be safe and want us to know they will be safe. Yet, as we have seen, teens tend to engage in unsafe driving behaviors in alarming numbers. Automobile crashes remain the leading cause of death for young people, despite the fact that 9 out of 10 teens (89 percent) consider themselves to be "safe" drivers!

Establishing expectations, praising (and modeling) safe driving behaviors, and setting and enforcing appropriate consequences for unacceptable driving practices all make cars less risky for teens. As I say in Chapter Five, reinforcing positive driving behaviors through increased freedoms, rewards, or even verbal praise (*"Great job sticking to the speed limit"*) make it more likely that those behaviors will reoccur. In particular, we know that the issues of speed, number of other teens in the car, hours of operation, distractions, impaired driving, and safety-belt use are incredibly relevant in any assessment of teen safety behind the wheel.

Thus, whenever you are talking about driving, it is helpful to stay focused on points about staying within the posted limits, avoiding driving late at night when he's likely to be tired, sticking to family rules—or state graduated licensing laws—about how many other kids, if any, may be in the car when she's driving, avoiding distractions that make crashes more likely, such as using a cell phone or fiddling with the radio, staying away from alcohol and other drugs, and avoiding getting into a car with a driver who has been using either, and buckling up.

While Decision Points are pretty easy to determine when it comes to driving (getting a permit or a full license), it is helpful to know that teen car crashes increase during the summer, when teens are unshackled from their school desks, homework assignments, and extracurricular activity schedules. They tend to have more free time and more freedoms. For example, young people spend 44 percent more hours driving in the summer each week than during the school year. So, while talking with teens about driving safety is always a good idea, it takes on a particular relevance come June.

Here are some examples of how to start a conversation about driving:

- *I guess a lot of kids are driving fast, and I want to let you know that there are some pretty big risks associated with that.*
- *Remember reading about those kids who died in a car crash because they weren't wearing their seat belts?*
- *I have heard that a lot of kids are text-messaging while they are driving. Do you know anybody who does that?*
- *I can recall that when I was a teen a lot of kids were driving after drinking alcohol. Do you think that is still a problem?*

Talking about Depression and Suicide

As discussed in Chapter Two, depression and suicide are major issues facing young adults, and the numbers of teens committing suicide—likely a small fraction of the number who are thinking about it or who have tried it—is on the rise. It's always important to carefully monitor our child's emotional state, not overreacting to normal variance in mood, but rather looking for signs and symptoms (see Chapter Three) that he is at risk.

Facing and talking about sadness is probably part of your regular routine with your child. Generally speaking, we are quick to notice shifts in mood and to pose questions or offer comment and consolation: "You seem out of sorts today. Is everything OK?" Or, "I'm sorry you had a bad day at school; you'll feel better tomorrow."

What is more difficult is facing the prospect that our child is actually depressed and may need professional help. We want our kids to be happy and healthy, and when they are not, it causes us no small amount of worry and pain. Physical injuries, such as a skinned knee, sprained ankle, or broken finger, are easier to spot and easier to treat. When it comes to the emotional well-being of our teen, we can be overwhelmed by feelings of inadequacy. Reflecting on a suicide by the teenage son of a friend, a New York mom says, "As difficult as losing a child in a car accident would be, how can a parent possibly live with a suicide? They'd be constantly wondering 'why?' and what they could have done to prevent it."

The motivations behind suicide are complex and varied, but often revolve around the fact that suicidal teens feel that they are without any other recourse to feel better, that there is no one who can help them, and that they will always feel this bad. They lack the life experience that we have, and thus don't always know that things will get better, even if professional intervention is required in the meantime.

In my own experience, as reported earlier, I have found that some parents are fearful of raising the issue of suicide because they believe it might plant the idea in their teen's head. In truth, teens know about suicide already, and not raising it poses the possibility that we will miss an opportunity to intervene if we don't know whether suicide is currently on their minds. If it is, we will likely need some immediate help to ascertain the degree of depression and the seriousness of the suicidal threat. (Is there a plan? Does he have the means to carry out the plan?)

On their Web site, www.aap.org, the American Academy of Pediatrics advises that if you think your child might be suicidal, you must act quickly.

- Ask your teenager about it. Don't be afraid to say the word "suicide." Getting the word out in the open may help your teenager think someone has heard his cries for help.
- Reassure that you love him. Remind him that no matter how awful his problems seem, they can be worked out, and you are willing to help.
- Ask her to talk about her feelings. Listen carefully. Do not dismiss her problems or get angry at her.

- Remove all lethal weapons from your home, including guns, pills, kitchen utensils, and ropes.
- Seek professional help. Ask your teenager's pediatrician to guide you. A variety of outpatient and hospital-based treatment programs are available.

When we suspect that our teen is in trouble, we can begin the dialogue in much the same manner as we approach the issues of alcohol, drugs, or sex—relying on what we observe or hear and how it makes us feel. Clearly stating our concerns and our desire to help is important.

- *You seem down lately, and I am wondering if you are feeling depressed.*
- *Many kids who get depressed think they will always feel that way and that is definitely not the case. I would like to help you feel better.*
- *I've been hearing about teens who commit suicide. Is that something you are thinking about?*
- *Are there things that you are thinking about or worrying about that you are having difficulty sharing with me?*
- *How would you feel about talking with a counselor who has experience helping kids with depression?*

The loss of a young life to suicide is one of the most disturbing and confounding events that adults have to confront. To us, she seems to have everything on her side, even in spite of temporary setbacks. Her whole life lies ahead of her, and the possibilities are infinite. But the truth is that many teens—even pre-teens—are depressed and suicidal. Thus, this issue needs to be a part of our ongoing dialogue about the real world that kids live in and the difficulties they face.

Talking about Bullying and Hazing

Often, one of the hardest things for kids to open up about is bullying and hazing—both because they are probably embarrassed about being victimized or witnessing another kid being victimized and also because they may fear further harm if they identify the perpetrators. Even so, we obviously cannot allow our kids to continue to be targets of abusive behavior at the hands of their peers.

Recognizing their natural reluctance to talk about being bullied or hazed helps us to address their concerns and offer supportive comments: "Being the victim of a bully makes a lot of kids feel weak and unable to respond." Or, "Kids who are hazed are often afraid to report it for fear of being labeled 'tattletales' or being subjected to something even worse when the kids responsible find out they have been identified." We can assure young people that they can respond by letting us know about the inappropriate, hurtful behavior and working with us to come up with a solution that addresses the situation without inciting further embarrassment or harm.

It is also helpful to knock down some of the commonly held beliefs about bullies that might make your child less likely to speak up, such as bullies will stop if they are ignored because all they are looking for is attention, bullying is just part of growing up and is to be expected, and that victims of bullies need to learn how to deal with the situation themselves.

Of course, many of the same fears and anxieties are common among young people who are being hazed—such as fear of "payback" for telling. These teens may also be worried that they will be left out of group activities in the future and have a hard time maintaining friendships. Here again, it is helpful to point out some of the truths about hazing: It is not harmless fun, but rather abusive, humiliating, and dangerous; agreeing to participate in the hazing does not mean you are not a victim; and even a little hazing is unacceptable—it does not teach respect or discipline.

Our dialogue with teens about bullying and hazing should reflect the realities of its inappropriateness and unacceptability, while offering support by acknowledging how hard it is for teens to talk about and to ask for help.

- *It hurts to be picked on by other kids, whether verbally, physically, or even on the Internet. And it's easy to feel intimidated, weak, and embarrassed.*

- *Many kids ask themselves, "Why does he hate me?"—even though the motivation behind the bullying is more one of wanting to control someone else than of their personal feelings about the other kid.*
- *I know that it is hard to figure out what to do when we're bullied or hazed, because we might feel that asking for help will only make the situation worse.*
- *Bullying is never acceptable, and it typically gets worse if it is not addressed. Tell me what you would like to do about this situation . . . and how I can help.*

Perhaps it goes without saying, but it's not only the victims of bullying and hazing that benefit from a thoughtful, guided discussion. The perpetrators, accomplices, and permissive bystanders need our help to understand the connection between behavior and consequence, for the victim and for themselves. As we saw in Chapter Two, victims can suffer in many ways, including having trouble in school, fighting with parents, or experiencing difficulty with sleeping or eating. They also may feel angry, embarrassed, or guilty.

We can use the very same communication techniques presented throughout this book to help them understand the motivations behind their behavior (or lack of action, in the case of the bystander) and how it affects everyone around them, including their family members and friends.

In *The Shelter of Each Other, Rebuilding Our Families*, Mary Pipher writes, "Raising healthy children is a labor-intensive operation. Contrary to the news from the broader culture, most of what children need, money cannot buy. Children need time and space, attention, affection, guidance, and conversation. They need sheltered places where they learn what they need to know to survive. They need jokes, play, and touching. They need to have stories told to them by adults who know and love them in all their particularity and who have a real interest in their moral development . . . families can be really healthy only when children once again have communities of real people who care about them."

It is easy to fall into the self-defeating trap of believing that we should instinctively know how best to talk with our own child and that it should come with the same ease that we experienced in conversation with him or her at a younger age. But it's harder. Remember, they're changing quickly and we, most likely, are not. But we'll probably have to change our communication patterns and styles to match their new interests, struggles, and needs.

Nine

Communication Counts

Steve, a 14-year-old sophomore from the suburbs of Chicago, sat to my left and settled in for a discussion about his life, his family, his choices. Steve explained that his parents "do a really good job" and said he wants to be like them when he is an adult. He described their relationship as "really good," and said he can go to them to talk about problems. He told me that they are the most influential people in his life and he can talk with them about anything, even alcohol and sex.

Steve has the type of relationship with his parents that many children and teens want: open, caring, connected. And his parents have the type of relationship with their son most of us wish for: honest, affectionate, involved. But that's not always easy to achieve.

When it comes to parenting, and parent-child communication, there are essentially four "styles" that parents tend to adopt: Indulgent, Authoritarian, Authoritative, and Uninvolved. These groupings are based on the research of psychologist Diana Baumrind and her work on families. They differ in the extent to which they are "demanding" and "responsive." In other words, they address what standards for behavior are established and expected by parents ("demandingness") and how warm and supportive the parents are toward their children ("responsiveness"). What kind of parent are you? This is important to consider, because each "style" has been shown to be predictive of how children perform academically and socially, and is closely linked to the amount of problematic behavior they will display as they grow and develop.

As you might guess from the label, Indulgent parents are responsive but establish few expectations for the behavior and responsibilities of their children. They're permissive and offer acceptance almost regardless of how their child acts. With few rules in place, their children are often prone to misbehavior.

Authoritarian parents rate high on control and low on responsiveness. In other words, they tend to establish strict standards for conduct and may react harshly when those standards are not met. On the other hand, they provide little supportive interaction. Children with Authoritarian parents are often anxious, depressed, and socially unsuccessful. They also may have trouble learning to think through choices on their own, as they have been brought up simply being told what to do and what not to do with few, if any, explanations.

Authoritative parents tend to be both demanding and responsive, holding children accountable for age-appropriate behavior, while engaging them in the process of understanding expectations, instead of simply adopting a "my way or the highway" approach.

Whereas an Authoritarian parent might say, "If you leave your bicycle in the driveway, you will not be allowed to use it for a month," an Authoritative parent may say, "When you leave your bicycle in the driveway, it means that I have to stop and get out of the car to move it out of the way. Even worse, I might not see it and run over it and damage it. So, please always leave it in the garage."

And, finally, Uninvolved parents are neither demanding (as are Authoritarian parents) nor responsive (as are Indulgent parents), leaving kids feeling disconnected, unwanted, or unloved. They neither set expectations for their children, nor do they pay them much attention or offer affection and support. In a sense, they're not really acting like parents at all.

Steve is flourishing under his parent's authoritative parenting style. He is socially adept and academically successful, and he stays out of trouble. He is self-confident in his abilities—including the ones that help him to make good decisions—and optimistic about his future. He has a high Sense of Self.

Like Steve, Mary, a 16-year-old 10th-grader from San Diego, enjoys a relationship with Authoritative parents—and also siblings. She says, "I don't drink because of my family. I'd be worried about their reaction and also what my older brothers and sisters would think."

These teens benefit from trusting relationships nurtured over time and maintained through regular dialogue, the expression by parents of expectations for behavior, and the certainty of consequence should they break the rules. Each of these is a common-sense step—and we've been discussing them a lot in this book—toward establishing a "triangle of trust" between parents and teens and that can effectively close the reality gap.

Building Blocks

These steps are hardly new, nor are they necessarily complicated. Rather, they are strategies reaffirmed by original research as effective means of taming the epidemic of underage drinking, other drug use, early intimate sexual behavior, and dangerous driving. Just as important, they can be tied in time to the specific Decision Points I discussed in Chapter Four, when such strategies are likely to be most meaningful.

First, communicate with your teens on a regular basis. As you know, communication is a fundamental building block in all human relationships. But communicating well, particularly with teens, requires a great deal of planning and effort (and even luck). Talking and listening can be intensive. But making the effort can yield volumes of information that we can use to help them choose responsible and rewarding behaviors.

As we have seen, parents and teens benefit from a renegotiation of roles during adolescence. Parents may become less directive and move toward becoming more of an advisor, consultant, or coach. Teens, on the other hand, may become less reliant on constant direction and move toward an internal locus of control, whereby they assume the ultimate responsibility for the decisions they make—within the broad structure of family rules and expectations.

Even with the best-prepared parents, many pre-teens and teens have a hard time communicating with the important adults in their world. For a variety of reasons (and often different ones), teenage boys and girls can have difficulty sharing their true feelings about the choices they are confronted with. Parents who are willing to take the time to talk, listen, and share their own experiences can do much to bridge the gulf that often lies between them and their sons and daughters.

Next, it is crucial for parents to establish expectations, making it clear where they stand on behavioral issues and what the penalties will be for violating any agreements. It's not easy to steer young people away from trouble, but again, "early" and "often" are important catchwords when it comes to communicating expectations to teens. Teens say they want to know where we stand—and when they know what we expect of them they are less likely to drink, use drugs, have sex, harass, bully, hit, or haze.

All this having been said, and said again, many families struggle to find the right approach to communication. Parents have difficulty raising sensitive issues with kids, and kids have trouble sharing thoughts, feelings, and decisions with parents. Different communication patterns need not be looked to as "right" or "wrong," but rather as "effective" or "ineffective." After all, it's the results that count. If parents and teens can communicate openly and honestly, share feelings, anxieties, concerns, and successes—everybody wins.

Nasha, who we met in Chapter One, had a good relationship with her mom, and it has helped her steer clear of alcohol. Much like the relationship Matt, who we met in Chapter Two, has with his parents and his older sister, Maya. Both kids are Avoiders.

The elements of successful communication:

Be calm.

Be supportive.

Be open.

Be aware.

Be active.

Fortunately, there are scores of communication tools available for families looking to get started on meaningful conversations. Social contracts can help lay out expectations for behavior and jump-start dialogue about choices. An example is the "Contract for Life" that was written by SADD. The "Contract for Life" was originally developed to help teens and parents "break the ice" about the issue of teen drinking and driving. As SADD developed a "No Use" message and then expanded its mission to include other destructive behaviors, the "Contract for Life" migrated toward a more general-purpose communication tool.

What's important about the "Contract for Life" is that it requires the participation of both parent and teen. Each must make a commitment to the other: the parent to seek to understand their teen's perspective; and the teen to do his best to avoid destructive behaviors. By its very nature, this "two-way-street" approach encourages candid conversation and helps parents and teens explore the right decisions. It acknowledges the reality that young people face tough choices, thus taking the issue of "if" off the table and replacing it with "when." The contract also encourages continued dialogue and specifies the steps that each party will follow should problems arise. It is on the following page:

CONTRACT FOR LIFE

A Foundation for Trust and Caring

This contract is designed to facilitate communication between young people and their parents about potentially destructive decisions related to alcohol, drugs, peer pressure, and behavior. The issues facing young people today are often too difficult to address alone. SADD believes that effective parent child communication is critically important in helping young adults to make healthy decisions.

Young Person

I recognize that there are many potentially destructive decisions I face every day and commit to you that I will do everything in my power to avoid making decisions that will jeopardize my health, my safety and overall well-being or your trust in me. I understand the dangers associated with the use of alcohol and drugs, and the destructive behaviors often associated with impairment.

By signing below, I pledge my best effort to remain alcohol and drug free, I agree that I will never drive under the influence of either, or accept a ride from someone who is impaired, and I will always wear a seat belt. Finally I agree to call you if I am ever in a situation that threatens my safety and to communicate with you regularly about issues of importance to us both.

_____

Young Person

Parent (or Caring Adult)

I am committed to you and to your health and safety. By signing below, I pledge to do everything in my power to understand and communicate with you about the many difficult and potentially destructive decisions you face. Further, I agree to provide for you safe, sober transportation home if you are ever in a situation that threatens your safety and to defer discussions about that situation until a time when we can both discuss the issues in a calm and caring manner. I also pledge to you that I will not drive under the influence of alcohol or drugs, I will always seek safe, sober transportation home, and I will always remember to wear a seat belt.

_____

Parent/Caring Adult

SADD and all SADD logos are registered with the United States Patent and Trademark Office and other jurisdictions.

While the "Contract for Life" has been remarkably successful in bringing families to the table to discuss difficult topics, other families struggle to get to the table at all.

"I get the fact that it's important to talk about this stuff, but don't really know what to say. Is there any place I can go to find help?" asked a dad, reclining on the floor of the school gymnasium along with other parents and teens waiting to ask me their questions on a warm, late June night in a town just north of Seattle.

Recognizing that not all parents, or all teens, possess the communication skills to make the "Contract for Life" a valuable tool right off the bat, SADD produced a companion guide called "Opening Lifesaving Lines" to aid those families motivated at least to try to talk. This tool paves the way toward the type of open, honest communication that connects, or reconnects, parents with teens and makes poor, potentially destructive, choices less likely.

Who does it benefit? Maybe you. Do you avoid talking about life decisions, peer pressure, and destructive behavior with your kids because you don't know how to start? You don't have time? It makes you uncomfortable? You don't want a confrontation? You don't want to face disappointment? Each of these is a common reason why both parents and teens sidestep important conversations.

On the next few pages, I outline five communication steps, along with my own commentary, from "Opening Lifesaving Lines": Breaking the Ice, Getting Started, Going Deeper, Making a Commitment, and Continuing the Conversation. Families don't have to complete the process in one sitting, or even follow all the steps laid out. And if you already talk about these issues in your family, you can even jump straight to a social contract. In either case, with regular and respectful conversation about these serious issues, both teens and their parents can achieve their shared goal: safe and healthy lives.

Breaking the Ice—Step One

Many parents and teens may actually begin the communication process by asking themselves, "Why talk in the first place?" The simple answer is that you both have a common interest—the health, safety, and well-being of your family. Thus, it is important for families to communicate about destructive decisions and the potential role they could play in a teenager's life. However, for a variety of reasons, and in many families, it is difficult to open a discussion of these issues. The parent or the teen must take the first step, answering the questions, "Why should we talk about destructive decisions?" and "How do we start the conversation?"

- Before responding, it is important to think about what destructive decisions are, what they mean to you, and what they mean from your teen's point of view. Of course, you may find a considerable difference of opinion between you and your teenager! And he might find the same! But that's OK.

- Knowing where the differences lie helps to bridge the reality gap while also pointing to areas of agreement, such as the most basic things in life that everybody wants or needs. Ask yourself, "How would a destructive decision by your teen affect the family?" That's something you are going to want to share with your teen, as well as ask of him.

Getting Started—Step Two

To proceed to step two, first find a time when you have your teen's complete attention—and remember not to interrupt her favorite activities to talk. That can doom conversation from the start! There are several ways to broach subjects such as underage drinking, impaired driving, sexual behavior, bullying, violence, and suicide. You could take the following steps:

- Show your teen the "Contract for Life," and explain that you would like her to take a look at it because you think it makes an important point about the value of parents and teens talking openly about issues such as drinking and driving.

- Ask your teen about his concerns about alcohol, drugs, sex, or suicide.
- Explain your thoughts about these issues, remembering, at least at the outset, to focus on your concerns for her health and safety.
- Tell a story from your youth or bring up a report in the news or an issue raised in a movie or television show involving a destructive decision, and ask your teen for his opinion of the issue.
- Decide which of these starters works best for you and makes you the most comfortable. You know your teen best and can anticipate how she is likely to respond. At this juncture, it's worth revisiting some of the conversation tips discussed in Chapter Eight, such as express your desire to hear each other's input or views and your wish to relate to each other; listen carefully; and don't lecture, give unwanted advice, or use scare tactics.

If your teen is disinterested or hostile and refuses to discuss the issues, tell him that it is something that *you* want to discuss, but you are willing to have the conversation when you can both voice your interests clearly. Let your teen know that you are concerned and you want his input. It is important to explain that you are not accusing him, but that you want to discuss things that are relevant to his life. Many parents find that it works best to ask their teen to listen briefly and have the conversation in small intervals over time.

It is easy to assume that it is always the parent who will begin the conversation. Yet, many times it's the teen who approaches his parent! So, it's best to be prepared. Some of the questions they may have in mind are: *What was life like when you were a teen? What do you consider to be bad choices? What do you wish most of all for me? What do you think of drinking, drug use, and impaired driving?*

Knowing your answers ahead of time will help facilitate a meaningful conversation with your teen.

Again, and this can't be stressed enough, we need to *always* be prepared to hear what our teen is trying to tell us, even if it comes in small snippets of conversation. The meaning behind the words—or the "meta-messages," including those conveyed nonverbally—can give us a lot of information about what our teen is thinking, doing, or considering doing. It can also tell us that she is asking for help!

Going Deeper—Step Three

Now that the conversation has started, it's time to take the discussion to a deeper level. To help each of you to understand the other, ask questions of your teen and of yourself.

- *How do you think destructive decisions pertain to you as a teenager, or to the family?*
- *As a teen, are you willing to acknowledge that there may be times in your life when you are tempted to make a poor choice?*
- *As a parent, are you willing to accept that your teen may be tempted to act this way?*
- *Are you both willing to recognize and accept that parents will feel upset and disappointed if a bad decision is made?*
- *Are you willing to deal with the consequences?*

Now it's time to drill further down. Ask your teen:

- *What are destructive decisions from your point of view?*
- *What potentially destructive decisions do you face every day?*
- *How do you handle these situations?*
- *Do you need advice from me?*
- *What do you do to avoid making destructive decisions?*
- *What do you perceive as the dangers associated with alcohol, drugs, and impairment?*
- *Do you feel that you have your parents' trust? Why or why not?*
- *Are you concerned that your parents might make dangerous choices?*
- *Do you think your experiences as a teenager are relevant?*

As the dialogue with your teen continues to unfold, it can be helpful to let him know the adolescent years can be very frightening for parents because they know what dangers are potentially lurking.

Explain that you wonder if he will develop a dependency; who her friends are and whether they are trustworthy; if he knows the consequences and dangers associated with drinking and drug use or other potentially destructive behaviors; whether or not she might be underestimating or not anticipating the bad things that can happen; how she handles peer pressure; how he's feeling about himself, his friends, or his family; whether or not he will be honest with you; and how you can best respond to him if he makes a decision that you don't approve of, or how you can help him if he needs it.

Airing your concerns reinforces the point of the conversation: your teen's health and safety . . . physical, social, and emotional. As you gather information and understanding, go back and answer some of the questions you had when you started:

- What potentially destructive decisions does your child face every day?
- How does she handle these situations and avoid making destructive decisions?
- Does he need advice from you or some other responsible adult?
- What does your teen perceive as the dangers associated with alcohol, drugs, or impairment?
- Does your child feel that she has your trust? Why or why not?
- Who does your child turn to for advice and feedback?
- How would you react to your teen if he made a destructive decision?
- Are you willing to answer questions about your own habits?
- How much of your behavior as a teen are you willing to discuss?

Stay on point, addressing the risks associated with certain choices.

Now, read the list of questions above to your child and answer them as you go along. Also, invite her to ask you questions. Tell her about the legal issues associated with destructive choices such as underage drinking and driving while impaired. Explain the physical issues associated with drinking and other drug use (e.g., losing judgment, getting sick, having hangovers, addiction, inability to focus, etc.) and the possible physical, social, and emotional risks of becoming sexually active too soon. Talk about how the adult decision to consume alcohol differs from the teen decision (e.g., it is legal; their bodies are more developed) and how it doesn't (they still need to worry about quantity, getting home safely, hangovers, addictions, and impairment). Tell your teen of an embarrassing or dangerous situation that happened to you, a close friend, or a relative as a result of drinking or drug use. Explain to him what your expectations are regarding his behavior.

As the *Teens Today* research points out, young people are often reluctant to disappoint parents. Ask how she would expect you to react to a destructive decision. Talk about how you think you might react if she makes a poor choice and violates your trust, or if he is being victimized or victimizing others, or if he told you he was stressed, depressed, or suicidal.

Remember 17-year-old Adam from Chapter Two? He was reluctant to tell his parents of his plans to kill himself, because he was afraid they would react by focusing on getting him the best doctor around, instead of listening and understanding what he was feeling and why.

Making a Commitment—Step Four

As you move to this stage of conversation, there are several things to keep in mind. Remember this is a dialogue, not an argument, lecture, or soapbox. Express your interests, including your beliefs, feelings, and wishes. Then, listen carefully and do not interrupt. Think about the issues from your teen's point of view. Realize that nego-

Always remember to **hear** what your teen has to say and to acknowledge your understanding; to **share** your thoughts about what your life is like, without lecturing or arguing; to **listen** to your teen's concerns and agree not to interrupt him; to **be honest** about your feelings; to **understand** that the teenage years can be a difficult, emotional time for both of you.

tiating does not mean "giving up" or "giving in." Instead, it means continuing to look for common ground. Maintain self-control if you hear something that you do not like. Don't get angry, and don't worry about other parents or teens and what they will think.

Brainstorm options together and make sure those options provide for mutual gains. Also, make sure that you treat each other fairly and that you both feel that you have been heard. And be sure to discuss the future as related to these issues, not the past.

The "Contract for Life" requests that teens avoid destructive decisions and refrain from using alcohol and drugs in order to stay alive and healthy. In reality, how do you accomplish this? One way is to help teens deal with peer pressure and feelings of embarrassment. They are overwhelming for teens and often influence their actions. Preparing them to respond to situations and the emotions that may come with them is essential.

Role-playing different ways to say no to drugs and alcohol may provide support in this area. Here are some recommendations of what a teenager could say or do. They could calmly say they're not interested, or simply, "No thanks." They can also say that they have to go home and don't want to smell like alcohol. They can hold the drink, but don't drink it (although remember they could be charged with possession). They can say they don't want to participate in illegal activities, or that they don't need alcohol or drugs to have fun. They can also say good friends wouldn't pressure them to do something they already said they don't want to do. Also, role-playing possible responses to requests for sexual behavior or for participating in orientation programs (such as athletic ones) that might include hazing will help prepare teens to stay safe.

Reinforce your commitment to your teen's health and safety by **letting him know** that he can ask you anything; **praising her** when she is honest with you; **establishing rules and guidelines** to display commitment; **being a good role model; offering alternative activities** for your teen and his friends to participate in; **spending time** with your teen; **listening** to your teen's concerns; and **accentuating her skills** to reinforce Self-Esteem and Sense of Self.

Despite our best-laid plans, our teens might still make a decision we wish they hadn't. Think about how each of you would react in the event that a destructive decision did occur, and what the consequences for this behavior would be. Say, for example, your teen tells you that she was drinking at a party, even though she said she wouldn't—much like what happened with 14-year-old Molly, whose mother had not only extracted a promise from her, but had also called ahead to make sure there was to be parental supervision (there was, but they allowed the kids to drink). Molly's mom was ready with a response (disappointment) and a consequence (grounding).

In addition to the legal and physical issues involved in dangerous choices, there are also emotional repercussions that involve the family. So, it is important that teens feel secure enough to inform their parents of their actions, and that parents are available for their teens and appreciate their teens' honesty. As a parent, how can you create a secure environment that will lend itself to honesty and openness? Setting rules may help.

Here are some recommendations:

- Discuss options for household rules regarding inappropriate behavior.
- Keep in mind age-appropriateness.
- Voice your reasons for wanting each rule, and outline its practical use.
- Make sure that the rules are mutually agreeable.
- Accept that there may be occasional "unforeseen circumstances."
- Discuss the consequences for breaking the rules.
- Write out the rules and consequences so that they are visible.

"Opening Lifesaving Lines" offers some additional advice with respect to the issue of drinking and driving. As we saw in Chapter Three, crashes resulting from impaired driving kill thousands of young people each year and often destroy the hopes and dreams of entire families. The "Contract for Life" requests that both parents and teen commit to the same concept—

calling for a ride home if you or your driver is not fit to drive. While this may seem like a simple idea, there are several questions to consider. Are you willing to drop everything and pick up your child if she calls? Are you willing to postpone discussions about the consequences until all parties can communicate calmly and clearly? (A group of 11th- and 12th-graders from Minnesota worry about this. One says, "The next day you wake up and they will be flipping out all day.") Are you willing to accept the fact that your child acted responsibly in calling you and praise him for that? Are you willing to follow through with any consequences that you and your child agreed upon for this behavior? Can you establish a simple rule that the driver of the vehicle you are in should not have had anything to drink? Remember that anger and punishment are temporary, but car crashes can have permanent repercussions.

There are some relevant questions for teens, too! Ask them: How do you determine when you or your driver is unable to drive? What if you are impaired and can't think clearly enough to carry out your pledge? How would you feel if you hit someone while under the influence? How would you feel if an impaired driver hit you? Are you willing to call for a ride despite the fact that it may be embarrassing and your parents may be angry? Are you willing to accept the consequences for being in this situation? Are you willing to discuss how you came to be in this situation in a calm manner when you are sober? Are you willing to show your parents appreciation for dropping everything, getting out of bed and getting dressed to pick you up?

You may wish to consider whether you want to agree to add another name to the list of people who can be called to actually pick up the teen. While the idea behind the contract is to promote safety through honesty and communication, the purpose of this is twofold: Many teens may feel that their parents won't refrain from showing their anger when receiving a phone call. This, in turn, may prevent the teen from calling if she has been drinking or is dependent for a ride on someone who has been drinking. Also, his parents may not be available when he calls. Another agreed-upon, responsible, and trustworthy adult who communicates well with you both and who would be willing, might also be considered as an option.

Of course, as we will see in a minute, a zero-tolerance approach to alcohol use is especially effective in helping teens to make good, legal choices.

Continuing the Conversation—Step Five

The "Contract for Life" and other social contracts are really just tools that are designed to open lines of communication, and should not be considered to have a beginning and an end. To ensure that the commitment to *ongoing* dialogue is upheld, frequently revisit the issues that affect your teen and your family. How will you manage this? Here are some recommendations: Make a commitment to have frequent conversations about your day-to-day activities; be sure to communicate before events that may pose the risk of destructive decisions; make sure that you both know that the "doors are always open" if there is a problem.

Advice and Testimonials

Here is some communication advice, straight from the mouths of teens and their parents:

- "Be straightforward; don't beat around the bush."
- "I wish more teens would be not as afraid to talk to their parents. You just have to approach them at the right time."
- "When you're not open with your parents, that is when they worry more and that is when they might come out of nowhere and question you. If you're open, it's easier."
- "Some parents refuse to acknowledge that their teens may drink. One did, until her son called for a ride and it saved his life."
- "Help your children by getting to know the parents of their friends, and call a parent of a child having a party to make sure that no alcohol will be served."

And here's what teenagers and parents say about the SADD Contract for Life.

- "[Discussing the contract] was positive because it was something concrete to have which had already been an unwritten understanding before."
- "Of course, they'll do it [drop everything and pick her up if necessary]. They're my parents. They agreed that they would do it under any circumstances."
- "My parents were willing to sign it, because they have seen the effects [of drunk driving]."
- "One father called his daughter for a ride, because he had made a promise not to drink and drive."
- "Kids who show the contract to their parents are saying, 'I'm going to be responsible, but if I'm not, I want your support if I call.'"

On the flip side, teens *want to know* they will be held accountable for their actions. Remember that after Stephanie's mom found out about her relationship with Craig, Stephanie reported a closer mother-daughter relationship, despite the fact that she was forbidden to see him anymore. Letting teens off the hook for bad behavior validates poor choices and allows them control they don't want or need over decisions they are not equipped to make on their own. Parents who adopt a zero-tolerance policy with their teens regarding destructive behaviors are able to positively influence their teens' decision-making.

For example, teens whose parents do not tolerate drinking are significantly more likely than other teens to say they do not drink (66 percent versus 43 percent). The statistics are equally positive when it comes to drug use and sexual behavior. On the other hand, parents of Repeaters tend to have tolerant—or indulgent—attitudes toward destructive behaviors, compared to the attitudes expressed by the parents of Avoiders. It is also interesting to note that punishment is more effective in preventing teens from repeating destructive behaviors when they have a close, open relationship with their parents—more evidence that closing the reality gap reduces the chances that teens will make dangerous choices.

* * *

A further obstacle in truly understanding teens is their propensity to hide the truth. In my 9th-grade discussion groups at summer camp, both boys and girls regularly raise issues of trust when talking about their relationships with their parents.

"Why don't they just trust us?" is a common refrain. A couple of years ago, I started taking an informal straw poll when this question emerged.

"How many of you would say it's important to you that your parents trust you about where you go, whom you're with, and what you're doing?" I would ask. Almost all arms would instantaneously shoot skyward. Then the follow-up: "How many of you lie about where you go, whom you're with, and what you're doing?" Almost two-thirds of the raised hands regularly remained in the up position.

How to explain this disconnect? These 14-year-olds had some answers.

"It's a game," said one.

"They expect us to lie," stated another.

"We're supposed to lie," offered a third.

Few of them sensed a contradiction.

Testing the phenomenon in a more rigorous way during a *Teens Today* study, I sampled nearly a thousand young people across the country via an online questionnaire. The results were startlingly similar. For instance, among high school teens almost all (89 percent) say it's important that they have their parents' trust. Yet significantly less than half (40 percent) say they tell them the whole truth. The "Contract for Life," along with the communication process outlined in "Opening Lifesaving Lines," can be enormously helpful in addressing dishonesty simply because they put the issue of open, honest communication on the table for parents and teens to talk about and to consider in relation to important health and safety issues, such as impaired driving.

Seventeen-year-old Brenda describes her relationship with her parents as "very good," and says she is generally honest, "except when I don't want to get into trouble." Sixteen-year-old Billy tells me he's dishonest, "when I think it will make things easier, such as with parents. Instead of getting my ass rode, I tell them a little white lie."

How are teens getting away with this? Many tell me that they speak in generalities, not answering completely or telling just enough of the truth to make their responses seem reasonable and believable. Remember, even the most engaged and informed parents do well by "drilling down"—asking follow-up questions, asking for specifics, looking for inconsistencies. As we saw in Chapter Eight, questions can help draw a teen into conversation.

Seventeen-year-old Anna, a junior in Houston, tells me, "It's not that I'm not honest with my parents. It's just that I don't always tell them exactly what I am doing. I don't lie, but I like to withhold information, because I am afraid they wouldn't like what I am doing." Sixteen-year-old Phil frames the issue this way: "I lie so I can do what I want to do."

If we make it easy for teens to lie, many times they will, even if they don't really want to. A startling number of teens say that if their parents came right out and asked them direct questions (such as, "Did you drink alcohol at the party?"), they would tell the truth. Remember the teen who said he'd tell his parents he was drinking at parties if they asked (and stop if they asked him to do so)! Too often, though, kids get off the hook by responding to a question like, "Were kids drinking at the party tonight?" without actually answering: "Oh Mom, get real!" for example. As we discussed in Chapter Eight, don't yell and don't threaten. That will just shut down communication. Ask the questions as calmly as you can, and be sure to listen carefully to the answers, reflecting back what you hear: "So, I'm hearing you say that you did not smoke pot, even though some of the other kids were?"

Ignorance self-perpetuates. If we don't know they're drinking with their friends in the basement, how will we know when they're drinking with their friends in the car? And if we don't know—or pretend not to know—they're drinking in the first place, will we pretend not to know that they're using other drugs or having sex?

Eighteen-year-old Robert's parents missed the alcohol and, subsequently, the marijuana and sex that followed. Seventeen-year-old Sam, who describes himself as "a good boy who likes to have a few," says he doesn't talk to his parents about his partying, but, "they know." And 15-year-old Mark's parents simply chose not to notice. Mark told me, "They know. They don't say anything, but they know. We were at the same New Year's Eve party and I got really drunk." As you might expect, his destructive behaviors escalated, as well.

Parents do much to create and sustain the reality gap, and young people often make it hard to close. More than a few teens regularly conduct a fairly sophisticated exercise of concealment, going to great lengths to make sure Mom or Dad doesn't really know what they're up to (remember the Seattle-area teens who used caller ID to throw their parents off the scent). It pays to have a watchful eye—especially around the key Decision Points times.

Effectively parenting teens means knowing what's going on, even when that entails actively pursuing an adolescent you suspect is up to no good. Parents should not be afraid to confront bad behavior, nor to insist on honesty and candor on the part of their teen. Both are important in adult-teen relationships. Kids need to understand that it is not OK to be evasive about what they're really doing. Good communication does not involve nuance. It's about sticking to the spirit of the dialogue, honestly and openly.

When her Mom asks Rachel who she went to the movies with, the answer should include *all* the people who were present that night. While it might be technically accurate to reply, "With Tina," candor would dictate a reply of, "Tina, Matt, and Joseph," regardless of whether Mom disapproves of Matt because she knows he drinks.

Cat and Mouse

As pointed out in Chapter Six, some parents find that the only way to get to the bottom of suspected alcohol or drug use by teens is to test them, or have them tested. Schools, too, often come to the conclusion that testing teens is the best deterrent to the onset of drug use, or the best intervention for a young person already using. President George W. Bush's call for increased federal funding of school drug testing programs in 2004 reignited debate over the efficacy and ethics of such potentially intrusive remedies to keeping kids safe. Most controversial are random tests not tied to a specific event or concern, such as a school dance or for a kid with red eyes who appears dazed and confused.

Random drug testing in schools began with student athletes and a "pay-to-play" philosophy that maintained participation in sports was a privilege extended on the condition of abstinence from substance use. In a practice upheld by the U.S. Supreme Court, this privilege principle quickly migrated to other competitive activities, from cheering to chess. And now, in its latest iteration, drug and alcohol testing is being applied more broadly to anyone simply enrolled in school.

This debate tends to be dominated by those having strongly held convictions about the issue one way or the other. It is anchored on one side by conservatives and on the other by civil libertarians, threading age-old arguments about privacy with newfangled applications of technology—so sensitive in some cases that it can, for example, detect alcohol use from several days before. In the middle of the debate remain a vast number of "undecideds" and the fundamental question of effectiveness. And here the data conflict.

University of Michigan researchers found virtually identical rates of drug use in the schools that have drug testing and the schools that do not (although a study author concedes that one "could design a drug-testing program that could deter drug use").

Meanwhile, a study of Indiana high schools by a Ball State University (BSU) researcher showed significant increases in drug use among students after drug testing was halted by a court order. According to BSU, about 85 percent of high school principals reported an increase of drug or alcohol use since random drug testing was stopped; the number of students suspended or expelled due to illicit substances jumped by 47 percent from 352 in 1999–2000 to 518 in 2000–2001; and about 55 percent of principals indicated they had received information that student-athletes were involved in more incidents of drinking after random drug testing ended.

Supporters of random drug testing may argue both the ethics (if we expect students to study and test them to find out, can't we also expect them to remain drug-free and test them to make sure?) and the outcomes (the Office of National Drug Control Policy cites results of drug testing programs in Oregon and New Jersey as proof-positive that they work). They also note the beneficial role that testing can play by giving young people "an out," blunting negative peer pressure with the threat of being caught. Not enforcement but, rather, reinforcement!

Even so, decisions about embarking on this path are difficult ones, requiring careful considerations. In an effort to inform those considerations, the White House Office of National Drug Control Policy in 2004 published two booklets as resources for those involved in this debate, "What You Need to Know About Drug Testing in Schools" and "What You Need to Know About Starting a Student Drug-Testing Program." In the introduction to the first, ONDCP director John Walters said, "Already, testing has been shown to be extremely effective at reducing drug use in schools and businesses all over the country. As a deterrent, few methods work better or deliver clearer results. Drug testing of airline pilots and school bus drivers, for example, has made our skies and roads safer for travel. Research shows that people who make it through their teenage years without using drugs are much less likely to start using them when they are older. So if testing can help keep kids off drugs and alcohol, if it can help free young minds for learning and allow growing bodies to escape the devastating cycle of dependence or addiction, it will be a valuable and important new tool."

* * *

Experience has taught us that people at the local level often know best how to deal with drug problems in their communities. But to combat this insidious threat, they need good information and the best resources available. The Supreme Court's ruling will help schools meet these needs. This is good news for students, parents, and teachers. And it is good news for America.

Detractors claim that such programs are ineffective as deterrents and fly in the face of civics classes on the appropriate balance between authority and individual rights.

In "Making Sense of Student Drug Testing, Why Educators Are Saying No," the American Civil Liberties Union (ACLU) and the Drug Policy Alliance maintain that not only is testing ineffective in deterring young people from using drugs, but it also can undermine relationships of trust between adults and children. While that could be true, *Teens Today* research suggests that the undermining may already be well underway. While 95 percent of parents say they trust their teens in making decisions about drugs, only 28 percent of teens report being completely honest with parents on the issue. And that says nothing of the often-elaborate steps teens will take to conceal, not just lie about, their drug use. In more than a few families, evasion blends with obfuscation—commencing a high-stakes game of cat and mouse that pits parents against teens and cripples the very trust and truth on which those relationships are based.

What seems to be lost in this debate is the perspective of those with the most at stake: the students themselves. Encouragingly, most teens (70 percent) say they are concerned about drug use. Yet, understandably, many see drug testing as a violation, not so much of civil liberties as much as of trust—at least absent some evidence of wrongdoing. They also seem to doubt its saliency as a deterrent, even when applied by Mom or Dad. In one *Teens Today* study, only 8 percent of students said that testing by parents would be effective in keeping them away from drugs, while more than 90 percent indicated that other parental measures would be effective. These include telling them about the dangers, letting them know you would be disappointed, restricting them from seeing their friends, and punishing them.

The good news in all of this is that young people recognize the dangers of drug use and seem to share adults' urgency in finding answers that will keep them safe. The better news is a solution that's been right in front of us all along: parents who talk regularly with their children about drugs and alcohol—as well as other dangerous, or potentially dangerous, behaviors.

Whatever the outcome of the spirited public discourse over random drug testing in schools, a surer bet may be some not-so-random drug prevention at home. Open communication and clear expectations are already proven deterrents to drug use among teens (just ask your kids if they are using them). So, too, is good-old-fashioned vigilance.

In this regard, it is helpful to remember what Ronald Reagan said about the Soviets: "Trust but verify." And, as we saw in the case of 16-year-old Justin in Chapter Five, taking aggressive action (checking his MySpace page in his case) can keep kids safe. Although such acts are not without their own thorny issues, under the right circumstances they can help to prevent kids from placing themselves in danger.

In what The Associated Press (AP) called, "a victory for rebellious teenagers," the Washington State Supreme Court recently ruled as illegal a mother listening in on her "out-of-control" daughter's phone conversation with an older boy suspected by police of involvement in an assault and robbery. Predictably, the case has rallied both privacy and parental-rights advocates to their respective causes. For the rest of us, it begs the question, "How far should we go to protect our children?" That is more easily asked than answered.

While federal law applies a broader interpretation of rightful parental intervention, Washington and 10 other states require the consent of all parties before a phone conversation can be intercepted or recorded, according to the AP.

No less contentious on the privacy scale are such detection methods as Breathalyzers (like those used by the Phoenix Youth Alcohol

Squad) and property searches, at school or at home. As is often the case when such divides exist, a common-sense middle ground can be found in the voices of those with a dog in the fight. In other words, parents and teens.

Few parents dispute the importance, if not the right, of privacy for teens . . . up to a point. And few teens quibble with parental inquisitiveness in the face of reasonable suspicion . . . unless they have something to hide. Indeed, parents tend to feel that building and maintaining trust with their teen means accepting, even fostering, a degree of independence and privacy. And, as we talked about in Chapter Five, most teens seem to agree that parents who believe their child is involved in, or headed toward, illegal or dangerous behavior have a duty to act—even if doing so entails investigative techniques that at other times would be deemed intrusive and unacceptable.

The communication tools and tips discussed earlier in this chapter offer parents a path to getting and staying involved. So, too, does the Office of National Drug Control Policy (ONDCP), which advises parents to take these now-familiar steps: Make a plan; organize your thoughts; decide what you want to say to your teen: listen; ask your teens for their response to the information you've presented; discuss the shared information; don't get lulled into "looking the other way" because it's easier; make it very clear that you will not tolerate drug or alcohol use; establish clear consequences and reward good behavior; let your teens know that you will be holding them accountable for their actions and that there will be consequences for not following the rules.

One thing is for certain and shows up in every piece of research that I do: Communication counts. Learning how to truly engage our children in ongoing, open, and two-way dialogue about the many issues they face and the many choices they must make helps us to better understand their world and helps them to make decisions with the benefit of knowing what our concerns are and what we expect of them. As we have seen, it is a time-consuming and at times exasperating task.

"I keep trying to talk with her," says the mom of 17-year-old Mandy, a high school junior from Ft. Lauderdale, Florida. "But she says if I don't lighten up, she won't be prepared to make decisions on her own when she is off at college. I don't know what to do."

Don't give up. Keep talking, explaining along the way that because you love and care about her, you have to keep your eye on the ball. It's your job to make sure she stays safe. It's quite likely anyway that Mandy secretly appreciates her mother's concern and, whether she knows it or not, is influenced by her mom's patient and repetitious dialogue.

Ten

Reason to Believe

The white sedan glided just above the surface of the long, straight two-lane road, jumping only slightly over some frost heaves the cold winter had brought to the Minnesota plain. The sun had already set off to my right, but an orange-red afterglow lends an almost mystical touch to the miles of snow-dusted farmland all around us. We were headed south—a town councilman ferrying me from a presentation I'd just given to middle and high school students and their parents. For years, the town had been grappling with the issue of substance use, and a recent survey of teen behavior convinced them they needed to do more to prevent an almost predictable tragedy from occurring.

It had been a remarkable evening: students and parents coming together on a cold, early-April evening to share ideas about what could be done to change kids' and parents' attitudes about alcohol, to prove that you can have a good time without drinking, and to learn how to talk more openly with one another. A large percentage of the senior class had already joined an alliance, each student committing to paper their pledge to remain substance-free. This was a great example of social contracts at work.

Each pledge card included promises from one student, one friend, and one network sponsor. The students pledged to live out their high school years without using alcohol, tobacco, or other illegal drugs. They also pledged to support their peers who abstain and to encourage peers who are struggling with these choices. In turn, a "great friend" pledges his or her support to help the student live chemical-free and to find help for them if they are making poor choices. Finally, an adult network sponsor pledged his or her support, and promised to help the student gain more friends within the network.

These cards were available at tables spread through the gymnasium, alongside copies of the SADD "Contract for Life." They made a powerful pair, and seeing them together validated, I thought, the importance of each.

I met with the seniors before the event began, heard first-hand of their commitment to creating positive change in their small community, and listened to their concerns that parents who provide alcohol are the biggest obstacle they face in moving their town's teen culture in a more positive direction. During the assembly, they sat together in the first few rows of seats, each wearing a brightly colored T-shirt that read, "Empower Today; Ensure Tomorrow," sending a strong message to their peers. At the end of the program, they stood with me in front of the stage in a semicircle that stretched from one side of the gymnasium to the other. Impressive. One-by-one, they spoke, encouraging their classmates and the school's younger students to take the same pledge they had. As 18-year-old Andrew put it, "I mean, why not? Whether we like it or not, we're role models."

The group also sent a firm, concise message to the parents: "Stop allowing parties in your house!" This sentiment is echoed by countless young people I meet as I travel and speak, such as the boy in New York who told me, "They don't even give us the chance to make the right decision."

These are the kids who give us a reason to believe, who see first-hand the results of destructive decisions and the adults who enable them. Much like the students at Wayland High School in 1981, these young people are setting a compelling example for their peers and, likely, for many of the adults in their community as well. They are leaders—even when it means making tough choices, or ones that are different from the ones their friends are making. It's easy to say the all right things and to merely call yourself a leader. What's more difficult is doing what these Minnesota teens are doing: standing up for their friends and classmates, and standing against the adults in the gym who don't have any problem with kids drinking in their homes. As I like to say, leaders lead.

Headed toward my hotel some 30 miles from the school, I recall some of the stories told to me that night. The woman who held on to my hand while she asked me to pray for her niece, who had been hit by a drunk driver and was on a ventilator in a faraway hospital. The young paramedic who told me that the worst night of his career was finding his best friend's daughter lying by the side of the road, her head crushed following an alcohol-related crash. And the student who said to his peers, "I know it seems like a pain to have your parents calling to find out where you are, but it's really a good thing. It's their job."

Most of all though, my mind keeps coming back to that group of seniors, all clad in matching T-shirts, who stood before their parents and schoolmates offering themselves up as role models, putting their ideas into words and their words into action. They were doing the right thing, even when doing the wrong thing—that is to say, *nothing*—seemed so much easier.

Just a week before this event, SADD had unveiled a new poster, which now adorns my outer office in Boston. It shows five teens standing in a school hallway with the words, "True leaders have the confidence to stand alone, the courage to make tough decisions, and the compassion to listen to the needs of others. They do not set out to be leaders, but they become leaders by the quality of their actions and the integrity of their intent."

This could certainly be said of the leaders at this Minnesota school, along with millions of other young leaders in schools and communities across the country.

They shine like the afterglow of the Minnesota sunset. Beautiful. Powerful. Teens on a mission to save lives. They give us a reason to believe that, by working together, young people and the significant adults in their lives—parents, teachers, coaches, aunts, and uncles, next-door neighbors—can find ways to embrace one another in communities of caring that are characterized by open, honest communication and a collective approach to helping young people enjoy their teenage years without turning to alcohol, drugs, and other dangerous behaviors.

For all the kids I meet who share frightening tales of alcohol and drug use, rampant sexual activity, and dangerous driving, I still encounter many who don't. Of course, that begs the question: *What makes the difference?*

Among other things, Decision Factors, parenting styles, and the choice of friends. These all play a role in determining which path our teens take. And, clearly, her Sense of Self—a measure of how she is doing with the developmental tasks of identity, independence, and peer relationships—guides her direction as well.

The popular notion of adolescence as a time of storm and stress has become almost cliché. Yes, it is true that teens live in an increasingly uncertain world. Alcohol, drugs, and sex are all too common components of their lives. Earlier and earlier, our children must find answers to important questions about who they are and what they will become. They do so in the face of disintegrating societal support, counterproductive and confusing messages from adults, and an overwhelming arsenal of corrosive messages unleashed daily in television, movies, and magazines.

In no small way, these factors, along with the current threat of terror for Americans at home and abroad, impinges on our teens' ability to move easily forward toward adulthood. True progress in mastering adolescent developmental tasks requires a nurturing family, school, and community environment, consistent messages about right and wrong, and the coexistence of freedom and safety, along with healthy doses of predictability, self-confidence, and trust. More than ever, teens need adult guidance to understand, temper, articulate, and make operational their thoughts, concerns, and hopes for the future—and to link them to the decisions they are making now. Anything is possible.

Jackie, the high school student we met in Chapter One as she described her hard-partying freshman year, recalls her dramatic turn-around: "Teachers talked about me and how irresponsible I was becoming, and I didn't like that. I knew from that moment that I had to change my lifestyle. I knew it would take a lot of work, but I was ready to put the time and effort into it. I want to be a role model for young adults and children. I want to show them that you can be 'cool' by just being yourself. My mother always told me that you must stand up for what you believe in even if you are standing alone."

The "storm-and-stress" analysis of the modern-day adolescent experience may miss the good news just below the fold: Teens aren't so unhappy after all. Despite what we may see on television or read about in newspapers, plenty of teens not only survive, but also thrive in today's society. The majority of teens, despite demanding schedules of schoolwork, extracurricular activities, and complicated relationships, feel good most of the time. Six-in-ten teens report that they feel happy almost every day, and say they enjoy a positive relationship with their parents. Even more describe themselves as smart, successful, responsible, and confident. That's important for young people navigating the path from childhood to adulthood. And examples of happy, successful, responsible, confident, and contributing teens abound, in every school and every community across the country. They stand as effective counterpoints to the presumption of storm and stress, and as important reminders of the resiliency, industriousness, and optimism of youth.

Maria, a high school student in Illinois is one such teen. "As I matured [I] began to stand up and voice my belief in life and what was important, and that was to make informed decisions. I noticed more and more students, even my close friends, were being drawn in and making some bad choices. I lost some friendships when I stood up for what I believe in, and it became known that I was not a 'partier.' I felt bad losing some of those friends, but stronger each time I could get the message out. I was there to listen and help when some of my lost friends did not make a good choice. It empowered me."

Professor Richard Lerner, the Bergstrom Chair in Applied Developmental Science and the director of the Institute for Applied Research in Youth Development at the Eliot-Pearson Department of Child Development at Tufts University, also offers rebuttal to definitions of this developmental stage that necessarily link it to conflict with parents, mood disruptions, and risky behavior. His book *The Good Teen* shares the results of his study of about 4,000 adolescents that found ample existence among young people of what he calls the "five Cs": competence, confidence, connection, character, and caring. These may coalesce, says Lerner, in a sixth C, contribution—something we will talk about later in this chapter. Lerner says, "All too often, parents have acted as if the only important aspects of their children's behaviors were those that caused problems. Scientists, too, have regarded young people as lacking, as deficient, as unable to behave correctly and in a healthy manner. We characterize them as dangerous to others and as endangered themselves (because of their self-destructive behaviors)."

* * *

Of course, not all young people are immune to the stress and sadness that so often surround them. About half of teens feel stressed at least once a week, and approximately 1 in 10 feels depressed almost every day. There's no question that keeping teens happy and stress-free is a tough job. And there's no doubt that Mom or Dad, along with wonderful mentors, can promote positive feelings and responsible decision-making among teens. In short, young people need, and want, active, involved parents who take the time to sit down and talk with them.

Lately, though, there has been a backlash against the self-esteem movement that many parents and schools have adopted in order to promote positive feelings of self-worth among our kids. The argument goes that we have been so busy trying to make our kids feel good about themselves that we have inadvertently created a generation of self-absorbed, anti-social, narcissistic malcontents incapable of becoming productive members of society.

A recent study by five psychologists rated more than 15,000 college students on a Narcissistic Personality Inventory over a 24-year period. What they found led the study's main author, San Diego State University Professor Jean Twenge, to conclude: "We need to stop endlessly repeating, 'You're special' and having children repeat that back. Kids are self-centered enough already."

Most parents and involved adults want children to develop positive views about their individual capabilities. It comes naturally to us. For years, those of us who work in schools, camps, and other education and youth organizations developed strategies to boost self-esteem in kids. In the meantime, we became afraid to point out weaknesses, permit defeat, or allow failure. (A colleague of mine told me the story of one community that was urging the elimination of the honor roll, fearing that students who didn't make it might resort to suicide. This is a sad commentary on the stress our children fear and on our disservice to them in occasionally failing to prepare them for anything less than perfection.)

Like most everything else involving kids, balance is important. We want to boost them up, give them confidence, and motivate them to succeed. At the same time, we don't want to go so far as to make them blind to their own shortcomings—and their poor choices—and thus hinder self-aware-ness and the work toward self-improvement it can prompt. We best pre-pare our children for their place in society by fostering self-esteem and, perhaps more important, sense-of-self, while allowing for the experiences that build resiliency against the setbacks and disappointments that life holds in store.

Resiliency

Eighteen-year-old Teddy found resiliency in the response of his grand-mother to an automobile crash involving a drunk driver. Teddy says, "Almost all of my life, I have had to deal with the effects of bad choices made by other people. When I was younger, my grandmother and great-grandmother were involved in an accident with a drunk driver. It was horrifying for me." Motivated by the loss of her mother, Teddy's grand-mother became active in MADD (Mothers Against Drunk Driving), and she in turn inspired him to take an active role with SADD in trying to prevent his peers from making costly, even deadly mistakes.

Simply put, resiliency is the ability to bounce back from adversity, to roll with life's punches, learn from them, and move on—better and stronger than before. When parents, teachers, coaches, or counselors work with young people toward building resiliency, we provide them with the mind-set and skill-set they need to avoid becoming undone, overwhelmed, or incapacitated by normative (e.g., the death of a grandparent) and non-normative (e.g., the death of a classmate) stressors in their lives. In short, we prepare them to deal with adversity.

According to researcher Bonnie Bernard in her study, "The Foundations of the Resiliency Framework: From Research to Practice": "Resiliency research documents the characteristics of family, school, and community environments that elicit and foster natural resiliency in children," altering or reversing potential negative outcomes.

Personal resiliency builders include the ability to form positive relationships, to distance oneself from unhealthy people and situations, to give of oneself to others, to have a positive view of one's personal future, to be good at something, to find faith in something greater, to persist in the face of challenges, to use creativity as a means of self-expression, and to make good decisions and exercise control over impulses.

Sixteen-year-old Bryan, whom we met earlier, is a resilient kid. When I first sat with him in a stuffy conference room at a research facility in New York, he described his depression, his father's alcoholism, his struggle to maintain a good relationship with his mother, and his thoughts of suicide. He agreed to seek help and—after five years of counseling, and with the strong involvement and support of his mom, he's finishing school and working at his first job. Bryan found the strength he needed to prevail against the anger, disappointment, and depression that were dragging him into drugs and drinking—and to the edge of suicide.

To help our children become resilient, it is especially important that we establish close ties with them and encourage supportive relationships with others (much as Bryan's mother did); place a high value on their education; set and enforce clear boundaries for behavior; look for opportunities for them to participate in community service; communicate high, but realistic expectations for their success; and convey a true appreciation for their unique talents. Despite the problems our friend Billy from Chapter Two was having with his mom, he went on to win her enthusiasm for his passion for music; she and Billy's father are helping him pursue a musical career.

* * *

Another important step in helping children become resilient is building nurturing relationships with peers. And most all teens need help from parents to successfully accomplish this critical task. Unfortunately, this need tends to come just at a time when parents are prone to give up their efforts at social engineering. While Mom or Dad no longer needs to arrange or supervise play dates, their attention, support, and intervention has never been more important.

Most teens are, of course, loathe to ask for help from parents in making or keeping friends. But, their neediness manifests itself in ways both subtle (anxiety) and overt (anger), and must be tended to with a sensitivity that matches.

How *can* we help our children to make friends? First, by **listening**. Parents can keep their ears tuned to what their teen is saying about their friends, their social plans, and their days at school. They can also keep grilling to a minimum, instead asking open-ended questions (such as ones that begin with, "Tell me about . . . ") that elicit dialogue as opposed to perfunctory one-word answers. Teens are then more likely to talk about their progress with peers.

Trey, who we first met in Chapter Two, had friends, but shied away from them because he didn't want to do what they were doing, namely drinking. And as he became more isolated, he became more depressed and less functional. His discourse on his trouble with his peers began innocuously enough with a simple, open-ended question from his mom: "What's up with the kids at school?" She could then guide him through his various reactions and emotions as to what he was encountering in his dorm and strategize with him to find solutions.

Second, by **watching**. Conflict, isolation, even physical manifestations of violence, mark many a child's social status and provide clues as to when parental intervention, such as notifying school officials about bullying or hazing, is most appropriate and most needed.

Many teens actually benefit from a parent willing to role-play responses to difficult social dilemmas. For example, it is difficult for teens to know what to do when a friend is picking on someone else. *Do I say something and risk making my friend mad at me, or do I just go along even though I know it's wrong?* Giving kids the words and the skills to use by modeling them helps them to respond appropriately.

And, lastly, by **waiting**. Teens will generally discuss the issue of peer relationships if they are allowed to do it on their own schedule and in their own way. Mom and Dad need to resist the temptation to jump in too soon. Look for opportunities to share a conversation, not deliver a lecture, with your teen. Doing so affords you the best chance to be supportive and helpful.

We can also guide our children by sharing our own adolescent struggles with peer assimilation. Parents can demonstrate to teens that they are not alone, and that there is a fluidity to the process of establishing meaningful relationships. Seeing where their parents are now, and the winding path they likely took to get there, can balance a teen's natural "short-sightedness" with a longer-term view of human socialization. Many parents remember the anxiety they felt on the first day at a new school, for example. *Will I make friends?* Or they may recall the nervousness that accompanies lunchtime: *Who will I sit with?* And, most assuredly, many can still feel the sting of being left out—*How come she didn't invite me to the sleepover?* Letting your teen in on your own discomfort is, well, comforting. It makes him feel more normal and also shrinks the reality gap by making clear that much of what he is experiencing, you have experienced, too.

Risk and Protective Factors

For anyone concerned about youth behavior surrounding such things as alcohol and drugs, it is logical to ask, "Who's at risk?" and, just as important, "Who's not?" According to researchers and prevention specialists, substance abuse, and the various social problems that often accompany it, has been associated with a series of risk and protective factors that answer those very questions.

According to SADD, risk factors are those that make a young person vulnerable to health and social problems. Researchers have found that the more risk factors a young person experiences, the more likely it is that she will experience substance abuse and related problems in adolescence and young adulthood. Like the Decision Factors discussed earlier, risk factors help us—parents and professionals—more accurately gauge which young people are most vulnerable.

Protective factors, on the other hand, offer great insights (and validation of much of what I have been discussing in this book) into how we can keep kids from being vulnerable in the first place. In other words, protective factors (also known as resilience factors) help safeguard youth from substance abuse and related problems, even if a young person is exposed to a substantial number of risk factors. Protective factors appear to balance and buffer the negative impact of existing risk factors. For example, even though Tommy may have poor impulse control and low self-esteem (risk factors), his parents provide a lot of structure, support, and communication about expectations and consequences (protective factors), thus "canceling out," in effect, the risk factors.

Both risk and protective factors exist at every level at which a person interacts with others and the surrounding world. Human interactions have been organized by researchers into six different life or activity domains and include biological, psychological/behavioral, and social/environmental characteristics, such as family history of substance use, depression or diagnosed mental health disorder, or living in an area where substance abuse and violence are tolerated and/or pervasive. The six domains are individual, peer, family, school, community, and society/environment.

Individual risk factors include a lack of impulse control (an inability to effectively manage feelings or actions), depression, low self-esteem, and anti-social behavior, while individual protective factors include good social skills, self-discipline, and the ability to form close, supportive relationships.

Peer risk factors include poor social skills and a peer group that is older or uses drugs, while peer protective factors include having friends who are involved in positive activities, such as sports or acting. This is consistent with the positive risk-taking research I discussed earlier.

On the family front, risk is related to a history of substance abuse or parents who simply allow their teens to drink or use drugs. On the flip side, protective family factors, not surprisingly, include consistent structure and open communication.

When it comes to school, teens are at risk when there are no clear behavior policies in place, when low expectations are placed on students, and when communication with parents is rare. Protective factors include a strong "do-not-use" message and procedures for referring at-risk students for professional help.

In the community, risk factors may be scarce resources for alternative activities, such as recreation or sports, a lack of involvement by adults, or a permissive approach to teen substance use. When community members collaborate to provide meaningful, fun, and safe activities for youth (such as those promoted in the Boston Market "Time for Your School" program), and when they support and enforce laws pertaining to alcohol and other drug use, teens are more likely to stay away from trouble.

Finally, as we saw in Chapter Six, the media messages young people see in our society can have a profoundly negative effect on the behaviors they choose. When those messages are filtered or limited, such as through policies that do not allow alcohol billboard advertising within 500 yards of a school, for example, teens are less likely to be at risk.

Here is what the domains and risk and protective factors look like all together.

Domain	Risk Factors	Protective Factors
Individual	Lack of impulse control; depressed; low self-esteem; rebellious, anti-social behavior	Strong social skills; enthusiastic attitude; self-disciplined; resilient temperament; ability to establish positive relationships/close bonds
Peer	Very few friends; friends who use drugs; friends who are much older	Friends are in SADD chapter; friends are involved with school activities (sports, music, art, theater, etc.); friends do not use drugs
Family	Family history of substance abuse or violence; parents tolerate teen substance use; parents lack clear expectations; family conflict; neglect	Parents provide consistent structure; open communication in family; positive bonding between family members
School	No clear behavior policy in school; low expectations of students; no opportunities for parent networking	Firm "No Use" policy enforced; strong, active SADD chapter; student assistance and referral systems in place
Community	Lack of youth recreation activities; lack of adult involvement or interest in youth; tolerance of teen substance use	Strong collaboration among parents, law enforcement, public health services, and schools; enforcement of purchasing ages for alcohol and tobacco; opportunities for youth participation in community activities
Society/ Environment	Alcohol use seen on TV commercials, shows, and movies aimed at teens; strong media influences to smoke cigarettes and use alcohol; alcohol-sponsored community events	No alcohol billboards within 500 yards of school facilities; strong impaired driving laws enforced; graduated licensing laws in place

As you can see, the equation is simple: Risk factors can increase a person's chances for substance abuse, while protective factors can reduce the risk. It is important to note, however, that most individuals at risk for drug abuse do not start using drugs or become addicted. Take 18-year-old Heather, a high school senior from New York. Heather's mom has a history of drug and alcohol abuse, but she has chosen another path. "I have had a life experience with the harm of a lifestyle influenced by drugs," she says. "This has given me the pride and great feeling to work toward keeping others drug-free and safe."

Seventeen-year-old Elizabeth, another high school senior, tells a similar story. "Vibrant, confident, beautiful, and hope-filled are adjectives I think of to describe my sister after her graduation from college," she says. "However, nearly six years later she returned to us looking gaunt, frail, tearful, and broken. I was only nine years old, but will never forget the impact of that awful change. A priority issue in my life is the need to address substance abuse and its powerful and adverse effects on our society." Elizabeth turned from crisis to action, reaching out in high school to educate her peers, work with law enforcement to stage a "mock car crash" before prom, and lobby Congress to restrict alcohol-related television commercials during certain times of day.

Also, much as we saw with positive risks in Chapter Four or important transitions (rites of passage) in Chapter Seven, what may be a true risk factor for one person—such as hanging out with older kids—may not be for another. Thus, we must always consider which risk and protective factors exist in our child's life, and if and how they appear to be influencing his choices. This is yet another reason why closing the reality gap is so important and why opening channels of communication can be such an effective deterrent to alcohol and drug use, risky sexual behavior, and dangerous driving, as well as anti-social behavior such as bullying and violence, or even suicide.

It is also important to point out that risk and protective factors can affect different children at different stages of their lives. At each stage, risks occur that can be changed through prevention or intervention. Early childhood risks, such as aggressive behavior, can be changed or prevented with family, school, and community interventions that focus on helping children develop appropriate, positive behaviors, including communication skills for interacting with other children and adults, respect for rules, and patience. If not addressed, negative behaviors can lead to more risks, such as academic failure and social difficulties, which put children at further risk for later drug abuse.

Obviously, there is a great deal of interrelatedness when it comes to behaviors and outcomes. One problem can easily lead to another. If Sandy has academic difficulties and problems making friends that prompt her to start smoking marijuana, for example, she may, in turn, experience more difficulty with school and damage her relationship with her parents, which might cause the drug use to accelerate or lead to other types of acting out, such as sexual promiscuity.

Prevention programs utilizing the paradigm of risk and protection focus on intervening early in a child's development to strengthen protective factors *before* problem behaviors develop, so early identification of them is important. A goal of prevention is to change the balance between risk and protective factors so that protective factors outweigh risk factors.

This body of research, along with the work on Decision Points, Decision Factors, positive risk-taking, Sense of Self, rites of passage, and mentoring all paint a positive picture of our ability—individually and collectively—to guide our teens toward safe, healthy behaviors that make their appropriate development, success, and happiness more likely. When we know what the dangers are, when they are most prevalent, what to look for, and how to help our kids meet their goals, we can live up to our potential as influential forces in their lives.

Empowered

We can really help our children—no matter what behaviors we fear they may be at risk for—by encouraging them to feel competent, connected, and capable of giving back to the people and places around them. In other words, empowered.

When I speak to young people in schools, I generally surprise them by spending little time on the dangers of alcohol and drug use or some of the other disturbing behaviors discussed throughout this book. Instead, I seek to empower them by explaining that they are extremely influential in their own lives, in their families, in their schools, and in their communities. That they have the power to make good things happen, and to help people.

This was also my message at a 2006 commencement address I delivered to the senior class at Tabor Academy in Marion, Massachusetts. I told the assembled students, "Young people have taught me the power of ideas and of action. That great good can come from the unbelievably bad. And that what is most important is not just the *good* decisions we make, but rather the additive impact of those decisions . . . on ourselves, our families, our friends, our schools, and our communities. In other words, it's not just about choices, but about change." Then I shared with them some words of *Boston Globe* columnist Brian McGrory, excerpted from a commencement speech of his own, called "Moving On, Forever Tied":

> "In ten years, twenty years, maybe sooner, maybe later, some of your teachers or the kids you hang out with are going to ask, 'Hey, whatever happened to Johnny or Jennifer?' Start thinking today what you want that answer to be.
>
> "I think you'll want them to say, 'I hear Johnny or Jennifer is a really great father or mother or the best electrician in town or a terrific stockbroker or someone who took wonderful care of their ailing mother.' I think you'll want that answer to be that he or she turned out to be one hell of a nice human being."

Brian was talking about building a legacy. It is important to remind young people that the choices they make today have an impact not only on their own lives but also on the people around them: parents, friends, siblings, teachers, coaches, and other caring adults. And, just as important, these choices become part of a legacy they'll be leaving behind.

Following on the exploding popularity of the LIVESTRONG bracelets developed by the Lance Armstrong Foundation, and inspired by his heroic fight against cancer, SADD, like many other organizations and causes, came up with its own version of the trendy wristwear. Ours are red (SADD's colors are red and black) and say, EMPOWERED. They come with a small, black card, with red and white writing. SADD students came up with a definition . . . and a description.

EM–POWER–ED: having the confidence to make the right choices in everyday life while positively influencing others

The other side of the card reads:

What is empowered? It's a word that doesn't have just one meaning. It's a word that means something different to everyone, but mainly it means having the ability to overcome. To today's youth, it means having the confidence to deal with life's everyday challenges, good and bad, and to prevail. As teenagers, we have many choices; we know we have the power to make the right ones. Being empowered, we can make a difference wherever we are in whatever we do. The power of you . . . changing many. Be empowered.

I ask teens, "What do you want your legacy to be? What do you want to be remembered for? Drinking, using drugs, bullying, fighting? Or something more positive, such as standing up to community norms that suggest everybody is drinking, using drugs, driving dangerously, or having sex? Do you want to be remembered for being self-centered or for being generous? Giving to yourself or giving of yourself to others?"

Because of their tendency to live in the moment, young people often fail to look at the bigger picture. This leaves them at risk for making decisions of which they will only later understand the consequences. And then it may be too late. When we can prompt teens to think ahead, and to think of others, we stand a better chance of igniting their natural proclivity to want to help and to want to do good things.

Doing good is clearly what high school senior Barrick had in mind when he offered to help out local children during the holidays.

"I volunteered at the mall where I worked at a store that was set up for young children to come and buy gifts for their parents," he says. "I was there to help the children budget their money, and I also wrapped the gifts for them. We also had large stockings that we made and in them we put toys and other items for needy kids and we distributed them out in the community." Barrick says he really enjoyed the experience of working with the younger children.

The desire on the part of young people to give something back is evidenced by an explosion of teen participation in community-service programs—which today more often than not take the form of "service-learning" opportunities. Service-learning differs from traditional community service in that it combines service to a community (let's say rebuilding schools and libraries after a hurricane) with a true learning component (perhaps lessons on climate conditions that tend to spawn the hurricanes).

The National Service-Learning Clearinghouse reports a rapid rise in such programs throughout communities, K-12 institutions, and colleges and universities, and defines the concept this way: "Service-learning combines service objectives with learning objectives with the intent that the activity changes both the recipient and the provider of the service. This is accomplished by combining service tasks with structured opportunities that link the task to self-reflection, self-discovery, and the acquisition and comprehension of values, skills, and knowledge content."

That so many of today's teenagers are drawn to the service-learning model of contributing to society while working toward self-improvement speaks volumes about their capacity for positive risk-taking and decision-making. Millions of young Americans participate in the National Youth Service Day every year, and, over the past decade, some 13 million people in communities nationwide have become involved. Significantly, one of the goals of National Youth Service Day is to promote young people as resources, rather than as problems, in their communities.

There is no greater hallmark of good news about our children than in the activism so many of them readily embrace and through which they are contributing mightily to improving the fabric of our society and other societies, as well. From Katrina relief in New Orleans to inner-city cleanups in Philadelphia, and from tending to the poor in South Africa, or South America, to building community centers in Mexico, our young people are speaking loudly about their commitment to making positive contributions in the world.

All the way back in 1981, SADD was started—remember, by *high school students!*—on the premise that "if the problem is ours, the solution is ours." And so it continues today.

In a special edition of *Newsweek*, a number of years back, about real teens in today's world, 17-year-old Brad wrote of the misperceptions that adults have about the direction teens are headed, stating that, "Against all odds, I'm just fine." Brad humorously rebutted a presumption of alcohol and drug addiction, Satan worshipping, unwanted pregnancies, and crime, poignantly reminding us of all that is right about our children and teens.

Brad wrote, "Actually, I'm doing quite well. I haven't fathered any children, I've never worshipped Satan, and I don't have a police record. I can even find Canada on a map, along with its capital, Ottawa. Call me a rebel, but I've stayed in school, and (can it be true?) I enjoy it. I'm looking forward to college and to becoming a productive member of society. I may not be America's stereotypical teen, but that only goes to show that there is something wrong with our society's preconceived image of today's teenager."

While we are right to focus on the challenges and problems young people face and to put in place strategies to inform and protect them, we are obligated, at the same time, to recognize and celebrate the wonderful children they are and the wonderful adults they are working hard to become.

Michelle, a high school student from Ohio, is another terrific example of a young person trying to make a difference, despite what some people think about kids. She says, "In this day and age, you hear the town elders talk about the younger generations making terrible decisions and how things aren't like they used to be. As I've learned throughout my high school career, making the right choices isn't always easy, but it's always right. Standing up to peer pressure, especially from those you thought were your friends, is tough and challenging, but it's not impossible . . . I did it."

In our struggle to be better parents—to keep our kids safe, alive, and moving toward independence, we must never lose sight of teens like Michelle, Brad, and Barrick, nor of the magic they create in our lives, homes, schools, and communities. Each and every day.

Lessons Learned

I have often suggested that understanding adolescence bears a resemblance to what I imagine it would be like to nail Jell-O to a wall—or at least the difficulty of achieving such a thing. Just when you think you've got it all figured out—surprise! The Jell-O jiggles away and the teen changes.

However similar today's teens might be to yesterday's, it is clear that the world in which we are all living changes much more frequently and sometimes more dramatically than the relatively benign era in which we were raised 20, 30, or 40 years ago. The choices that lie ahead of our kids are more numerous and, in some ways, of greater importance, because some choices, like smoking marijuana or having unprotected sex, are physically more dangerous and also because the stakes are higher: Laws in many states have been strengthened. And, in many communities, they are more likely than in the past to be enforced!

Yet, because of their new ability to think abstractly, teens are compelled to consider those choices and ultimately make decisions that will define their place in the world. Our assignment ("should we choose to accept it") is to help them.

Long discussed and debated, the period of adolescence is one of transition from childhood to adulthood, and has been described by parents in many ways: interesting, dreadful, tough, incredible! Many of us still seem to be looking for the keys to unlock the mysteries (or perhaps the vagaries) of this fascinating time in an increasingly unpredictable and treacherous world.

At camp, I co-host a Sunday-night variety show modeled after *The Tonight Show* on NBC and *The Late Show* on CBS. Borrowing from David Letterman, part of my weekly shtick is to share a "Top Ten" list of something current in camp life, such as "The Top Ten Ways to Tell It's Parents Weekend" ("The 'Turn Around Here' signs are changed to 'Welcome, Please Come In'") or "The Top Ten Most Requested Changes at Camper Council" ("Personal golf carts for every camper!").

In that spirit, I have attempted to construct a Top Ten list for raising teens. Its contents reflect not research or professional practice, but rather some simple grains of truth I have gleaned from all these years spending time with other people's children. Some of the same ideas and threads of understanding are presented more thoroughly in earlier chapters, but this list is more personal—I refer to it myself from time to time.

In any event, I hope that you will find in them some kernels of common sense that will help you as you work to raise, love, and protect your teen.

There is no question that parenting teens is a risky business, especially emotionally. Emotional risk sort of goes with the turf, because our love, concern, and aspirations for our kids are so high. Through instruction or instinct, adults have a natural tendency to pull away from the emotional connections they used to share with their child. While doing so may save considerable consternation and heartache, it also tends to steal both self-discovery and the pure enjoyment of maintaining close, caring relationships with our children.

In a recent conversation with my sister-in-law, she told me about a friend's frustration that most of the parenting books she has

Countdown—My Top Ten Tips for Raising Teens

#10 You know more than you think you do (and they know less).

#9 Everybody has a role to play.

#8 You can learn a lot by listening . . . or nothing at all.

#7 Pay attention.

#6 Don't take yourself too seriously.

#5 The imaginary audience is Standing Room Only.

#4 Rules were made to be broken.

#3 Where there's smoke, there's (usually) fire.

#2 Mental health is a fleeting thing.

#1 Take risks.

looked through do not offer exact dialogue for her to use with her daughter.

"Why can't they say, 'If she says that, say this'?" In truth, imparting exact dialogue that perfectly fits each family, each situation, and each interaction would be an impossible task—there are simply too many interlocking issues and factors. But, that having been said, there are many rules-of-thumb to help us, some of which I've listed in this chapter, many more of which are contained throughout the pages of this book.

Most important, when all is said and done, it is our love and genuine concerns for our children that will best guide us.

When in doubt, leave it out.
Communication is so important to all healthy relationships. But it sure can be difficult at times. Remember that it is important to

- communicate carefully (verbally, nonverbally, and physically)
- err on the side of brevity
- forgo sarcasm
- seek honest dialogue
- share your own perspective
- respect views and feelings that are different from your own

ACKNOWLEDGMENTS

When I began working on this book more than four years ago I underestimated the degree of difficulty in navigating the circuitous—and lengthy—path to publication. Translating my experience as a "writer" into the art form of being an "author" proved to be a big, and at times terrifying, task. Often, I would seek solace in the acknowledgment section of books already published, either those in my office or others I would visit the bookstore to read. Invariably, they contained references to the help and support of family and friends who nurtured the author through "the dark times," who boosted the author's spirits when he thought he would never finish, or who provided that little bit of insight or humor that enabled her to fight through the writer's block and continue apace. Misery loves company.

Now it's my turn to acknowledge those who have helped me, though surely they are too many to name. Nevertheless, I offer heartfelt thanks to my family, friends, colleagues, and other passersby for their words of encouragement and genuine interest in the topics I feel so passionately about. In particular, I want to thank my friend, novelist John Urban, whose love of fiction has taken him on a journey instructive to mine. He unfailingly preached patience, determination, and, most important, optimism.

Also, I want to thank my cousin Mike and my friends Alison and Larry for loaning me their quite-perfect writing retreats. Escaping the hectic pace of my life (not to mention the cold) in Boston allowed me to clear my head and focus on the people who matter most, the children.

My good buddy (and accountant) Jim Thompson also deserves huge credit for keeping the books straight and keeping me out of jail—although, in truth, he was doing that long before I became consumed with writing *Reality Gap*.

Many thanks to my agent-extraordinaire, Nancy Stauffer Cahoon, who signed on to this project mid-stride and offered so much support and expertise it would be difficult to quantify here. Also, I want to thank my editor, Lela Nargi, for her professionalism and perseverance. She pushed me to do better and work harder—even sending me off to tackle another round of rewrites one early June morning with some wise Italian counsel: "La forza!" I am grateful as well to Marlene Conelly who patiently proof-reads almost everything I write.

Of course, you wouldn't be reading this book at all were it not for the good folks at Union Square Press/Sterling Publishing who believed in the concept and worked diligently to bring it to life. In particular, I want to thank Philip Turner and Iris Blasi. Kudos as well to Christine Zikas who also did a masterful job making edits to the manuscript.

I also owe a debt of gratitude to SADD's executive director, Penny Wells, to our partners at Liberty Mutual Group, and to the talented researchers and analysts at Guideline, especially Peter Hooper, Kelly Basile, and Seth Hardy. Each contributed greatly to the backbone of this book: the data.

Most important are the young people who have graciously allowed me to participate in their lives or who bravely agreed to take part in my research. I am enormously grateful to each and every one of them. Similarly, I am thankful for the many families who have generously wel-comed me into their homes for meals, holidays, birthdays, graduations, and other special events. My time with them and their children fuels my interest in helping young people make good decisions and occupies my many sleepless nights with a flood of new ideas for research, education, and prevention.

April 2008
Boston, Massachusetts

RESOURCES

American Social Health Association
www.iwannaknow.org
The American Social Health Association site iwannaknow.org answers questions about teen sexual health and sexually transmitted diseases.

Centers for Disease Control and Prevention
www.cdc.gov
The Centers for Disease Control and Prevention, as the sentinel for the health of people in the United States and throughout the world, strives to protect people's health and safety, provide reliable health information, and improve health through strong partnerships.

Community Anti-Drug Coalitions of America (CADCA)
www.cadca.org
CADCA's mission is to strengthen the capacity of community coalitions to create and maintain safe, healthy, and drug-free communities. CADCA works on behalf of over 5,000 community coalitions from across the country to realize its vision.

Governors Highway Safety Association (GHSA)
www.ghsa.org
GHSA is the states' voice on highway safety. The nonprofit association represents state and territorial highway safety offices. Its members implement programs that address the behavior of motor vehicle drivers and road users. Areas of focus include occupant protection, impaired driving, speed and aggressive driving, motorcycle safety, pedestrian and bicycle safety, as well as highway safety issues relating to mature and younger drivers, drowsy driving and distracted driving. In addition to the behavioral aspects

of driving, GHSA also represents other aspects of highway safety, such as traffic records and training.

i-SAFE

www.isafe.org

Founded in 1998, i-SAFE Inc. is a leader in Internet safety education. Available in all 50 states, Washington, D.C., and Department of Defense schools located across the world, i-SAFE is a nonprofit foundation whose mission is to educate and empower youth to make their Internet experiences safe and responsible. The goal is to educate students about how to avoid dangerous, inappropriate, or unlawful online behavior. i-SAFE accomplishes this through dynamic K-12 curriculum and community outreach programs to parents, law enforcement, and community leaders.

Leadership to Keep Children Alcohol Free

www.alcoholfreechildren.org

Leadership to Keep Children Alcohol Free, a unique coalition of Governors' spouses, federal agencies, and public and private organizations, is an initiative to prevent the use of alcohol by children ages 9 to 15. It is the only national effort that focuses on alcohol use in this age group.

Liberty Mutual Group

www.libertymutualinsurance.com

Liberty Mutual offers *The Road Ahead: Stay Safe at the Wheel*. The *Road Ahead* kit includes a powerful video of teens discussing their driving attitudes and behaviors before and after viewing the HBO Family documentary *Smashed: Toxic Tales of Teens and Alcohol*, a family discussion guide and a family safe-driving pledge. For your free copy, call toll-free 1-800-4-LIBERTY, contact your local Liberty Mutual office, or visit Liberty Mutual's Web site.

National Campaign to Prevent Teen Pregnancy

www.teenpregnancy.org

The mission of the National Campaign is to promote values, behavior, and policies that reduce both teen pregnancy and unwanted pregnancy among young adults.

National Campaign to Stop Bullying

www.stopbullyingnow.hrsa.gov/index.asp

The US Department of Health and Human Services, Health Resource and Services Administration, sponsors this site offering information about bullying and tips to reduce and prevent it.

National Highway Traffic Safety Administration (NHTSA)

www.nhtsa.dot.gov

NHTSA's mission is to save lives, prevent injuries, and reduce economic costs due to road traffic crashes, through education, research, safety standards, and enforcement activity.

National Institute on Drug Abuse

www.nida.nih.gov

The National Institute on Drug Abuse (NIDA) is a federal agency responsible for bringing the power of science to bear on drug abuse and addiction. NIDA's Web site contains special sections for parents and educators, and for teens.

National Organizations for Youth Safety (NOYS)

www.noys.org

NOYS is a collaborative network of national organizations and federal agencies that serve youth and focus on youth safety and health. Through this network, NOYS influences more than 80 million young people ages 5 to 24 and adult advisors and supervisors. Their mission is to promote youth empowerment and leadership and build partnerships that will save lives, prevent injuries, and promote safe and healthy lifestyles among all youth.

National Youth Violence Prevention Campaign

www.violencepreventionweek.org

The National Association of Students Against Violence (SAVE) and GuidanceChannel.com, a brand of Sunburst Visual Media, are founding partners of the National Youth Violence Prevention Campaign. The goal of this campaign is to raise awareness and to educate students, teachers, school administrators, counselors, school resource officers, school staff, parents, and the public on effective ways to prevent or reduce youth violence.

NoStigma.Org

www.nostigma.org

Nostigma.org is dedicated to battling the stigma, shame, and myths surrounding mental disorders that prevent so many people from getting the help they need.

NotMyKid.Org

www.notmykid.org

Notmykid.org is dedicated to facilitating improved understanding about youth behavioral health issues including suicide, drug abuse, eating disorders, and depression.

SADD (Students Against Destructive Decisions)

www.sadd.org

SADD (Students Against Destructive Decisions) is the nation's preeminent peer-to-peer youth education, prevention, and activism organization, with thousands of chapters in middle schools, high schools, and colleges. With a mission of promoting positive decision-making and addressing attitudes that are harmful to young people, SADD sponsors programs that address issues such as underage drinking, other drug use, impaired driving, and teen violence and suicide.

StopAlcoholAbuse.Gov

www.stopalcoholabuse.gov

Stopalcoholabuse.gov is a comprehensive portal of federal resources for information about underage drinking and ideas for combating this issue. People interested in underage drinking prevention—including parents, educators, community-based organizations, and youth—will find a wealth of valuable information here.

White House Office of National Drug Control Policy (ONDCP)

www.whitehousedrugpolicy.gov

www.theantidrug.com (for parents)

www.freevibe.com (for teens)

The White House Office of National Drug Control Policy (ONDCP), a component of the Executive Office of the President, was established by the Anti-Drug Abuse Act of 1988. The principal purpose of ONDCP is to establish policies, priorities, and objectives for the nation's drug control program. The goals of the program are to reduce illicit drug use, manufacturing, and trafficking, drug-related crime and violence, and drug-related health consequences. To achieve these goals, the Director of ONDCP is charged with producing the National Drug Control Strategy. The Strategy directs the nation's anti-drug efforts and establishes a program, a budget, and guidelines for cooperation among federal, state, and local entities.

Youth Service America (YSA)

www.ysa.org

YSA is a resource center that partners with thousands of organizations committed to increasing the quality and quantity of volunteer opportunities for young people, ages 5–25, to serve locally, nationally, and globally. Founded in 1986, YSA's mission is to expand the impact of the youth service movement with communities, schools, corporations, and governments. YSA envisions a global culture of engaged youth who are committed to a lifetime of service, learning, leadership, and achievement.

INDEX

Abstinence programs, 38, 273–79
Acker, Dana, 90
Addiction. *See* Drug dependency/addiction; Substance abuse
Adolescence. *See also* Teen culture
  choices & personal goals, 129–31
  communicating during, 155–61
  consequences & outcomes, 131–33
  decision points, 140–45
  decision-making, 134–36
  developing Sense of Self in, 124–26
  emotional & cognitive development, 82–85, 127–29, 136–40
  "Five C's" of, 278
  gender differences, 120–24
  learning independence, 110–15
  lessons learned about, 293–95
  mentoring relationships in, 207–13
  the peer group in, 114–20
  rites of passage in, 213–18
  sexual identity formation in, 93, 107–10, 120, 125
  "storm-and-stress" of, 276–79
  "Three C's" of, 131–33
  what parents can do during, 126
Adults. *See also* Parents
  building a coalition of, 167
  destructive examples from, 204–06
  double standards, 206
  facilitating underage drinking, 78–82
  as mentors, 207–13
  role in creating protective factors, 283–87
  role in creating teen resiliency, 279–82
  role in empowering teens, 283–87
  as role models, 5–7, 131–33, 201
  teen abstinence programs and, 273–79
  unspoken messages, 202–03
Advertising, media, 183–91

Aggression/aggressive behavior
  bullying and hazing, 55–58, 65–66
  gender differences, 56, 121
  media impact on, 186, 191
  prevention & intervention, 286–87
  suicide and, 69–70
  while driving, 92, 299
AIDS/HIV, 12
Albanese, Matthew, 190
Alcohol. *See also* Substance abuse; Underage drinking
  accessibility of, 4, 26–28
  advertising, 189–91
  binge drinking, 28, 30, 81, 138, 197
  categories of behavior toward, 21–26
  combined with drugs, 36–37, 89
  how parents can talk about, 231–33
  impaired driving behaviors and, 48–53
  MADD and, 279
  media impact on, 7–8, 183–87
  sending the wrong message about, 149–50
  teen-parent relationships and, 83–84
  testing as a deterrent, 265–71
  underestimating risks of, 78–82
  warning signs, 167–70
Alcoholism, 11–12, 82–83
Alfred University, 62
Alliance for Consumer Education, 90
Alternative aggressions, 56
American Academy of Pediatrics, 69, 194, 240
American Civil Liberties Union (ACLU), 268
American Foundation for Suicide Prevention, 71
American Medical Association (AMA), 189
American Pie (movie), 195
American Psychiatric Association, 88
American Social Health Association, 299

America's Promise Alliance, 209
Anti-Drug Abuse act of 1988, 303
The Arizona Republic, 75
Armstrong, Lance, 289
Arnold, Kevin (television character), 107
The Associated Press, 98, 269
Athletes/athletic performance. *See*
   Sports/athletes
Attention deficit disorder, 89
Avoider behaviors, 21–26, 131, 143,
   150–52, 213, 248, 262

Ball State University, 266
Baumrind, Diana, 245
Bernard, Bonnie, 280
"Big Brothers Big Sisters," 207
Binge drinking, 28, 30, 81, 138, 197
Birth control. *See* Teen pregnancy
Blake, Henry, 224
Blodgett, Jonathan W., 198
Blood-alcohol content (BAC), 48, 76, 85,
   269
Boston Globe, 188
The Boston Herald, 36
Boston Market (restaurant), 34, 284
Boundaries
   adult role in setting, 65, 173
   "bail-out" strategy for creating, 147
   communicating & enforcing, 131–32,
      222–24, 238, 280–81
   media assault on, 191–92
   safety & security of, 110–12, 178
Brain structure. *See also* Maturity and
   emotional development
   decision-making and, 136–40
   gender differences, 120–21
   media impact on, 186
Breathalyzer. *See* Blood-alcohol content
   (BAC)
Brizendine, Louann, 121
Brown, H. Jackson, Jr., 202
Brown, Jane D., 192
Bullying and hazing

alcohol and, 82
epidemic of, 54–56
how parents can talk about, 241–44
increasing use of, 30
myths about, 58–60, 63–64
parental awareness of, 2–3
in today's teen culture, 10
what parents can do about, 57–58,
   65–66
Burns, Scott, 52
Buscaglia, Leo, xii
Bush, George W., 31, 266
Bush, Laura, 123

Cancer, 89, 289
Cape Cod Sea Camps, xiii–xiv
Carnegie Council on Adolescent
   Development, 113
CASA. *See* National Center on Addiction
   and Substance Abuse (CASA)
Center for Science in the Public Interest,
   31, 190
Center on Alcohol Marketing and Youth,
   189
Centers for Disease Control and
   Prevention (CDC), 29, 299
Century Council, 82
"Change agents," SADD students as, ix
Child molestation, 98
Child Trends, 207–08
"Club drugs," 4, 26, 37, 90, 171, 212. *See
   also* Substance abuse
Cocaine. *See* "Hard" drugs; Substance
   abuse
Code of conduct. *See* Rules of conduct
Cognitive development. *See also* Maturity
   and emotional development
   alcohol and, 82–83
   decision-making and, 136
   impact of media messages on, 183–87
   marijuana use and, 88–89
Cognitive dissonance, 28–30
Collins, Rebecca, 192

Columbia University, 27, 127, 233

Commitment, contraception, consequences (the "Three C's"), 192

Communications
advice from teens on, 181, 261–65
"bail-out" strategy for, 147
control-freedom continuum and, 224–26
"conversation clogging," 147–49
creating trust, 247–49
destructive messages, 204–05
double standards, 206
"early and often," 77, 141, 173–74, 228, 237–38
effectiveness of parent-child, 5–6
essential elements of, 248
family time, 16–18, 164–66
family tips for, 227–31
how to talk about alcohol, 231–33
how to talk about bullying & hazing, 241–44
how to talk about driving, 238–39
how to talk about drugs, 233–35
how to talk about sex, 235–38
how to talk about suicide, 239–41
lessons learned about, 293–95
"Opening Lifesaving Lines" steps, 252–61
parenting styles of, 245–47
risk & protective factors, 283–87
in today's teen culture, 12–16, 155–59
understanding teen behavior for, 21
unspoken, nonverbal, 202–04
what parents can do about, 159–61, 174–77

Community Anti-Drug Coalitions of America (CADCA), 299

Community service
mentoring relationships and, 212
as positive risk-taking, 151–53
teen participation in, 290–91

Competence, confidence, connection,
character, caring (the "Five C's"), 278

Contraception, 39–40

Contract for Life, 250–52, 261–62, 274

"Contract for Life: The SADD Story" (CBS), ix

Corliss, Richard, 188–89

Cosby, Bill, 200

Cosmopolitan (magazine), 102

CSI (TV program), 189

The Culture of Adolescent Risk-Taking (Lightfoot), 149–50

Culture of cruelty, 55–56, 123

Curfews
advice from teens on, 181
as boundary, 111
creating & enforcing, 164, 167, 177, 218
as punishment, 160

Cutting, behavior, 4, 72–73

"Cyber-bullying," 56

Date-rape drugs. See "Club drugs"

Deaths
chronology of an auto crash, 86
drug abuse, 35–36, 89–90
from suicide, 12, 67
from traffic accidents, 47, 49
from violence and weapons, 29–30

Decision Factors, 126–34, 137, 234, 276, 283, 287

Decision Points, 140–47, 230, 238–39, 247, 265, 287

Decision-making
adolescent development and, 107–15, 126–29, 201
adults as role models in, 5–7, 138–39
advice from teens on, 181
brain structure and, 136–38
categories of behavior in, 21–26
control-freedom continuum, 223–26
empowering teens for, 287–92
enabling poor, 149–50

facing the consequences of, 75–78,
131–33
having a "bail-out" strategy for, 147
"helicopter parents" and, 219
learning to make, 220–23
mentoring relationships in, 207–13
"Opening Lifesaving Lines" steps,
252–61
peer pressure and, 19–20
protective factors in, 283–87
resiliency to adversity, 279–82
risky behavior and, 134–36
in today's teen culture, 10–18
zero-tolerance policies and, 53–54,
261–62
Depression. *See also* Stress; Suicide
epidemic of, 66–68
how parents can talk about, 239–41
lookout for the signs of, 167–70
parental awareness of, 2–3
recognizing, 69–70
sexual behavior and, 40
in today's teen culture, 10
underage drinking and, 82–85
Desperate Housewives (TV program),
188–89
Dilemmas of Desire (Tolman), 101
Discipline
Contract for Life, 261–62
failure of parents to, 5–7, 132
hazing is not, 64, 242
punishment is not, 161–67
Distracted driving, 44–48, 91–92, 299.
See also Driving behaviors; Impaired
driving
Disturbia (movie), 188
Double standards, 56, 101, 205–06,
228
Douglas, Michael, 2
Driving behaviors. *See also* Impaired
driving
adolescent perception of, 138
alcohol & drug-impaired, 48–50

attitudes in teen culture toward,
44–48
chronology of an auto crash, 86
as concern in today's society, 13
how parents can talk about, 238–39
marijuana use and, 52–53
negative reinforcement, 160–61
parents as role models for, 45–47
"safe-rides" program, 50
setting consequences for, 50–52
teen perceptions about, 44–45
what parents can do about, 48, 53–54
Drug Abuse Warning Network (DAWN),
35–36
Drug dependency/addiction
alcohol and, 12, 83
drug abuse and, 35
drug testing and, 267
marijuana as "gateway" drug to, 88
Drug overdose, 36
Drug Policy Alliance, 268
Drug testing, 170, 265–71
Drug use. *See* Substance abuse

Ecstasy. *See* "Club drugs"; Substance
abuse
Edna McConnell Clark Foundation, 207
Education. *See also* School
adult failures, 5–7
on danger of inhalants, 90
destructive behavior programs, 138
in making healthy choices, 140–41
in media literacy, 193
role of television in, 194
Elkind, David, 8–9, 179
Emotional abuse, 87–88
Emotional development. *See* Maturity and
emotional development
EMPOWERED, SADD program, 289
The Enterprise (newspaper), 103
*Epidemic: How Teen Sex is Killing Our
Kids* (Meeker), 96, 101
Erikson, Erik, 108

Expectations
about driving behavior, 48, 50–51, 238
about drugs, 269
about sexual activity, 44, 99, 105
adults create, 133, 178–79, 181, 205
create outcomes, 131, 280–85
create structure, 111, 161–62, 246–48
establishing, 8–9, 15, 18, 22–23, 43, 145–46, 149, 192, 248–49
failure to establish, 117, 173, 234, 245–46
failure to meet, 69, 160–61
gender differences, 120–24
holding on vs. letting go, 219–20, 226
mentoring creates, 208
negative, 195
Experimenter behaviors, 21–26

Facebook, 197
Family/family values. *See also* Parenting; Parents
communication styles, 245–47
communications, 16–18, 99, 164–65
communications tips, 227–31
Contract for Life, 249–52
"core-values statement," 166
enforcing accountability, 77–78
media impact on, 187–88
media literacy and, 193–94
"NIFTY syndrome," 29, 177
risk & protective factors, 283–87
rites of passage and, 213–18
Federal Bureau of Investigation, 197
Federal Communications Commission, 187–88
Federal Office of Legislative and Policy Analysis, 30
Federal Trade Commission, 185, 196
Feig, Paul, 201
The Female Brain (Brizendine), 121

Fighting. *See* Aggression/aggressive behavior
"Five C's" of adolescence, 278
Focus groups, *Teens Today*, xv–xvii
Freud, Sigmund, 109
"Friends Don't Let Friends Drive Drunk," ix
Friendster, 197

Gammill, Andy, 119
Gangs, 62–63, 167–70
Gender/gender stereotype
brain structure and, 120–21
media impact on, 188, 191–92
puberty and, 121
self-esteem and, 41–42
sexual behavior and, 95–96, 100–102
in today's teen culture, 98, 120–26
Get Out of My Life... (Wolf), 5, 113
GHB. *See* "Club drugs"; Substance abuse
Girls Gone Wild (movie), 195
"Go along to get along," 65–66
The Good Teen (Lerner), 278
Governors Highway Safety Association (GHSA), 299–300
Grayson, Randall, 162
Grodner, Allison, 200

Haber, Joel, 60–61
Hacker, George, 31
Hallucinogens/LSD, 4, 29, 37, 171, 180
Hannibal Rising (movie), 188
Happy Days (television show), 140
"Hard" drugs, 4, 26, 36–37, 88–90, 149, 170–72, 212, 232. *See also* Substance abuse
Harmful to Minors: The Perils of Protecting Children From Sex (Levine), 102
Harris, Judith Rich, 201
Harris Interactive, 81
Hazing. *See* Bullying and hazing
Hein, Jon, 140
Heinrichs, Jay, 148

"Helicopter parents," 219–26
Henry J. Kaiser Foundation, 188
Heritage Foundation, 40
Heroin. *See* "Hard" drugs; Substance abuse
Hersch, Patricia, 113
HIV/AIDS, 12
Homosexuality, 44, 122, 237
Honesty, parent-child, 14–18
"Hooking-up" (recreational sex), 40–44
Hoover, Nadine C., 62–63
Howe, Neil, 221
The Hurried Child (Elkind), 8, 179

Identity: Youth and Crisis (Erikson), 108
ImpacTeen Illicit Drug Team, 90
Impaired driving. *See also* Distracted driving; Driving behaviors
    epidemic of, 48–52
    legal consequences of, 92–93
    marijuana use and, 52–53
    SADD campaign toward, ix–xiv
    what parents can do about, 53–54
In-depth interviews, *Teens Today*, xv–xvii
Inhalants, 4, 26, 90, 168, 171–72. *See also* Substance abuse
"Initiation Rites in American High Schools" (Hoover & Pollard), 62–63
Internet. *See also* Media
    cyber-bullying, 56
    impact on sexual behavior, 102
    impact on teen culture, 183–87, 195
    pornography, 198
    restricting access to, 132
    SADD surveys, xviii
    safety online, 198–200
    social networking, 10, 196–98
Internet resources
    anti-drug education, 174
    bullying and hazing, 63
    inhalant abuse, 90
    ONDCP website, 37
    SADD website, 90–91

social networking safety, 198–200
suicide and depression, 240
website addresses, 299–303
Intimacy
    consequences & responsibility of, 94–95
    maintaining parent-child, 115, 214
    role models for, 235
    teen sexual activity and, 42
i-SAFE, 200, 300

Jackass (movie), 135, 149
Jackson, Janet, 191
"Jump the shark," 140

Kaiser Family Foundation, 55
Ketamine. *See* "Club drugs"
Kick Me: Adventures in Adolescence (Feig), 201
Kindlon, Dan, 55, 121–22
Knight, James L., 192
Koplewicz, Harold, 67

The Late Show (TV show), 293
Leadership to Keep Children Alcohol Free, 300
Lerner, Richard, 277–78
Lessons learned, 293–95
Letterman, David, 293
Levine, Judith, 102
Liberty Mutual Group, xv, 179, 227, 298, 300
Lightfoot, Cynthia, 149
LIVESTRONG, 289
Living, Loving & Learning (Buscaglia), xiii
Lost (TV program), 189
LSD. *See* Hallucinogens/LSD

Marcia, James, 109–10
Marijuana. *See also* Substance abuse
    accessibility and potency, 4
    declining use of, 29
    as "gateway" drug, 88–89

Marijuana, *cont.*
   impaired driving and, 52–53
   lookout for the signs of, 172
   sending the wrong message about, 149–50
Martin, Karin A., 105
Maturity and emotional development. *See also* Brain structure; Cognitive development
   in adolescence, 107–10, 127–29
   alcohol and, 83–84
   childhood decision-making and, 201
   diminution of childhood, 8–10
   gender differences, 120–26
   lack of life experience and, 7–8
   media impact on, 183–87
   rites of passage to, 213–18
   self-control/self-gratification, 106
   sexual activity and, 93–95
   "storm-and-stress" of, 276–79
McGrory, Brian, 288
Media. *See also* Internet
   glamorizing unhealthy behavior, 7–8
   impact on teens, 98–99, 101–02, 183–87
   movies, 195–96
   risk & protective factors, 283–87
   Teens Today and, xviii
   television, 187–94
Media literacy, 193–94
Meeker, Meg, 96, 102
Mentoring, 207–13
Methamphetamines. *See* "Hard" drugs; Substance abuse
Millennials Go to College (Howe & Strauss), 221
Mimicked behaviors, 8–10
Mineta, Norman, 52
Monday Night Football (TV program), 189
Monitoring the Future (University of Michigan), 29
Moore, Kristin A., 208
More Than Moody (Koplewicz), 67

Moritsugu, Kenneth, 32
Mother's Against Drunk Drivers (MADD), 279
Movies, 195–96
MySpace, 10, 196–98
Myths about teen behavior, 177–81

Napoleon Dynamite (movie), 58
Narcissistic Personality Inventory, 278
National Campaign to Prevent Teen Pregnancy, 39, 301
National Campaign to Stop Bullying, 301
National Center on Addiction and Substance Abuse (CASA), 27, 127, 233
National Clearinghouse for Alcohol and Drug Information (NCADI), 174
National Highway Traffic Safety Administration (NHTSA), 47, 301
National Institute of Child Health and Human Development, 192
National Institute of Mental Health, 67, 137
National Institute on Alcohol Abuse, 32
National Institute on Drug Abuse, 88, 301
National Mental Health Association, 69
National Organizations for Youth Safety (NOYS), 301–02
National Service-Learning Clearinghouse, 290
National Transportation Safety Board, 91
National Youth Service Day, 290
National Youth Violence Prevention Campaign, 302
Negative expectations, 195
Negative reinforcement, 160–67
Negative risk-taking, 140–49
Negotiation, "giving in" is not, 257–60
The New Brain (Restak), 186
New Line Cinema, 195
Newsweek (magazine), 291
Nickelodeon, 55

"NIFTY syndrome", 29, 177
"No Use" message, SADD, 249, 284
Nostigma.org, 302
Nothin' Much, Just Chillin' (Perlstein), 42–43
Notmykid.org, 302
The Nurture Assumption (Harris), 201

Obesity, 191
Odd Girl Out (Simmons), 56
Office of National Drug Control Policy (ONDCP). *See* White House Office of National Drug Control Policy (ONDCP)
"Opening Lifesaving Lines", SADD, 252–61
Oral sex. *See also* Sexual activity
    as no big deal, 19, 94–95, 103–04
    as non-intercourse alternative, 93
    parents talking about, 18, 28, 236–37
    prevalence of, 38, 41–42, 83, 98–100, 134
    in today's teen culture, 4, 24, 117
    viewed as "safe sex," 97
Over-the-counter (OTC) drugs, 89. *See also* Substance abuse
Oxycontin, 29, 36

Parade (magazine), 123
Parental rights, 269
Parenting. *See also* Family/family values
    advice from teens on, 181, 261–65
    challenge of, 5–10
    communication styles, 245–47
    control-freedom continuum, 224–26
    discipline vs. punishment, 161–63
    enforcing accountability is, 75–78
    "helicopter parents" and, 219
    holding on vs. letting go, 110–15, 159–60, 163–67, 220–24
    it's not just other people's children, 10–18
    lessons learned about, 293–95

listening, watching & waiting as, 281–82
    overcoming myths of, 177–80
    peer-to-peer relationships and, 116
    setting consequences, 50–52
Parenting Tips Newsletter, 174
Parents. *See also* Adults
    abdication of responsibility, 5–7
    adolescent separation from, 110–15
    cognitive dissonance in, 28–30
    diminution of childhood by, 8–10
    getting to know other, 167
    how to talk about alcohol, 231–33
    how to talk about bullying & hazing, 241–44
    how to talk about driving behaviors, 238–39
    how to talk about drugs, 233–35
    how to talk about sex, 235–38
    how to talk about suicide, 239–41
    lack of awareness by, 1–4
    as role models, 14–18, 44–48, 121–23, 131–33, 201
    Teens Today methodology and, xv–xviii
    warning signs for, 174–77
    what to do during adolescence, 126, 129–31
    what you can do about alcohol, 33
    what you can do about bullying, 57–58
    what you can do about driving behavior, 48, 53–54
    what you can do about drugs, 37–38
    what you can do about hazing, 65–66
    what you can do about internet safety, 198–200
    what you can do about negative behavior, 145–49
    what you can do about sexual activity, 99, 105–06, 192–93
    what you can do about suicide, 70–72
    what you can do to cope with silence, 159–61

Parents Television Council, 188
The Patriot Ledger (newspaper), 103
PCP. *See* "Hard" drugs
Peer group
    abstinence programs, 273–79
    adolescence and the, 114–20
    importance of, 20, 108, 223
    making and keeping friends, 281–82
    parents and the, 201, 226
    risk & protective factors, 283–87
    risk-taking and the, 284
    Sense of Self and, 125
    sports as, 66
    what parents can do about, 116
Peer pressure
    alcohol and, 83–84
    to belong to the group, 65–66, 129
    drug testing as deterrent to, 267
    ostracism for taking a stand, xii
    role-playing to prepare for, 146, 258,
        282
    sexual behavior and, 100
    in today's teen culture, 10–14
Perlstein, Linda, 42
"Pharming," 36–37
Physical abuse, 87–88
Pipher, Mary, 101, 124, 129, 243
Pollack, William, 101, 123
Pollard, Norman J., 62–63
Ponton, Lynn, 101
Pornography, 198
Positive behaviors/risk-taking, 149–53
    abstinence programs, 273–75
    decision-making in, 276–79
    empowering teens for, 287–92
    protective factors, 283–87
    resiliency to adversity, 279–82
Positive reinforcement, 160
Pregnancy. *See* Teen pregnancy
Prescription drugs. *See also* Substance
    abuse
    increasing abuse of, 89
    increasing use of, 29

"pharming," 36
prevalence and variety, 4
The Pressured Child (Thompson), 12–13
Prevention and intervention
    advice from teens on, 261–65
    building blocks for, 247–49
    Contract for Life, 249–52
    drug testing, 265–69
    listening, watching & waiting in,
        281–82
    "Opening Lifesaving Lines" steps,
        252–61
    parental rights in, 269–71
    protective factors, 283–87
    suicide and depression, 70–72
    understanding teen behavior for, 21
    when warning signs appear, 167–70
The Primal Animal (Strauch), 136
Privacy, rights to, 169, 266, 269–70
Protective factors, 283–87
Puberty
    gender differences, 121
    maturity and emotional development
        at, 138
    as rite of passage, 213–16
    sexual awareness and, 43
    teen sexual activity and, 97, 235–36
*Puberty, Sexuality, and the Self: Boys and
    Girls at Adolescence* (Martin), 105
Punishment. *See also* Discipline
    for behaviors, 132–33
    following through with, 60, 77, 260
    imposing effective, 160–61, 181–82,
        262
    as legal consequence, 90–91

R. Adams Cowley Shock Trauma Center,
    180
*Raising Cain: Protecting the Emotional
    Life of Boys* (Kindlon & Thompson),
    55–56, 121–22
RAND Corporation, 192
Random drug testing, 265–71

Reagan, Ronald, 269
Real Boys and Real Boys Voices (Pollack), 110, 123
The Real Cancun (movie), 195–96
Reality Gap
  creating & sustaining, 265
  diminution of childhood, 7–10
  drinking and drug use, 1–4
  overcoming the myths of, 177–81
  parental lack of awareness, 2–5
  parental responsibility, 5–7
  in today's teen culture, 10–18
Recreational sex
  "buddy sex"/"friends with benefits," 44, 104
  "hooking-up," 40–42, 208
Reinforcement and support, 21–26
Relational aggression, 56
Relational sex, 41–42
Religion/religious beliefs, 22, 144
Repeater, behaviors, 21–26, 171, 262
Research, *Teens Today*, xv–xviii
Resiliency to adversity, 279–82
Resources. *See* Internet resources
Restak, Richard, 186
Reviving Ophelia: Saving the Selves of Adolescent Girls (Pipher), 101, 124, 129
Risk factors, 283–87
Risk-taking. *See* Negative risk-taking; Positive behaviors/risk-taking
Risky behavior
  distracted & impaired driving, 44–48, 91–93
  emotional distress and, 19–20
  facing consequences of, 75–78
  how to talk about alcohol, 231–33
  how to talk about bullying & hazing, 241–44
  how to talk about driving, 238–39
  how to talk about drugs, 233–35
  how to talk about sex, 235–38
  how to talk about suicide, 239–41
  legal consequences of, 85

marijuana use and, 52
media impact on, 186–87
"Opening Lifesaving Lines" guide, 252–61
risk vs. protective factors, 283–87
sexual activity, 93–104
social networking as, 196–200
substance abuse, 87–91
teen abstinence programs and, 273–79
underage drinking, 78–84
what parents can do about, 85–87, 105–06, 145–49, 281–82
zero-tolerance policies, 53–54, 261–62
Ritalin, 89
Rites of passage
  destructive behavior as, 32
  hazing as, 32
  to healthy behaviors, 286–87
  recognizing importance of, 213–18
  risk-taking as, 25–26
  underage drinking as, 32
The Road Ahead: Stay Safe at the Wheel, 179
Robinson, Glen, 187
Rogers, Carl, 129
Rohypnol. *See* "Club drugs"
Role models. *See also* Adults; Parents
  adolescent, 133–34, 202–05
  adult failure as, 5–7
  for boys, 121–22
  celebrity figures as, 204
  mentors as, 207–13
  teens as, 273–79
Role-playing, 146, 156, 229, 258, 282
Rules of conduct
  abdication of responsibility, 5–7, 14–16
  for adolescents, 113–15
  advice from teens on, 181
  communicating & enforcing, 77–78, 131–32, 159–61, 247–48

Rules of conduct, *cont.*
  in a "culture of cruelty," 55–56, 123
  discipline vs. punishment, 161–67
  for driving, 48, 238
  facing the consequences of, 131–33
  family "core-values statement," 166
  family responsibilities in, 15, 93–94, 98

SADD. *See* Students Against Destructive Decisions (SADD)
"Safe sex"
  education and awareness of, 100, 138
  oral sex viewed as, 97
  STDs/STIs and, 38–39
  teen pregnancy and, 40
"Safe-rides" programs, 50
School. *See also* Education
  drug testing, 266
  finding positive risk-taking in, 152
  as part of "letting go," 221–22
  peer pressure and, 11–13
  risk & protective factors, 283–87
  sexual behavior at, 103
Self-asphyxiation, 4
Self-control/self-gratification, 106
Self-esteem/self-respect. *See also* Sense of Self
  bullying and, 58–60
  decision-making and, 276
  gender differences, 41–42
  media impact on, 185–87
  vs. self-absorption, 278–79
  sexual behavior and, 13, 38–40
  what parents can do about, 258
Sense of Self, 124–27, 130, 134, 211–12, 287. *See also* Self-esteem/self-respect
Service-learning projects, 290–91
Sessions Strepp, Laura, 41–42
The Sex Lives of Teenagers (Ponton), 101
Sexual activity. *See also* Oral sex
  abstinence from, 38, 144
  adolescent perception of, 138

  decision points for beginning, 140–45
  emotional vs. physical maturity, 93–94
  epidemic of, 38–44
  gender stereotypes and, 95–96, 98, 100–102, 120–26
  how parents can talk about, 235–38
  legal consequences of, 97–98
  media impact on, 183–87, 192
  parental awareness of, 2–3
  parental expectations and, 99
  "safe sex," 40, 96–97, 100, 138
  self-control and, 106
  in today's teen culture, 10–18
  underage drinking and, 82–85
  what parents can do about, 99, 105–06, 192–93
Sexual assault, 24, 37, 78, 82, 139–40, 191, 197–98, 231
Sexual identity formation
  adolescence and, 93, 102, 108–12, 120, 125
  media role in, 186
  mentoring programs for, 207–13
  rites of passage in, 213–17
  role models in, 133–34, 202–05
Sexuality
  homosexuality, 44, 122, 237
  importance of role models, 43, 99, 120, 235
  media exploitation of, 190
  societal confusion over, 93, 122, 236–37
Sexually transmitted diseases (STDs), 12, 29, 38–39, 96–97
Shapiro, Arnold, 200
The Shelter of Each Other, Rebuilding Our Families (Pipher), 243
Simmons, Rachel, 56
"Six C's" of adolescence, 278
Smashed: Toxic Tales of Teens and Alcohol (HBO documentary), 179–80
Smoking. *See* Marijuana; Tobacco
Sober Truth on Preventing (STOP)

Underage Drinking Act of 2006, 31–33
Social aggression, 56
Social networking sites, 10, 196–200
Somers, Patricia, 221
Sports/athletes
    alcohol advertising and, 190
    alcohol and, 83–84
    destructive behavior in, 202–05
    drug testing, 266–67
    effects of abuse on performance, 84,
        96, 142–43, 234
    hazing in, 62–63
    as peer group, 66
    teen participation, 119, 151–53, 212
Statutory rape, 97–98
STDs/STIs. See Sexually transmitted dis-
    eases (STDs)
Steinberg, Laurence, 138
Stimulants, 89, 171
STOP Campaign, 31–33
Stopalcoholabuse.gov, 303
Strauch, Barbara, 136
Strauss, William, 221
Stress. See also Depression
    adolescence and, 110–14, 127–28,
        157–58, 164–65, 217, 220, 276–80
    alcohol and, 82–85
    destructive behavior and, 19–20,
        142–43
    personal goals alleviate, 129–31
    pushing children creates, 8–9
    shelter from, 107–08, 118–20
    substance abuse and, 127–29,
        171–73
    teen sexual activity and, 40–41, 44
Students Against Destructive Decisions
    (SADD)
    Contract for Life, 249–52
    EMPOWERED program, 287–92
    family communications tips, 227–31
    formation and message of, ix–xii, 291,
        302
    Lifetime Achievement Awards, 200

"No Use" message, 249, 284
"Opening Lifesaving Lines" guide,
    252–61
    research on bullying, 58–60
    STOP Campaign and, 31
    teen behavior resources from, 174
    Teens Today project, xiii, xv–xviii
Students Against Driving Drunk (SADD),
    ix
Substance abuse. See also Alcohol
    abstinence programs, 273–79
    adolescent perception of, 138
    categories of behavior toward, 21–24
    cognitive dissonance toward, 28–30
    decision points for beginning, 140–45
    epidemic of, 34–37
    how parents can talk about, 233–35
    looking for warning signs of, 170–73
    lookout for the signs of, 167–70
    media impact on, 183–87
    parental lack of awareness, 1–5, 26–28
    risk & protective factors, 283–87
    SADD campaign toward, ix–xiv
    stress as trigger for, 127–29
    testing as a deterrent, 265–71
    in today's teen culture, 10–18, 87–91
    types/variety in today's culture, 26
    what parents can do about, 37–38,
        174–77
Substance Abuse and Mental Health
    Services Administration (SAMHSA),
    32, 191, 193–94
Suicide. See also Depression
    alcohol and, 82
    epidemic of, 66–70
    how parents can talk about, 239–41
    lookout for the signs of, 69, 167–70
    SADD campaign toward, ix–xiv
    sexual behavior and, 40
    in today's teen culture, 10–12
    use of weapons, 69, 71, 241
    what parents can do about, 70–72
Surveys, Teens Today, xvi–xvii

Teen culture. *See also* Adolescence
  facing accountability in, 75–78
  gender stereotypes, 95–96, 98,
    100–102, 120–26
  growing up in today's, 10–18
  lessons learned about, 293–95
  overcoming the myths of, 177–80
  overlooking destructive behavior in,
    19–20
  risk & protective factors, 283–87
  risk-taking as rite of passage, 25–26
  survival in today's, 13–14
Teen leadership
  in abstinence programs, 273–79
  Cape Cod Sea Camps, xiii–xiv
  examples of, 286, 289–92
  peer ostracism toward, xii
Teen pregnancy
  contraception/birth control, 40, 100,
    236
  declining rates of teen, 29
  early sexual activity and, 38–39
  societal-emotional impact of, 39–41
  U.S. rate of, 43
Teen stories of behaviors
  Adam's suicidal thoughts, 69, 71, 129
  Billy's struggle with depression, 68,
    108–09, 219, 263–64, 281
  Brad's advice to parents, 15, 291–92
  Connor's avoidance of risk, 22, 104
  Jackie wanting to "fit in," 11, 276–77
  Jared's drug use, 1–2, 11, 16
  Matt's risk avoidance, 35, 134, 148,
    248, 265
  Nasha's relationship to mother, 18,
    248
  Robert's alcohol use, 11–12, 16, 21,
    52, 84, 188, 196, 265
  Stephanie's sexual activity, 16, 38–39,
    43, 262
  Tracy's loneliness & depression, 23,
    84

Trey's sex & alcohol use, 32, 38, 43,
    128, 281
  Zach's risk avoidance, 22–23, 98
"Teens, Sex, and TV" (survey), 188
Teens Today project
  categories of behavior, 21, 24–25
  on Decision Points in teen life,
    140–45
  on depression, 40–41fig.
  on driving behaviors, 45fig., 46fig.,
    50fig., 51fig.
  on drug use, 35fig., 143fig., 233
  on drugs & alcohol, 27fig., 78fig.
  on drugs & sexual activity, 25fig.
  on online pornography, 198
  parental guidelines, 53–54
  programs & methodology, xiii, xvi–xviii
  on risk-taking, 130, 151fig., 152fig.,
    214
  on Sense of Self, 210–12, 216fig.
  on sexual behavior, 38–39, 144fig.
  on suicide, 66–67, 71
  teen vs. parent concerns, 13fig.
  on trust & communications, 257, 263,
    268
Television. *See* Media
Thank You For Arguing... (Heinrichs),
    148–49
THC. *See* Marijuana
Thompson, Michael, 12, 55, 121–22
Thomson, Michael, 9
"Three C's" (commitment, contraception,
    consequences)
  adolescence and, 131–33
  consequences, 50–52, 75–78, 85,
    92–98
  contraception/birth control, 40, 100,
    236
  media impact on, 192
Timberlake, Justin, 191
Time (magazine), 188–89
Time for Your School program, 34, 284

Tobacco, 138, 172, 193, 232, 273. *See also* Marijuana
Tolman, Deborah, 101
The Tonight Show (TV show), 293
"Top Ten" tips for raising teens, 294
Traffic (movie), 2
"Triangle of trust"
    building blocks of, 247–49
    Contract for Life, 250–52, 261–62
    steps in creating, 253–61
A Tribe Apart (Hersch), 113
Tufts University, 277
Twenge, Jean, 278

Underage drinking
    adolescent perception of, 138
    decision points for beginning, 140–45
    emotional & developmental risks of, 82–85
    epidemic of, 30–31
    facing the consequences of, 75–78
    media impact on, 189
    parental cognitive dissonance and, 28–30
    SADD campaign toward, ix–xiv
    STOP Campaign, 31–33
    in today's teen culture, 10–18
    underestimating the risks of, 78–82
    what parents can do about, 33, 53–54

Unhooked, How Young Women Pursue Sex... (Sessions Strepp), 41–42
University of California, 136–37, 147, 194
University of Maryland, 180
University of Michigan, 29, 266

University of North Carolina, 192
U.S. News & World Report, 188
U.S. Surgeon General, 31–32

Villani, Susan, 186
Violence/violent behavior
    increasing use of weapons in, 29–30
    "numbing" effect of media on, 183–87
    SADD campaign toward, ix–xiv
    television and, 187–94
    in today's teen culture, 10
"Violent TV ads leave parents wincing" (*Boston Globe*), 188
Vocelle, Daniel, 33
Volunteering for community service, 153

The Wall Street Journal, 81
Walters, John, 52, 267
Weapons, 29–30, 69, 71, 241
Websites. *See* Resources
Welcome to the Dollhouse (movie), 58
When Good Things Go Bad (Hein), 140
White House Office of National Drug Control Policy (ONDCP), 29, 36–37, 88, 90, 159, 174, 267, 270, 303
Who's Raising Whom (Thomson), 9
Williams, Robin, 100
Wolf, Anthony, 5, 113
The Wonder Years (television show), 107

Xanga, 197

Youth Service America (YSA), 303
YouTube, 10, 196–98

Zero-tolerance policies, 53–54, 261–62

ABOUT THE AUTHOR

Stephen Wallace is an expert when it comes to child and teen issues. In his multiple roles as SADD chairman and CEO, school psychologist, camp director, and college professor, he has gained unique insight into youth development and decision-making. Since 2000, he's conducted groundbreaking research that has shed new light on the most difficult issues facing young people and their families. Stephen is a regular contributor to regional and national broadcasts and has appeared on CNN, NBC, PBS, and the Fox News Channel. His columns, opinion-editorials, and articles appear in newspapers and magazines across the country. Stephen has been formally recognized by the White House and the American Camp Association for his tireless work on behalf of the nation's youth. He has also held senior positions in business and government. For more information about Stephen and his work, visit www.stephengraywallace.com.